ACKNOWLEDGING RADICAL HISTORIES

ACKNOWLEDGING RADICAL HISTORIES

Conversations with Gerald Horne

By Gerald Horne &
Chris Time Steele

INTERNATIONAL PUBLISHERS, New York

Description: Communism, African American History,
Biographical History, Radical and Political History:
20th Century Communism—Communist Party, USA—Race
Relations—Anti-Apartheid Struggles—
Internationalism—History—Pan-Africanism—Fascism—
Anti-Colonialism

Cover art design by Joaquin Gonzales II
Instragram: @Joaquin_Gonzales_Art

ISBN-10: 0-7178-0942-0   ISBN-13: 978-0-7178-0942-4
Typeset by Amnet Systems, Chennai, India

Table of Contents

Foreword

A lifetime of excavating the links between capitalism and white supremacy
By Gerald Horne

I appreciate the tireless labor of Chris Steele and International Publishers for bringing these words to the attention of a larger audience.

At this point in my life, I have witnessed more yesterdays than I shall see tomorrows. So, it is appropriate to reflect on how we reached the present conjuncture and what that may tell us about what is around the corner and just over the horizon.

My writing life has been the inverse of how my life has proceeded chronologically. That is, it is only recently that I began to write in depth about the roots of settler colonialism in North America—the system that continues to persist along with its evil handmaidens: capitalism and white supremacy.

Somehow, I wish that I had begun decades ago writing about the 16th century—instead of recent years. For it was in that faraway era I sought to expose the ineffable ties between religious conflict—Protestant vs. Catholic; Christian vs. Islam and Judaism—and the rise of 'race' and its close cousin, racism, a peculiar form of "identity politics" that has yet to disappear. Indeed, this pestilence continues to infect pandemically.

If I could turn back the hands of time I would have tackled the Haitian Revolution, 1791-1804, much earlier in my writing life—as opposed to recent years. Like most revolutionary processes, this erupting Caribbean volcano continues to instruct, as it ignited a general crisis of the entire slave system that could only be resolved with its collapse.

It was a mighty blow to the white supremacy that began to flourish in the 16th century and, as well, was a shot of adrenalin into the bloodstream of labor as these unpaid workers served as a premonition of what was to unfold in the 20th century with the rise of various socialist projects. More precisely, it is hardly accidental that with the abolition of slavery in North America, union organizing accelerated along with its complement, struggles for the eight-hour day.

But, alas, I began my writing life decades ago reflecting on the Cold War and the Red Scare. Therein, inter alia, I sought to limn a lingering contradiction: the stiff price exacted for an agonizing and halting retreat from the more egregious aspects of Jim Crow / U.S. apartheid was the bludgeoning of the tallest trees in our forest: W.E.B. Du Bois; Paul Robeson; William Patterson; Shirley Graham Du Bois; Ben Davis; Ferdinand Smith; John Howard Lawson; Koji Ariyoshi (the persecution of those of Japanese ancestry has been a particular concern of mine) and Frank Marshall Davis (the latter two sited in Hawaii with Davis exerting influence on a future U.S. president who hailed from the archipelago)—all of whom I subjected to biographical scrutiny. Eventually I was able to expand this excavation to Southern Africa, where I examined the South African Communist Party, including the former leading members Nelson Mandela and Thabo Mbeki (former presidents both of this estimable nation). My study of Africa also involved detailing settler colonialism in both Kenya and pre-1989 Zimbabwe (Rhodesia), which at once enhanced my understanding of North America.

This survey also included scrutiny of the Caribbean, including the nation now known as Guyana (therein I examined the heroism of the late Communist, Cheddi Jagan, which led me to traverse his ancestral homeland, i.e., India and this giant's potent pre-1947 entanglement with African Americans): as ever, the impact of the export of the Cold War / Red Scare there was a focus on these Caribbean explorations, not to mention the backstory of the monumental Cuban Revolution.

Therein I arrived early on at a conclusion that I have yet to discard: 1917 and the Bolshevik Revolution ignited a general crisis of the capitalist system that will only be resolved with its collapse and / or overthrow. The disintegration of the Soviet Union did not destroy this thesis insofar as this catastrophe involved a post-1972 anti-Soviet entente with China that created a juggernaut in Beijing now in the passing lane, a point I have made repeatedly in various interviews and journalistic forays, including the slim volume, *Blows Against the Empire*.

Indeed, post 1991—unlike many—instead of dancing on the grave of the Soviet Union or even pursuing the healthier option of divining what went wrong in the socialist bloc, what captured my imagination was simply why there existed a maniacal obsession with Communist parties that would lead U.S. imperialism to execute a deluded policy that—ultimately—has placed Washington's hegemony in jeopardy?

Inexorably, this led me to excavate further the sedimented layers of U.S. history back to the origins of settler colonialism and Indigenous dispossession in the 16th century, then the rise of enslavement of Africans in the 17th century and the slaveholders' revolt of the 18th century and then the long reach of the Haitian Revolution culminating in abolition in 1865. The latter, quite revolutionarily, also involved one of the largest uncompensated expropriations of private property in world history (to that point), involving the bodies of enslaved Africans.

At once this served to engender a demented compulsion to destabilize socialism—thought to represent yet another lurch toward an even more massive uncompensated expropriation of private property, sparking hysteria shadowed by 1865. The fact that the presumed avatars of 20th century socialism in North America included those of African descent (see above) only caused the compulsion to metastasize.

Needless to say, these excavations involved deep dives into the excrescences of U.S. imperialism, including land grabs from Mexico that created the dual engines of the U.S. economy: Texas and California and the smashing of Indigenous rule—and further land grabs, for example, in Hawaii in the late 19th century. How this system of malevolent misrule manifested domestically—and how it generated unique forms of class struggle—I explored in works on Hollywood, boxing, the music we call jazz, the Negro press and aviation.

As I begin the process of passing the torch on to a younger generation, embodied in the talented Chris Steele, I would be remiss if I failed to acknowledge what is haunting my nightmares and shaping my writing life: the specter of U.S. fascism. It does not beggar belief to suggest that a nation grounded in Indigenous dispossession and enslavement of Africans has a fertile womb allowing for an emergent fascism, a subject detailed in my biography of the intellectual leader of U.S. fascism—Lawrence Dennis—and the origins of the 28th U.S. state: Texas, born in a massive land grab in order to facilitate enslavement of Africans.

Still, the existence of a vibrant socialist bloc, which continues to persist, not to mention the stubbornness of domestic antifascism, reassures that my nightmares will not escape my slumber.

ACKNOWLEDGING RADICAL HISTORIES

Introduction

Curiosity and Care—Fractals for Justice
By Chris Time Steele

Honesty and openness is always the foundation of insightful dialogue.

—bell hooks, *All About Love: New Visions*

There's something magical about a good conversation. Linear time seems to break open. Everyone involved feels seen, felt, and heard. A good conversation is transformational. When I first contacted Dr. Horne, I was surprised he was so giving of his time. When we spoke on the phone, I was grateful for his kindness and willingness to dig deep into topics. The hospitality of Dr. Horne offering his time, listening, and sharing knowledge is an act of love. T. Storm Heter explains listening takes improvisation like seen in jazz. It nurtures "empathy, inquiry, dialogue, and perhaps most importantly, respect."[1]

One of my goals with this book was to showcase the big heart Dr. Horne has and ask him to dive into his research while also highlighting his personal story and the legacy of activism and mutual aid he has provided for decades. Dr. Horne has been all over the globe as an activist, journalist, scholar, and historian, armed with curiosity. From taking part in anti-apartheid struggles to occupying buildings at Princeton, to becoming the head of the National Conference of Black Lawyers, to representing the New York Hospital Workers Union, to being a journalist for *Freedomways*, penning articles for the Nation of Islam newspaper, the Black Panther's newspaper, helping mediate the Sudanese Civil War, haunting archives around the world, authoring more than 30 books, and being a revered professor, Dr. Horne has a boundless heart.

What first enthralled me about Dr. Horne was reading his book *Black and Brown: African Americans and the Mexican Revolution, 1910-1920*. He tells the story of the boxer Jack Johnson, who was denied food in Mexico City by a US store owner thinking he could uphold

---

1. T Storm Heter, *The Sonic Gaze: Jazz, Whiteness, and Racialized Listening*, Lanham: Rowman & Littlefield, 2022, xi

Jim Crow laws.[2] Jack left the store and returned later with three or four generals who revoked the store owner's license, made him apologize, and told him that Mexico was "not 'white man's country.'"[3] These are histories seldom heard to which Horne gives a voice. Horne's analysis of the legacy of white supremacy and the refusal of mainstream US history and education to acknowledge colonialism shows us how Empire continues to survive. Horne also points at the cracks in these systems and the power of coming together.

While teaching political science in the community college circuit in Colorado, I was faced with preassigned textbooks that presented history from a Eurocentric male perspective, devoid of a critique of capitalism, gender, patriarchy, and colonialism. On the first day of teaching comparative government, a student in the course asked why the textbook didn't cover any of the genocides in Africa, such as Belgian King Leopold II's genocide of an estimated ten million in the Congo for rubber, or Germany's genocide of the Herero and Nama in 1904. I reflected on my white colonial mind and my college education and realized I was never assigned readings that had to do with genocides in Africa. I decided to rework the course readings with student input to change this pattern of reproducing global white supremacy in the classroom, as well as the cultural, intergenerational, and historical trauma that students of color often endure throughout education / pedagogy by not receiving the whole picture of history. This is what led me to first email Dr. Horne and ask if he would do an interview on this topic, he graciously agreed.

Dr. Horne offers a sober perspective that is indispensable. He seeks to stab through hagiography and dismount from historical mythology, allowing his readers to see the connection to capitalism, slavery, the genocide of Indigenous peoples, Pan-Africanism, and liberation struggles with a worldview that is often absent in the classroom and mainstream discussions. When looking at a panorama of Dr. Horne's work he explains that the history of white supremacy is illusive but can be traced back to the Crusades where it wound its way into philosophy, Christendom, colonialism, and capitalism. For example, when looking at early European philosophy, particularly the Enlightenment and Liberalism and its relationship with global white supremacy, John Locke was invested in the Royal African Company

---

2. Gerald Horne, *Black and Brown: African Americans and the Mexican Revolution, 1910-1920*, New York: New York University Press, 2005

3. Ibid., 34

and wrote much of South Carolina's constitution justifying slavery.[4] Montesquieu deemed Islam despotic. Voltaire blamed the slave trade on Africans. Kant's anthropology lectures were filled with racist vitriol supporting racial hierarchy. And Hegel argued that even the flora and fauna of the America's were inferior to Europe's.[5] As Grant Morrison said, "It's not so much that history is simply cyclical, it seems to progress via recursive, repeated fractal patterns with minute variations."[6] These fractals of the past are present today and become further normalized when they aren't questioned. Dr. Horne's underlying message is coming together with internationalism and solidarity. Perhaps this is a futurism that creates fractals in the present for a future with more justice?

At times our conversations feel like Errico Malatesta's book *At the Café: Conversations on Anarchism*, where each dialogue introduces a new character, where different political positions and perspectives are discussed, particularly Dialogue Seventeen, when Luigi, a socialist enters the book. With my interest in anarchism many of my questions intersect with Dr. Horne's experience and expertise on socialism, such as Paul Robeson in the Spanish Civil War and direct actions that jazz musicians took against the exploitative industry. Note, these interviews are conversational, and they take place over five years. Dr. Horne often interjects numerous points simultaneously. Some of the conversations may seem repetitive. However, the conversations are largely unchanged and reflect Dr. Horne's vast knowledge and expertise.

My hope for this work is to aid current and future researchers, historians, and listeners. I hope this work will be used in publications, theater, poetry, art, wherever needed. I hope this book acts as an introduction or an addendum to Dr. Horne's vast work. With citations, I sought to cite many of his mentions of his other books

---

4. Charles M. Mills, *The Racial Contract*, Ithaca: Cornell University Press, 1997

5. Gerald Horne, *The Apocalypse of Settler Colonialism: The Roots of Slavery, White Supremacy, and Capitalism in Seventeenth-Century North America and the Caribbean*, New York: Monthly Review Press, 2018; Grégoire Chamayou, *Manhunts: A Philosophical History*, Princeton, Princeton University Press, 2012; Charles M. Mills, *The Racial Contract*, Ithaca: Cornell University Press, 1997; Enrique Dussel, *The Invention of the Americas: Eclipse of "The Other" and the Myth of Modernity*, New York, Continuum, 1995

6. Grant Morrison, *Supergods: What Masked Vigilantes, Miraculous Mutants, and a Sun God from Smallville Can Teach Us About Being Human*, New York: Spiegel & Grau, 2012, 294

and articles and created a type of personal annotated bibliography of many of his works. I hope these interviews will help push back on public memory and propaganda, these dangerous myths that continue to uphold, as bell hooks would say, white supremacist, imperialist, capitalist, patriarchy. My biggest hope is that this project inspires more conversations. I hope it inspires others to record stories from youth, elders, and loved ones in their life, so their voices and stories can be passed down and shared, creating intergenerational solidarity. As carla joy bergman wrote about breaking down intergenerational hierarchies, "solidarity begins at home."[7]

We need to hear from each other, not algorithms. When I first started interviewing people, I quickly learned that all you need to do is be present, hit record, and listen with curiosity and care.

---

7. carla joy bergman, *Trust Kids: Stories on Youth Autonomy and Confronting Adult Supremacy*, Chico: AK Press, 2022, 146

Chapter 1

Decolonizing the Classroom: Embracing Radical Internationalism
June 24, 2017

Chris Time Steele: What is one's role in the classroom as an educator and framer of history?

Gerald Horne: With regards to the United States of America, since the United States of America is a nation that was built on slave labor, particularly of Africans, it is mandatory to have that story embedded in the basic narrative, and it is mandatory for the teacher to frame the narrative of the construction of the United States of America through the lens of the African Slave Trade and the enslavement of Africans.

CS: Can you speak about how professors can avoid the pitfall of just describing atrocities of colonialism instead of also addressing the perseverance, resistance, and complexities of people of color throughout history such as the 1712 revolt in Manhattan and other slave revolts?

GH: Well, I think even today in 2017, you have historians who consider themselves to be progressive who tend to downplay the question of resistance, which I think does a disservice to history. Certainly, it does a disservice to Black people. In some ways, it reminds me of the reaction to Trump in liberal and left circles. There's a lot of denunciation of Trump, which is fine. I can resonate with a denunciation of Trump. But what we really need is an explanation of how this happened. Likewise, if you don't have a story of resistance along with the story of enslavement you really can't provide an explanation of how we got to this point and therefore you are doing a disservice to history and you're doing a disservice to those who are trying to resist today.

CS: Can you speak about representation and resistance in the classroom, tying in Indigenous history, which is American history, or other issues such as patriarchy, throughout US history?

GH: Well, certainly if you look at the revolt of 1776 that led to the creation of the United States, in my book *The Counter-Revolution of*

1776 I stress the question of slavery and only mention the Royal Proclamation of 1763 in passing. The Royal Proclamation of course was London's attempt to avoid expending more blood and treasure fighting Native Americans for their land, but the settlers of course resisted this Royal Proclamation and led directly to kicking London out of what is now the United States. Certainly, in the state of Colorado where you are sitting, Native American resistance has shaped the history of that state. Unfortunately, in terms of writing about the U.S. Civil War, many historians do not engage the question of how that led directly to more expropriation of Native American land. I'm thinking of the Sand Creek Massacre in Colorado, for example. Certainly, we need an integrated history of the United States that braids and threads the question of African suffering and African resistance, Native American suffering and Native American resistance, the question of patriarchy, the question of ethnic cleansing, all of that needs to be incorporated into a grander narrative history of North America.

CS: Two of the principles you routinely talk about are organization and what Paul Robeson called "Radical Internationalism." Can you talk about how these can be applied to education?

GH: With regard to radical internationalism, I would say that given the unsavory origins of the United States, which led to the empowerment of powerful white supremacists and right-wing forces, then in order to overcome that tendency, the victims of capitalism and white supremacy have had to reach across the oceans and reach across the borders. In order to reach across the oceans and reach across the borders for solidarity and assistance you need organization. I mean otherwise it doesn't work very well and certainly that's a central lesson that needs to be imparted in the classroom.

CS: Have you researched how this colonizer form of history in the classroom can reproduce cultural or intergenerational trauma?

GH: Oh, sure. I haven't researched it, but I have an opinion, which is that if those who are the victims of white supremacy and ethnic cleansing are not told in the classroom about the history that has led us up to the present moment then there might be a tendency to feel that their present unfortunate circumstance is a personal, individual issue as opposed to the result of the tides of history. Obviously, that can lead to a kind of individual trauma, which I would say could be avoided if there was more engagement with an accurate portrayal of history in the classroom.

CS: You are working on a new book about anarchists, communists, and Black nationalists and how they have confronted the seat of national power. What is your perception of anarchism and American history?

GH: It's complicated. I haven't begun to research deeply into this project, but I wrote a book a couple years ago on William Patterson—it was titled *Black Revolutionary*—who was a Black communist and he was inducted into the communist movement through his engagement with anarchists, particularly with the Sacco and Vanzetti case of the 1920s in Massachusetts. From my past reading I also know that in Mexico and in Spain in particular there's been a strong anarchist movement. Now, of course, there have been tensions between and amongst these three forces that I've mentioned—anarchists, Black nationalism, and communism—but one of the purposes of my project when I finally get lift off and take off is to try to deal with those differences because I think if we're going to build a more stable and more productive and more progressive environment, we're going to have to grapple honestly with these differences so that we can build that more productive environment.

CS: With the rise of the right-wing can you speak about how the KKK were in Cuba and Fiji?[1]

GH: It's interesting. I guess you're familiar with my book *The White Pacific*, where I deal with the KKK in Fiji, which of course was in the context of the attempt to revive Black slavery this time focusing on Melanesians as opposed to Africans with the site of the exploitation being Queensland, Australia, and Fiji. I'm doing a book on Southern Africa now and of course there are many ties between the masters of apartheid in South Africa and the KKK and white supremacist organizations here in the United States. I mean there's been this sort of white international, this white right-wing international more precisely, and it certainly needs more attention particularly nowadays because as you know in the United States there has been a resurgence of what's euphemistically called the Alt-Right and what could be more accurately called white supremacist, white nationalist organizations. Now more than ever, we need close scrutiny of these organizations and their history so we can better defeat them.

CS: Throughout your research have you studied the so-called Doctrine of Discovery and the implications it had on the Indigenous population?

GH: Yes, it is sort of ridiculous. It's like if I come to where you are staying in Colorado and bust into your apartment and say, "I think I discovered your laptop and under the right of discovery I'm going to claim it." I mean the arrogance of the ridiculous nature,

---

1. Gerald Horne, *The White Pacific: U.S. imperialism and Black Slavery in the South Seas after the Civil War*, Honolulu: University of Hawai'i Press, 2007.

but obviously it was deadly serious. Obviously the Christian church, particularly the Roman Catholic church has a lot of explaining to do as they say in the United States, a lot of apologies to craft since we know that the rise of that doctrine has been congruent with the expansion of Catholicism and, in particular in the Americas, but of course this takes place in the context of religious conflict. I have a book coming out early next year on the 17th century, *The Apocalypse of Settler Colonialism*, and of course the 17th century, that is to say the 1600s, marks the rise of the expropriation of the Indigenous population and enslavement of the Africans and this is taking place against the backdrop of religious conflict, particularly between Christians and Protestants and the reconciliation ultimately between Christians and Protestants, or an attempted reconciliation I should say reaches its zenith in North America, in the trade union movement in the United States. This used to be called pork chop unity. That is to say that folks would bury their contradictions and intentions in order to get those pork chops, with the pork chops being in this case the land of the Native Americans and the bodies of the Africans and certainly that whole Doctrine of Discovery the more I think about it is obviously utterly ridiculous.

Chapter 2

Fighting Fascism by Acknowledging Histories and International Solidarity
July 13, 2018

> What is euphemistically referred to as "modernity" is marked with the indelible stain of what might be termed the Three Horsemen of the Apocalypse: Slavery, White Supremacy, and Capitalism, with the bloody process of human bondage being the driving and animating force of this abject horror—
> —Gerald Horne, *The Apocalypse of Settler Colonialism*[1]

CS: When I spoke to you last time we spoke about representations of resistance in the classroom. Can you speak about teaching philosophy and how this relates to the work you do?

GH: Well, I accept wholly and fully the predicate of your question. I think that particularly with regard to students of African descent, but not exclusively students of African descent, it's very important for them not to see Black people only in the role of slaves. For example, and even in dealing with the inextricable unavoidable history of enslavement in North America—which by the way also ensnared millions of Indigenous people—it is important to portray them as actors. That is to say, as seeking to collaborate with the enemies of their enslavers. Of that there is abundant evidence. One of the many scandals of US historiography is not dealing with that history, which I think leads to a misimpression that the slave population was inert or as the designer / rapper Kanye West said: "400 years of slavery is

1. Gerald Horne, *The Apocalypse of Settler Colonialism: The Roots of Slavery, White Supremacy, and Capitalism in Seventeenth-Century North America and the Caribbean*, New York: Monthly Review Press, 2018, 9

a choice." Basically, that kind of opinion comes clearly from this idea of presenting enslaved people as passive.[2]

Now, with regard to teaching, particularly the history of North America, I think number one, students need an explanation of why we're speaking English in the first instance, particularly given that as I say in my book *The Apocalypse of Settler Colonialism*, that in the early 1600s, England was fundamentally a minor power in Europe. And students need to understand how this minor power in the early-1600s became a major power by the late-1600s and of course the answer in brief is slavery. I think that it's important in talking about settler colonialism and European settler colonialism in North America to also deal with the conflicts and contradictions in Europe, not least the Ottoman Empire. That is to say Turkey. And not least the religious conflict between Muslims and Christians and Jewish people and between Protestants and Catholics and between Catholics and Jewish people and somehow all of those conflicts in the 17th century get resolved on the basis of the common altar of race. It reminds me of the Michael Jackson music video "Beat It." You have the two gangs and Michael Jackson comes between them and sort of reconciles them. This is what happens between the Protestants and the Catholics. They say "Why are we fighting? We should unite under this common banner of whiteness, and we can loot everybody." Basically, that's what happened. Let the transcript show the speaker is now chuckling. That's part of what I try to impart to my students.

CS: You spoke about when the Dutch, French, English, and Spanish came over they all kind of homogenized into this structure of whiteness as you were mentioning.

GH: Oh yeah, you have this transition from religion as the axis of society, to race, and what's interesting is you have many bourgeois analysts and scholars, they laud the United States. They say look at the First Amendment. The United States moved away from religious conflict of Europe and guaranteed freedom of religion, which is true, but they don't go to the next statement, which is that there was basically a switch from religion to race. So, these scholars and analysts, they glorify the First Amendment because it guarantees Freedom of Religion, but what they don't mention is that this was a maneuver by the settlers to gain more numbers by downplaying religious conflict

---

2. Benjamin Lee and Ben Beaumont-Thomas, "Kanye West on slavery: 'For 400 years? That sounds like a choice.'" *The Guardian*, May 02, 2018, https://www.theguardian.com/music/2018/may/01/kanye-west-on -slavery-for-400-years-that-sounds-like-a-choice

and hoping to attract more settlers by guaranteeing that they would not be bedeviled by religious conflict. The flip side of that, of course, is that they could then benefit from seizing the land of Native Americans and enslaving Africans.

You have a shift from religion to race at the axis of society in North America. What's striking is that you have scholars today talk about what they call the Enlightenment, and you would think that the Enlightenment—that is to say this movement away from religion and towards what might be called a rational or materialist approach—came solely and exclusively from the heads and the brains of geniuses as opposed to being an adaptation to facts on the ground in North America in particular and in colonial settings whereby you needed to broaden the base for settler colonialism by extending and expanding it beyond religion and then drawing upon a population pool that stretches from the Atlantic to the Ural Mountains in Russia.

That is to say, a population that could be defined as white and even dipping down into the Arab world to define them as white, too. Danny Thomas, a popular comedian in the 1950s, was of Syrian origin. Ralph Nader, a consumer advocate, of Lebanese origin. Even dipping into Persia, the head of Uber is of Iranian origin; he's considered to be white. There's a new book from Stanford Press called *The Limits of Whiteness* that deals with Iranians being defined as white in North America. Of course, what happens, instead of being seen as an adaptation of settler colonialism to generate enough numbers to overawe and overmatch Indigenous populations and Africans, this is seen as some stroke of genius, liberalized so to speak.[3]

What is even more ironic is that the so called Enlightenment scholars and debutants of the Enlightenment talk about a rational approach to phenomenon, but when it comes to responding to what I just articulated they're all caught off guard. As I said, they don't talk about how this move away from religion and how it was a created adaptation to the perils of colonialism and settler colonialism in particular. It wasn't until the Haitian Revolution, 1791 to 1804, that you got some of this pushback against this construction of race and slavery, which was then complemented in the 20th century by the rise of socialism, the Bolshevik Revolution, etc., and this is where we are today.

---

3. Neda Maghbouleh, *The Limits of Whiteness: Iranian Americans and the Everyday Politics of Race*, Stanford: Stanford University Press, 2017

CS: You've said that the $64,000 question is elusive of the origins of global white supremacy. You and Roxanne Dunbar-Ortiz have suggested that it lay in the Crusades. In one of your footnotes, you say a scholar dates the word "race" back to 1508. Do you find its origins with Christendom, colonialism, capitalism, or a combination of all three?[4]

GH: Well, I would say a combination of all three. You know, it's interesting. I mean I'm working on a book now on the 1500s.

CS: That's *The Dawning of the Apocalypse*?

GH: Exactly, and you begin to see—like if you look at the Crusades, which you can plot from the late 11th century—these are pan-European projects from the inception. They're taking Christians from all over western Europe to march to what might be called the Holy Land and to oust the Muslims. Then of course, we all know that slavery is a phenomenon during that period, not only enslaving of Africans but of course enslaving of other Europeans, galley slaves, for example. We need more research on galley slaves, that is to say, the people who were propelling vehicles on the seas, were enslaved. We all know about the roots, that the term of slave in general in terms of how people in the Slavic world were heavily subjected to enslavement.

So, I would say that the Crusades would be one root of not only slavery but a pan-Europeanism, which then bleeds into whiteness. I would also suggest that looking at the Iberian Peninsula and the fact that Muslims were ruling in Spain from about 711 in the so-called Christian era A.D. until they were formally ousted circa 1492 and then expelled altogether in 1609. This conflict in Spain between Muslims and Christians, it seems to me, is a predicate for the construction of whiteness, not to mention the expansion of Spain across the Atlantic. What befalls the Muslim population on the Iberian Peninsula in the 1500s is strikingly similar to what befalls the Indigenous population of the Americas and Africans as well in the 1500s. That is to say, falling victim to enslavement and then of course whiteness being the vehicle that propels that.

Another aspect that I think we're going to have to deal with is what's happening in the 1300s with the African leader Mansa Musa. The story is well known about how he's a Muslim and then of course

---

4. Roxanne Dunbar-Ortiz, *An Indigenous Peoples' History of the United States*, Boston: Beacon Press, 2014; Gerald Horne, *The Apocalypse of Settler Colonialism: The Roots of Slavery, White Supremacy, and Capitalism in Seventeenth-Century North America and the Caribbean*, New York: Monthly Review Press, 2018, 195

starts dealing with the rise of the enslavement of Africans and the rise of whiteness. You have to contemplate that some of the earlier areas subjected to enslavement in so-called Sub Saharan Africa were heavily Muslim dominated as they are today, what is now present day Senegal, what is now present day Guinea.

Guinea of course used to be a sort of synonym for all Black people. What is now present-day Mali, for example, Mansa Musa is well-known; he was a Muslim ruler and his trans-Saharan voyage across Africa on his Hajj was a major event of the 1300s and this idea of African wealth that he exhibited attracted the dedicated attention of many potential colonizers. Which actually when I think of Mansa Musa, I also think about the movie *Black Panther*, where you have this African kingdom and how they're to keep their wealth shrouded so to speak. I think that Mansa Musa might have been better off if he had not made such an exhibition of the vast wealth that he was controlling because it attracted the ravenous attention of outsiders to the detriment of his people. In any case, I think that in terms of explaining and shedding light on the dawning of the apocalypse or the dawning of settler colonialism, it is important to understand the Crusades. It's important to understand what was going on in the Iberian Peninsula, particularly Spain, and it's also important to understand the phenomenon that was Mansa Musa.

CS: This next question ties into the 1400s. In your book *The Apocalypse of Settler Colonialism*, I'm going to read a part because it's so well-written: "What is euphemistically referred to as 'modernity' is marked with the indelible stain of what might be termed the Three Horsemen of the Apocalypse: Slavery, White Supremacy, and Capitalism, with the bloody process of human bondage being the driving and animating force of this abject horror." I wanted to tie in Enrique Dussel, the philosopher. In his work *The Invention of Americas*, he says the birthdate of modernity is 1492 and "with it the myth of a special kind of sacrificial violence which eventually eclipsed whatever was non-European." Do you agree that this is when modernity began in 1492?[5]

GH: Well sure. I mean that's as good a date as any. You could also say 1095 with the origins of the Crusades, but 1492 is as good a time as any. Not only because it leads to Christopher Columbus—who by

5. Gerald Horne, *The Apocalypse of Settler Colonialism: The Roots of Slavery, White Supremacy, and Capitalism in Seventeenth-Century North America and the Caribbean*, New York: Monthly Review Press, 2018, 9; Enrique Dussel, *The invention of the Americas: eclipse of "the other" and the myth of modernity*, New York: Continuum, 1995, 12

the way had significant experience in West Africa where he crossed the Atlantic. If you look at his diaries and journals, he's repeatedly comparing the Indigenous populations that he encounters with West Africans to the determinant of both. So, certainly that voyage—which leads to the enslavement of the Indigenous populations, forcing them to work in mines and produce wealth, the defeat of the Aztecs and the Incas, and Mexico and Peru, and then the gradual extension of enslavement to Africans—is as good a date as any.

The Spanish in the 16th century were also involved in the Philippines and had begun a Filipino slave trade as well, bringing them to Mexico to work as bonded laborers. This is a fact that's often neglected and unmentioned. Then 1492 not only marks the origins of that horrific process but it also marks an acceleration of the Inquisition and the expulsion of the Jewish population from Spain. I deal with that in my book *The Apocalypse of Settler Colonialism* and, of course, as I said before the beginning of the final defeat of the Muslims and their final expulsion by about 1609. So yes, I think 1492 as a turning point is quite appropriate.

CS: Well, I want to move up a little to 1676 with Bacon's Rebellion. You wrote, "This was a turning point creating a cross-class collaboration between and among Europeans that has yet to disappear in North America, the headquarters of settler colonialism." As you point out, some on the left and some historians are split on this and they portray this as you wrote, "a revolt from below targeting an elite is ipso facto righteous." Can you speak on this interpretation of Bacon's Rebellion?[6]

GH: Well, you know, it's interesting. Let's look at the United States in 2018, when you have a vulgar alleged billionaire as president, actually a conman, who obviously receives significant support from the Euro-American working class and middle class—even though some of our friends on the left torture the numbers until you would think that the only people who voted for Donald Trump were Ivanka and Eric and Donald Jr. Obviously false. He had 63 million votes. He won Wisconsin, Michigan, not to mention Dixie, where routinely the right wing wins 90 percent of the Euro-American vote with an amazing cross-class coalition.

What I am suggesting is that obviously we need a new interpretation of the history of the United States. The history of its origin as a settler colony and Bacon's Rebellion is something of an exemplar

---

6. Gerald Horne, *The Apocalypse of Settler Colonialism: The Roots of Slavery, White Supremacy, and Capitalism in Seventeenth-Century North America and the Caribbean*, New York: Monthly Review Press, 2018, 28, 145

because it represents the kind of class forces that you see then materializing in 2016 November. That is to say, in Bacon's Rebellion you see that those increasingly defined as white are rising up against London and the colonial structure because they don't think the colonial structure is moving rapidly enough and aggressively enough to seize the land of the Native Americans. Of course, that's an impetus also for 1776, a scant century later when per the Royal Proclamation of 1762-63, London expressed exasperation at continually moving west expending blood and treasure, seizing the land of Native Americans so it could be turned over to real estate speculators like George Washington.

Admittedly, there was a trickle down to poor Europeans. Though, I think it would be a mistake to act like there wasn't something called the "American Dream," that is to say people starting off relatively poor and becoming wealthy. I mean that did happen, but once again like our discussion on the First Amendment, you have to turn that coin over and see how that comes at the expense of other people. It comes at the expense of seizing the land of Native Americans, enslaving Africans, etc.

London was faced with a real dilemma in 1676 because at the same time the Caribbean, particularly Barbados and Jamaica were quite typically on fire. The Native Americans in what is now New England were rebelling and it was easier to try to accommodate the European settlers in Virginia, where Bacon's Rebellion takes place, as opposed to conciliating the Africans whose unpaid labor you needed from a colonial point of view in the Caribbean or the Indigenous population in what is now New England because their land was "needed."

So, this leads of course to the accelerated move away from religion as an axis of society to race whereby you could accommodate and conciliate poor Europeans. You could give them a social promotion through the device of whiteness and also try to seize more Native American land to accommodate them and also move away from indentured labor—which was quite horrific in terms of its exploitation and move more towards enslaved African labor—which you also see after 1676. As I explain in *The Apocalypse of Settler Colonialism*, 1676 is a real turning point in the history of settler colonialism in North America.

CS: This is also when a lot of the new legislation was introduced into Virginia that gave more of a foundation of what whiteness was to be.

GH: Oh sure, you know fortunately we have a substantial literature on whiteness. It's been one of the major innovations I would say in scholarship in recent decades. You can trace this quite adequately through the existing literature.

CS: My next question: you already touched on that Nathaniel Bacon was from a wealthy family. He created this bridge to colonize Indigenous land. Do you see intersections between him and Donald J. Trump, his attack on the Latinx / Chicano population, and his instant approving of the Keystone and Dakota Access Pipelines?

GH: Well, clearly. Obviously. And it's becoming more ominous by the day. What Donald J. Trump is doing—which sadly and unfortunately many of our progressive friends have not done—is that he's globalizing and internationalizing his movement. If you notice, as we speak he's castigating Prime Minister Theresa May in London and touting as a potential successor Boris Johnson, her recently defrocked foreign secretary, who is to her right.

In Germany, he's been castigating the traditional conservative Angela Merkel and his ambassador in Berlin. Richard Grenell has gone on record as saying that he sees part of his job as boosting forces to the right of traditional conservatives, sort of these neo-fascists who now rule in both Rome and Vienna.

And what's remarkable is that despite this tremendous electoral victory in Mexico just days ago I don't see a parallel movement of our progressive friends to try to send delegations immediately, if not sooner, to Mexico City to confer with our counterparts and the progressive movement in Mexico City in light of the election of López Obrador, the next president of Mexico. Of course, not only that individual, but then you have comrades around him who are actually to his left.

Certainly, there is a parallel between Nathaniel Bacon and Donald J. Trump. In fact, I'm awaiting one of our creative artists to either do poems or paintings or plays drawing parallels between Nathaniel Bacon and Donald J. Trump.

CS: My next question involves 1688. When I teach the beginning of U.S. History to Reconstruction to check the box on the Glorious Revolution all the textbook says is William III and his wife Mary II became co-rulers in the "relatively bloodless" Glorious Revolution.[7] In your books *The Counter-Revolution of 1776* and *The Apocalypse of Settler Colonialism* you talk of something much more sinister going on—the deregulation of the slave trade, can you elaborate on this?

GH: Well, what's basically happening as I talk about in *The Apocalypse of Settler Colonialism* is that you have the slow but steady rise

---

7. James Roark, Michael Johnson, Patricia Cohen, Sarah Stage and Susan Hartman, *The American Promise: A Concise History*, 5th ed., Boston: Bedform/St. Martin's, 99

in the 17th century of the merchant class. They have what might be called a premature victory with the rise of Oliver Cromwell in the 1640s and the beheading of a king. One of the turning points comes in 1655 when under Oliver Cromwell and the English are able to oust the Spanish from Jamaica, which opens up more land for European settlement, opens up more avenues for enslavement of Africans.

This leads to the sugar boom, creating more wealth pouring into the coffers of London, which allows London to build more ships to bout with the Dutch, who are a preeminent power at that time. More ships to transport the sugar across the Atlantic, build other ports for ships to transport settlers into the Americas, more ships to transport enslaved Africans. Of course, you have a working class building these ships, and planting the seeds of capitalism in England. You have the rise of a banking industry because voyages of the slave ships and financing of all this industry has to be financed through banks. You have the rise of an insurance industry because there are shipboard insurrections, you have to insure against the Africans taking over a ship and throwing the crew into the sea.

So, you have a circle devoid of virtue being created generating tremendous wealth, which is in some ways at odds and in contradiction with the power of the monarch who is seeking to keep the African slave trade in particular under the thumb of the monarch per the organization of the Royal African Company in 1672, but all along you have merchants who are seeking to end that monopoly and clamoring for deregulation of the African slave trade. "Free trade" in Africans was their cry and finally in 1688 you see a triumph of the merchants.[8]

You see a clipping of the wings of the monarch with the monarch on a glidepath to where Queen Elizabeth is today. That is to say, quite wealthy and quite powerful but certainly not as powerful as earlier monarchs. You have the rise, the acceleration I should say, of the African slave trade with the deregulation of the African slave trade with the monarchs descending upon Africa with the maniacal energy of crazed bees manacling and handcuffing every African in sight, dragging them across the Atlantic to produce even more wealth. Then of course, you have the rise of parliamentary power as well with merchants claiming a portion of political power to the

8. Gerald Horne, *The Apocalypse of Settler Colonialism: The Roots of Slavery, White Supremacy, and Capitalism in Seventeenth-Century North America and the Caribbean*, New York: Monthly Review Press, 2018, 127

detriment of the monarch through the rise of parliament. That in sum is how I represent 1688.

CS: When I had first read *The Counter-Revolution of 1776* it really opened my eyes, and I started integrating that into the early US North American history class. So, thank you for your work. The next question is in response to migrant families being separated. Director and Ojibwe, Jesse Wente, tweeted, "Colonial states separate children from parents because they know it works. It destroys and traumatizes for generations. It's an attack on the future as well as the present. It's not partisan issue, it's a colonial one."[9] Can you speak on this and this long legacy of colonialism and white supremacy?

GH: There's a young historian at Emory University in Atlanta by the name of Dawn Peterson who has just written a book on the inglorious history of Native American adoption into European settler colonial families.[10] You can draw a straight line from that dastardly history to recent scandals, for example, not only on the Texas Mexico border, because what's going to happen now is that the alleged inability to find parents of some of these youth who have been sequestered, due to their being doled to U.S. families.

Simultaneously, look at what's been going on in El Salvador for years now. You've had a kind of fraudulent adoption industry taking place where youth from El Salvador are being adopted by US settler families. Often times by means that are hardly fair, mostly foul. It reminds me—actually I think this is one of your fellow Coloradans—of the US military officer in the 19th century who most infamously said, "Nits make lice," and so therefore you not only have to deal with Native American adults you have to deal with Native American infants.[11]

CS: Is that Chivington?

GH: Yes, I think that was Chivington. Because they grew up to be adults. So, given this history and also given the history of US foreign policy, for example in the 1970s, US imperialism supported the Argentine junta of which was "notorious" for seizing the children of

9. Everyday Feminism, Twitter post, June 20, 2018. https://twitter.com/EvrydayFeminism/status/1009466069378125824?s=20&t=Zsd4VH9heE7 3LfqRAeHWqg

10. Dawn Peterson, *Indians in the Family: Adoption and the Politics of Antebellum Expansion*, Cambridge: Harvard University Press, 2017

11. Brenden Rensink, "The Sand Creek Phenomenon: The Complexity and Difficulty of Undertaking a Comparative Study of Genocide vis-à-vis the Northern American West," 2009: https://digitalcommons.unl.edu/historydiss/26

leftists and dissidents, throwing the parents into the Atlantic Ocean and then dulling out the children to be adopted by military officers in the junta. In fact, that policy was so notorious it led to a quite affecting film, which I recommend called *The Official Story*, it's an Argentine film.

Then, of course, we don't even have to talk about the African slave trade, which quite notoriously, the images are rampant of slave owners and slave traders ripping infants from the arms of weeping mothers and selling the mother down the river while selling the infant down another river. In fact, it was so notorious it was a key in the penultimate scene in the TV series *Roots*, which played on US television and of course there was a second version that came out a few decades later. These are shall we say open secrets. They're not secrets at all. In fact, they're open scandals. I think that's the better phrase that can be used.

CS: These atrocities tie right back into the Carlisle School of separating Native Americans and trying to take away their culture as well. It was cultural genocide that took place.

GH: Clearly. It is a clear case of appropriation. It's interesting, doing this research on the 1500s and dealing with the Muslim population in Spain, for example, after the Muslims are ousted after ruling for hundreds of years, the new Christian authorities ban certain dances that the Muslims engage in, certain food and recipes that the Muslims use, and it's a very curious form of not necessarily cultural appropriation but cultural liquidation, which is also a phenomenon that we have witnessed under settler colonialism in North America.

CS: And you also had European philosophers' kind of aiding that right? You wrote about Montesquieu who said, "Islam created despotism."[12]

GH: Yes, right. This whole conflict, circa 1512. It's fair to say that the Ottomans, the Ottoman Turks probably had the most powerful military and in *The Apocalypse of Settler Colonialism* I posit that the defeat of the Ottomans in 1683 at the gates of Vienna was a turning point in terms of the rise of Western European settler colonialism because up until the early 19th century you still had cases of US nationals, Euro-Americans being kidnapped and enslaved off the coast of North Africa.

---

12. Gerald Horne, *The Apocalypse of Settler Colonialism: The Roots of Slavery, White Supremacy, and Capitalism in Seventeenth-Century North America and the Caribbean*, New York: Monthly Review Press, 2018, 69

Although it begins to decline after 1683, and once Western Europeans ran less risk of being enslaved themselves, they fell southward into Africa—that is to say, being enslaved in Algeria or sold into the slave markets in Istanbul. With 1683 there is less of a chance for that, even though as I said it continues up until the 19th century. This whole question of Islam is a major factor that is not only rearing its head in the 21st century but this conflict between Muslims and Christians has been a staple of European history stretching back to the founding of Islam in what might be called the 7th century.

CS: This is my last question. I think you have already tapped into your famed crystal ball with where you went with your last response, but the underlying message I see in your work is internationalism and you end your book stating: "This impact of global currents on nefarious domestic trends should remind today's strugglers that their interests would be better served by spending less time debating with the American Civil Liberties Union about the 'rights' of fascists and more time conversing with potential and actual allies in Beijing, Moscow, Havana, Brussels, Pretoria and elsewhere."[13] Can you speak about how throughout US history, such as in Chile or Guatemala, the US has supported fascism in its foreign policy, the roots it laid, and the current attack on Antifa, such as anti-mask legislation in the US and current anti-fascist movements?

GH: Well, I've been thinking about Chile a lot lately. I'm quite familiar with the overthrow of the socialist government on 11 September 1973 of Salvador Allende and the rise of Augusto Pinochet and one of the reasons I've been thinking about it is because many progressive Chileans were just shocked by the rise of fascism. They thought that their democratic structures were less fragile and brittle than they actually were.

It reminds me of the United States because people in the United States were shocked by the rise of Donald Trump and his neo-fascist trends. They overestimated the strength of their "democratic" institutions. Although I must say that people in the United States have less reason to be shocked than the people of Chile even though, of course, you have settler colonialism in Chile and you had a certain level of enslavement in Chile as well, but not to the dimensions that you had in North America.

It's shocking to me that in a country built upon genocide of Native Americans and enslavement of Africans to whom the constitution and the Bill of Rights did not apply, that people could be shocked,

13. Ibid., 192

that might serve as a precursor and a precondition for the rise of neo-fascism in 2018. Obviously, there's been an overestimation it seems to me of democratic traditions in the United States, which of course brings us to Guatemala and the overthrow of the Arbenz government in 1954 and the subsequent studies that suggested that US imperialism helped the Guatemalan military execute a kind of genocide against the Indigenous population of Guatemala. My next book deals with Southern Africa and the neo-fascist trends that proceeded in 1994 in the election of Nelson Mandela, supported all along the line by US imperialism and then of course I've already spoken about how the Trump team is bolstering neo-fascists in Rome and Vienna and Berlin and elsewhere. So, obviously we have a lot of work to do, that's for sure. But I think our work could be facilitated if we had a clearer understanding of how we got to this point and if we cast aside these fantasies and illusions that masquerade as US history.

CS: And you're calling for working with anti-fascists in other countries as well, with this internationalism that you describe?

GH: Absolutely, reference what I just said about delegations to Mexico City to begin with.

Chapter 3

Race and Religion, the Embryos of Whiteness
December 12, 2020

CS: This first question digs into your history. I was wondering if you could describe a pivotal moment in your history or transformative experience that helped you see through the propaganda of US history and settler hegemony. Also, what made you question what was being taught in your K-12 education and dominant culture as a whole?

GH: Well, it's difficult to point to one moment. I was born and raised in St. Louis, Missouri, during the era of Jim Crow, and certainly from an early age it became very difficult to accept the mythology of the United States as a shining city on the hill and this epicenter of democracy. When you can't go into certain restaurants and are treated like a third-class citizen, you don't have to be a genius or an Oracle to begin to suspect that there's something awry. So, I would say that growing up under those conditions was pivotal in terms of my own evolution, as a scholar and a thinker.

CS: I remember in one of your works, you had spoken about one of the political leaders of India who came to the US and was persecuted in the South. You compared that to Angela Davis notifying people she spoke French to combat this Jim Crow South.[1]

GH: Well, that point was speaking to how the rules work in the United States. They tend to have a particular animosity towards the descendants of mainland enslaved Africans. They have an animosity, of course towards Black people who have roots in the Caribbean and Africa. But they have a heightened animosity, at least historically—it'll be interesting to suggest whether or not there has been an evolution since Jim Crow began to retreat. But certainly, during the heyday of Jim Crow, that was the case. When Angela Davis was in

---

1. Gerald Horne, *The End of Empires: African Americans and India*, Philadelphia: Temple University Press, 2008

Birmingham, Alabama, seeking to escape Jim Crow by speaking French, she was reflecting what I'm referring to, because that meant that she was not a descendant of mainland slave Africans.

Now, today, with the erosion of Jim Crow, and the concomitant heightening of anti-immigrant hysteria, it's not clear if that old trope still persists. I think that's one of the reasons why some of us study history. It's because things change, things evolve. That's something everybody acknowledges in the abstract. You know, the song "Everything Must Change"? But when it comes to the concrete, people can sometimes have difficulty in understanding that things do change and that things evolve and that may be an example of what I'm referring to.

CS: Now, going back and talking about this evolution through colonialism and whiteness: as you write about in your work, *The Dawning of the Apocalypse*, you speak of the conversion from religion to race, that foments whiteness under class collaboration and I really see this embodied in the long project of the Doctrine of Discovery, papal bull, that sent over Columbus. Then this Doctrine of Discovery became the legal precedent in Johnson vs. Mcintosh in 1823, which went into the Supreme Court ruling, which was further cited by the late Justice Ruth Bader Ginsburg in the City of Sherrill vs. Oneida Indian Nation of New York, where she actually used the Doctrine of Discovery in her ruling.[2] Can you speak about the far reaches of this precedent? In your book, *The Dawning of the Apocalypse* you talk about the 1551 decree by Charles V of separating races. There is a long history and legacy of white supremacy and it's obvious how it pans out with these precedents today.

GH: Well, with regard to the book itself, in some ways, the starting point of the book—at least in the loose sense, not in the rigid sense—is about 1,300 years ago with the rise of Islam, which takes off like a rocket and by 1095, you have Western European Christendom that's uniting in what's called a crusade to reclaim the area they call the holy land, from what they consider to be Muslim domination. Therein, I suggest you begin to see the roots of what emerges as whiteness, that is to say, it's originally grounded not necessarily in the concept of race, but in religion and with Christian versus Muslim.

A further step along this rocky road takes place in 1453 when the Ottoman Turks who are predominantly Sunni Muslim, oust the

---

2. Steven Newcomb, *Pagans in the Promised Land: Decoding the Doctrine of Christian Discovery*, Golden: Fulcrum Publishers, 2008; Kevin Bruyneel, *Settler Memory: The disavowal of Indigeneity and the Politics of Race in the United States*, Chapel Hill: University of North Carolina Press, 2021

Christians from Constantinople, today Istanbul, which injects and induces existential fear in Western European Christendom. They suspected that the Vatican, now sited in what we call Italy, would be next. That further unites them and further helps to underscore the roots of this phenomenon that we refer to as whiteness.

Indeed, it's in 1492—a pivotal year in world history—when not only are the Muslims ousted from their final place of rule of the Iberian Peninsula, speaking of Spain, this is after a real fear that Muslims would take over a good deal of Western Europe, just like they had taken over Constantinople. Ultimately of course, Muslim people altogether were expelled from Spain—as a people, each and every one it was thought—by 100 years later. But 1492 also marks the acceleration of the Inquisition, whereby sharper lines are drawn, shall we say, between Catholics and non-Catholics, which particularly hits the Jewish population, very hard, and very rigorously. Many of them are expelled and of course, 1492 also marks Columbus sailing the ocean blue and perhaps not surprisingly, it's suspected that there were escaping Jewish folk on the ship that Columbus was sailing across the Atlantic, although many of them wound up in Ottoman Turkey. Many of them wound up in North Africa. Many of them wound up in what we would call the Netherlands and of course, many of them wound up in London, which is curious because London had expelled its Jewish population by 1291. I'll explain in a moment or two why London would absorb and accept the Jewish population after they've expelled their own Jewish population 200 years before Spain did.

So, therefore, in 1492 you see Columbus, sailing across the Atlantic. Of course, they begin to expropriate the Indigenous population of the Americas, inflicting a bloody genocide upon them. You also begin to see the beginnings of an African slave trade, although of course, there's also enslavement of the Indigenous population as well in addition to liquidating them.

Another turning point comes in 1517 with the rise of Martin Luther and the Protestant secession from the Catholic Church. Martin Luther and those who followed him thought that the Catholics were corrupt, for reasons that need not detain us here, and the Protestant faith spread like wildfire throughout Europe by the 1530s. It had become the state religion in London and that's still the case to a certain degree today. I'm sure you know the story about Henry VIII, and how he wanted a divorce and how he couldn't get a divorce because he was a Catholic and I won't dispute that story. Although I will add that when Henry VIII seceded from the Catholic Church, it allowed him to expropriate a good deal of Catholic property and it also, of course, allowed him to get a divorce. With the secession of London from the Catholic Church, it ignites these religious wars between Catholics and Protestants throughout the 1500s throughout, the 16th century and to make a long story short, and to give you opportunity to inject your own intelligence, what happens is that Spain has religion as a qualifier for settlement.

As late as the 19th century when Steven F. Austin and his comrades wanted to settle in what is now Texas or Tejas about 200 years ago, they had to profess Catholicism. Whereas London, the scrappy underdog, when it began to try to challenge Spain for the right to claim the territory of the Indigenous population in the Americas they moved away from religion as a qualifier to race, which gets me back to why they began to absorb the Jewish population after expelling them in 1291. In other words, they drew sharp lines of demarcation between those who were of European ancestry and those who were not of European ancestry and on the other side of that line, of course, were the Indigenous population and the African, whereas the Spanish for example, they would allow for Black conquistadors, if they professed Catholicism.

Historically, you had a substantial free Negro population in Spanish Cuba, for example, who had their own military brigade as early as the 1500s. This was not necessarily the case, to put it mildly in the English settlements, they drew a sharper line of demarcation between Blacks and those defined as white. And therein you begin to see the roots of our dilemma in the revolting spawn of London speaking of today's United States of America, because settler colonialism, the system under which we are still laboring, which involved initially English, and those they have been warring with, meaning Irish and Scots crossing the Atlantic, magically rebranding themselves as white once they land on these shores and beginning to seize the land of the Native Americans.

Settler colonialism, that system involves class collaboration, that is to say, it involves collaboration between wealthy Europeans and non-wealthy Europeans, with the non-wealthy being the foot soldiers and the non-wealthy feeling that if they go along with the program, they can become wealthy, which may help to explain, for example, the US Civil War 1861 to 1865 when the Confederate states of the South, fought the United States because they wanted to preserve African slavery, enslavement of Africans forevermore. Their army was overwhelmingly and disproportionately comprised of non-slave owners. So, there was class collaboration between slave owners, who were at the wheel of the locomotive, and those defined as white, who we're non-slave owners, but the latter thought that if they went along with the program they could become slave owners too, which made the project worthwhile.

Then, in 2020, in a phenomenon that I'm afraid to say, me and my friends on the left still, they can't believe is happening: You have 73-74 million people, mostly defined as "white," mostly not of the one percent. It's mathematically impossible, if not imprecise, for 70 million people shall we say, to be part of the one percent in a nation of 330 million. The numbers don't add up and I think you can't understand this phenomenon unless you understand class collaboration and settler colonialism. Or to use another example that I've started to use of late: in 1991, David Duke in Louisiana, a Nazi won 55 percent of the Euro-American vote in a race for governance. Now, the sardonic and bitter joke that I tell is that when our friends on the left start to comprehend that phenomenon, they'll say something like, "Well, the voters, they saw that he was a member of the National Socialist Party. So, they thought he was a socialist. That's why they voted for David Duke." Well, you know, the joke may be on me because I'm afraid to say that, you know, this attempt to rationalize the strength of the ultra-right in the United States, ultimately, is going to have people like myself, although not exclusively me, of course, as the ultimate victim.

CS: That's an extreme example of cognitive dissonance to say it mildly. You brought up so much when you were talking about how the Jewish community was expelled from England in 1291. Going back to this project of whiteness, you said that they were in some circles referred to as new Christians?

GH: That's right.

CS: Okay, and then to kind of hone this conversation on the genealogy of whiteness. One work I read long ago was Theodore Allen's *The Invention of the White Race*. He wrote about the legislation of whiteness in Virginia. You eloquently wrote how the history of settler colonialism has strong roots in Florida and New Mexico: "The history of Virginia and New England, which wrongly deems either or both to be the seedbed of settler colonialism in what is now the United States—and, in the long run, the United States itself has to be adjudged with this point firmly in mind."[3]

So, when you're breaking this open more and tracing this, you also mentioned that this embryo of whiteness was seen with Queen Isabel, who was said to have English blood in her veins; you also wrote

---

3. Gerald Horne, *The Dawning of the Apocalypse: The Roots of Slavery, White Supremacy, Settler Colonialism, and Capitalism in the Long Sixteenth Century*, New York: Monthly Review Press, 19

of Lepanto fever and the great naval battle. In addition, you wrote about how Italian colonialism inspired Iberian colonialism, which you succinctly put into settler colonialism as a pan-European project containing this germ of whiteness. Building on what you were saying, from going to 2020 to your previous books with Bacon's Rebellion where you were talking about class collaboration, you really bring this timeline into a longer narrative. Can you speak more about this misconception of Virginia being the seedbed of settler colonialism, which I think you've already spoken to, but to break it open more?

GH: Basically, if you look at North America, it's obvious that the Spanish created a settlement in St. Augustine, Florida in 1565, and Augustine, Florida still exists. If you look at my footnotes, you'll see that I did quite a bit of research at the St. Augustine Historical Society. I recommend St. Augustine, Florida; it's right on the Atlantic Ocean, it's very scenic; you have buildings, including a slave market that is still in existence from the bad old days; you still have these very narrow streets and ancient architecture. But in any case, it's clear that Florida is the origin of settler colonialism in the United States of America. And indeed, when the English sail into what they call Virginia, in 1607, named after the so-called virgin queen, Queen Elizabeth, that the Spanish from their perch in St. Augustine want to stop them but they're too busy fighting the Indigenous population and their African allies. So, they're tied down. One of the reasons why we're sitting here speaking English, is a result of the successful venture of the English in 1607, is because the Africans and the Indigenous in Florida were so adept at battling the Spanish. Then, of course, if you look across the continent at the US state we now refer to as New Mexico, it was about 30 years after St. Augustine that the Spanish conquistadores began moving north from New Spain or Mexico, as we now call it, Mexico City in particular, to settle to use that euphemism, New Mexico. What's interesting about that, to connect it to our previous discussion, is that it's suspected that the conquistadores who invaded, what we now call New Mexico, we're probably of Jewish origins, but they were passing, they were actually so-called new Christians. The new Christians played a pivotal role with regard to this new era that was opening with Columbus's voyage as noted, some of them might have been on the ships with Columbus.

They played a pivotal role, because many of them were expelled to Africa, for example, from the Iberian Peninsula, and many of them became cartographers or map makers in Africa and drew up maps that proved to be essential when the moment arrived for the Western

Europeans to sell into Africa to take Africans and transport them across the Atlantic to be enslaved. So, I like Theodore Allen's book. I recommend it—the *Invention of the White Race*, Volumes 1 and 2. But I think that in focusing on Virginia, which I understand—I guess what you could say is that of Virginia, it carries the roots of Anglo settler colonialism to be more precise. It's just like the *New York Times* 1619 project, where the idea was put forward, August 1619 marks the date when enslaved Africans were brought to Virginia, when in fact, as my book suggests, in the 1520s, from their perch in Santo Domingo, the Spanish brought enslaved Africans to the area north of Florida, but the enslaved Africans rebelled, joined the Indigenous comrades and sent the Spanish fleeing and packing back to the Caribbean. So sometimes there's a sort of making an equivalent of settler colonialism and Anglo settler colonialism when actually we're talking about two distinct phenomena. It was the Spanish who were the pioneers.

CS: That's an important distinction. Going back to St. Augustine, you said that Spain's defeat on August 7, 1588, was the origins of the USA because of that defeat Spain suffered. I was really interested reading in your book about Jacques de Sores and when you wrote about how he struck fear into Menendez de Aviles, who you say is the founding father of settler colonialism in the US. It reminded me of Thomas Jefferson's fear after Toussaint Louverture and the Haitian Revolution, as kind of the same fear that was struck into Menendez. I was wondering if you could tell more of the story on Jacques de Sores, who you refer to as John Brown of the Pan-Caribbean?

GH: Well, it's a very interesting story. So, you have all this contestation, particularly between the English, the Spanish, the Portuguese, and the French. Then you have contradictions, those splits amongst those groups. For example, you have splits between French Catholics and French Protestants; the French Protestants known as the Huguenots. And to make a long story short, what happens is that the Huguenots, the French Protestants tried to gain an advantage over their French Catholic competitors, and over other European competitors, by cutting deals with enslaved Africans who are under the jurisdiction of Spain, for example. So, Jacques de Sores or de Soria, and you can check my book for the different spellings of his name if you're interested in gaining more information about him. He was a French Protestant mariner or corsair.

The Spanish will call him a pirate, who would sail into Spanish territory, including Cuba, by the way, and try to overthrow Spanish rule by promising to give a better deal, to the Negroes. I have a piece coming out in *The Nation*, the New York based publication in a few weeks, where I talk about Jacques de Sores; Jacque de Soria is sort of a template for what happened subsequently.[4] Because what happened subsequently, is that the Africans in South Carolina in 1739, they ally with the Spanish to try to overthrow London's settlement in South Carolina, Stono's Revolt, the bloodiest slave revolt in British North American, colonial North America. Then, in August 1814, during the War of 1812, when London and the United States were at war, you have the Negroes in Washington, DC, who align with the red coats, and send President James Madison and his garrulous spouse, Dolly, fleeing into the streets. Then they hop on British vessels and flee to Trinidad and Tobago, where their descendants continue to reside.

Then we're turning to Florida, which about 200 years ago becomes US territory. But Britain, like Jacques de Sores, thought it could gain an advantage by cutting favorable deals with the enslaved population under US rule. So, in northern Florida as the US is about to take over, the British helped to establish what's called the Negro fort, where you had one of the most well-armed encampments of Black people in North America, making the Black Panther Party of the 20th century seem tame by comparison. Indeed, Andrew Jackson, the favorite president of the 45th US president, Mr. Trump, he gains his reputation waging war against the Negro fort, which was eventually liquidated. Jacques de Sores begins an example, then it continues in the 20th century, with many Black people aligning with Japan, as I talk about in my book *Facing the Rising Sun*.[5]

Many Black people align with Moscow during the Cold War as discussed in my book on Paul Robeson.[6] W.E.B. Du Bois wrote a number of books on that subject. So, the issue being that even for the oppressors, it's dangerous to engage in oppression because the oppressed will cut a deal with your antagonists and seek to overthrow you and I think that lesson has not been learned sufficiently by the US ruling class, which is not necessarily renowned for its political intelligence and its political acumen. That's one of the reasons I've spent so much time on the 16th century book talking about this French corsair. Speaking of the Protestants and the Catholics in France, that illustrates another theme of this book that's still relevant. Because there was murderous war between the French Protestants

---

4. Gerald Horne, "A Poisonous Legacy: New York City and the persistence of the Middle Passage," *The Nation*, February 24, 2021, https://www.thenation.com/article/society/john-harris-last-slave-ships/

5. Gerald Horne, *Facing the Rising Sun: African Americans, Japan, and the Rise of Afro-Asian Solidarity*, New York: New York University Press, 2018

6. Gerald Horne, *Paul Robeson: The Artist as Revolutionary*, London: Pluto Press, 2016

and the French Catholics culminating in the early 1570s, with St. Bartholomew's Massacre, when the Catholics invited the Protestants to meetings all over France and then fell upon them and massacred them by the thousands in Rwanda style genocide.

Now, what's interesting, number one, is that this kind of approach was oftentimes used against Native Americans. Actually, it was also used against Toussaint Louverture in Haiti when he was captured in 1802. When he was fighting the French invaders, they had invited him to a meeting and then they arrested him and then sent him into exile in Europe, where he died. Of course, it was oftentimes the settlers in North America, they'd invite Native American leaders to have meetings, and then fall upon them and massacre them. That particular strategy is echoed in what one set of Europeans often did to another set of Europeans. But as noted, that kind of antagonism between and amongst Europeans began to dissipate as they crossed the Atlantic and decided that the better part of wisdom was to rebrand themselves as "white" and to unite under one umbrella so as to better combat the Indigenous who, of course, are many different ethnic groups. Just speaking of my part of North America, the Kiowas, the Comanches, the Lipan Apache, the Arapaho in your part of North America, the Caddos. The Cherokees are forced to evacuate from Georgia to Oklahoma, during the Trail of Tears. So, the Europeans, they unite under this one umbrella of whiteness, even though before they were split, between French Protestants, French Catholics, English versus Irish, English versus Scots, British versus German, German versus Poles, Pole versus Russian, Serb versus Croat, Northern Italian versus Southern Italian. Once they cross the Atlantic they're all united under one identity politics, militarized identity politics is what I call it. It's quite a story and then you mention Lepanto, this is a pivotal war, because recall that just a few moments ago we were discussing the ascendancy of the Muslims, particularly the Ottoman Turks, and how it was that they began to be eclipsed.

Part of the reason that they were eclipsed was because of Lepanto. This is where the Catholics in particular unite in the early 1570s to inflict a stinging defeat upon them. But also, London, one of the reasons we're speaking English today is that London cut deals with the Ottoman Turks against the Spanish Catholics in particular, who they see is the more formidable foe and I think the Ottoman Turks underestimate London. And in fact, in the 1530s when Henry VIII, as noted, expels the Catholics and liquidates a goodly number of them. As I say in the book, on one day you see these monks in Catholic robes walking the streets of London, the next day they're gone, liquidated, get out of here. And then what happens is that Henry

VIII sends a good deal of the wealth expropriated from the Catholics to Ottoman Turkey to solidify the alliance against the Catholics. Over the last 500 years, you've had the story of the decline of the Muslim power that was Ottoman Turkey that culminates of course in 1918 when they're on the losing side during World War I, but you may have noticed that with the rise of—I'm not going to draw an equivalence between the forces I'm about to mention, and Ottoman Turkey—but as noted, it's unavoidable that today you have the rise of the Islamic State, al Qaeda, and from their point of view and their way of thinking, they feel that they're trying to revive and relive the glory days of Ottoman Turkey. Certainly, if you look at the African continent, which has some of the weakest political structures on this small planet, they're making significant gains in northern Nigeria, Sahel region, Mali, Burkina Faso, Niger, Chad, even in Mozambique, so that's something to keep your eye on.

CS: Speaking of that: this new report just came out by *The Intercept* as well, about these CIA backed Afghan death squads, that have been accused of massacring children in Afghanistan.[7]

GH: Well, what's interesting about that is that the International Criminal Court in The Hague just a few months ago opened a case against the United States to investigate the US for war crimes in Afghanistan. So, what happens is that the US per Secretary of State Michael Pompeo immediately slapped sanctions on leaders of the International Criminal Court, including the chief prosecutor, the Gambian barrister, Fatou Bensouda, and the United States reach was so extensive, that it not only froze her bank account, although she doesn't live in the United States, it froze the bank accounts with many of her relatives. The United States takes this idea of being investigated for war crimes, for some reason, they take that very seriously.

CS: Just like when the US pulled out of the International Criminal Court when they were accused in the 1980s with Nicaragua.

GH: Oh, mining the harbors? Precisely.

CS: Thank you for going into all those topics. I was really interested in Amador who fought against slavery in São Tomé. You wrote about him stating: Amador "should be seen as part of the Pantheon that includes Nat Turner and Hatuey in Cuba, they slaughtered

---

7. Andrew Quilt, "The CIA's Afghan Death Squads," *The Intercept*, December 18, 2020: https://theintercept.com/2020/12/18/afghanistan-cia-militia-01-strike-force/

Europeans in churches, including priests and an army of thousands under his leadership destroyed virtually all of the despised sugar mills."[8]

GH: Well, you know, it's interesting. As some may have inferred from my remarks thus far, there is a critique in this book of the bloodier aspects of organized religion, particularly Christianity, and that helps to shed light about Amador, because of course, as you know, I did some books on Hawaii some years ago, *The White Pacific* and then *Fighting in Paradise*.[9] The Indigenous alliance, at least many of them, part of their folklore is that in the 19th century, the European and Euro-American missionaries began to arrive, and we had some land, and they had the Bible. But it wasn't long before we were missionized, and we had the Bible, and they had the land. Obviously, there is a critique to be made of the bloodier aspects of settler colonialism and of colonialism itself because Amador for example, what he was fighting was taking place in Africa itself, actually in São Tomé and Príncipe to be more precise.

What was happening is that in the late 1500s, the Europeans were trying to establish these sugar plantations in São Tomé and Príncipe, and then have enslaved African labor work that land, but then Amador rose up and began to lead an army of thousands. You chase them out, and then at that point, you begin to see the Portuguese in particular, began to focus on Brazil. They say, "you know what, maybe we should just cross the Atlantic, set up our sugar plantations in Brazil, and then drag the Africans further away from the African continent, as opposed to enslaving Africans on their own soil." Of course, there's an analogue to the Indigenous population because even though there was an enslavement process of the Indigenous population, oftentimes in the Americas, they were liquidated, or they were shipped out to be enslaved in the slave markets of Ottoman Turkey, Algeria, or even the Caribbean.

Then Africans were brought over from the Atlantic to be the major bulk of the enslaved labor force. So, Amador, as noted, needs to be celebrated because he helped to rescue Africa from an even more horrible fate and let me also say that with regard to the comment you

---

8. Gerald Horne, *The Dawning of the Apocalypse: The Roots of Slavery, White Supremacy, Settler Colonialism, and Capitalism in the Long Sixteenth Century*, New York: Monthly Review Press, 192

9. Gerald Horne, *The White Pacific: U.S. Imperialism and Black Slavery in the South Seas After the Civil War*, Honolulu: University of Hawai'i Press, 2007; Gerald Horne, *Fighting in Paradise: Labor Unions, Racism, and Communists in the Making of Modern Hawai'i*, Honolulu: University of Hawai'i Press, 2011

made about how he was attacking the missionaries: there's this New Zealand film that I recommend, I think it's on YouTube, although I'm sure you could find it, it's called *Utu*. It's about the Europeans or the British invading what they call New Zealand, in the middle of the 19th century, and the Maoris who are expert fighters. So, there's a scene in *Utu* where this Indigenous leader, he comes into this church where the Europeans are trying to missionize as they say, the Indigenous population and the Indigenous population is sitting in the pews and the leader, he marches up to the pulpit, takes out a hatchet and attacks the missionary. It's a remarkable scene.

CS: I'm going to check out that film.

GH: Check it out, *Utu*. Let me digress. I've done books on film history and so for the longest time I've been watching various films. I also recommend in that regard, *The Chant of Jimmie Blacksmith*. It's an Australian film about Indigenous resistance in Australian. I would also recommend *The Killing of Angel Street*. That's another Australian film. It deals more with contemporary Australia, but of class struggles in Australia. Let's see, I probably could think of a few more, but those are the ones that come to mind immediately.

CS: Okay. Awesome. I'll check those out. I love your books on Hollywood, as well.

GH: Oh good.

CS: Along with Amador I was really interested when you wrote about how in 1522 that there was a large-scale uprising during the Christmas holiday, where a sugar mill belonging to the son of Christopher Columbus and his comrades was burned down and also there was this revolt led by a man named Miguel or was that a different revolt?

GH: Yes, that's a different revolt. You know, I talk about so many revolts in that book that I understand why they all sort of run together. But what's interesting about that revolt is that it's replicated. If you were to do a typology of slave revolts, one of the things you would find is they often take place around this time of year—hint, hint—that is to say, during the so called Christmas holiday, when there was this feeling that the settlers would be inebriated, distracted, celebrating, and the oppressed would seize that opportunity to rise up. I mean, that happens, not only the 1500s, but the 1600s, 1700s, 1800s. It's quite remarkable.

CS: Thanks for sharing that and breaking open that history on those revolts. Speaking of revolts and internationalism, I want to ask you about May 25, 2020, when George Floyd was murdered. You saw this internationalism with people protesting at US embassies. I believe some African nations filed a UN inquiry into US racism and I was wondering if you could talk about this internationalism and where we are at right now with the fight against global white supremacy.

GH: Well, it's interesting that the United Nations Human Rights Council investigation is ongoing. In fact, and it walks in the footsteps of previous efforts such as the effort spearheaded by the late great Paul Robeson in 1950 when he and an organization now defunct called the Civil Rights Congress (CRC), filed a petition with the United Nations charging the United States with genocide against Black people. You can still find the book, *We Charge Genocide*, at various libraries—and it is still available through International Publishers. Then in 1978, there was another effort led by the National Conference of Black Lawyers. As a young lawyer, I was part of that effort to file a similar sort of petition against the United States, at the highest bodies of the United Nations. As you suggest, after 25 May 2020, with the lynching on camera of George Floyd, there was quite a remarkable display of international solidarity with the Black American community in Australia, New Zealand, London, Berlin and elsewhere.

We really need organizational forums, certain organizational forums to capitalize on that kind of solidarity because one of the themes of my work has been the importance of international solidarity and propelling struggle forward in these United States of America. Because class collaboration has been so potent, it reminds me, it's like the silent gas that kills, it's potent, but it's oftentimes not seen or perceived. It's like you see these stories occasionally in the newspaper, about how a person would leave their car running in the garage then the carbon monoxide escapes that kills the family and such. Well, obviously, the family is not aware of this gas that's killing them. That's how class collaboration works. It's oftentimes not visible to the naked eye. It's almost like it's normal. Reference, the comment I just made about David Duke, a Nazi getting 55 percent of the Euro-American vote in 1991 for Governor of Louisiana.

That was a clear example of class collaboration. But it was not necessarily problematized in that sense. And so, because of the potency of this class collaboration, it makes all the more important our attempt to forge global solidarity, which is even more possible now given the rise of the Internet, you can find out what's happening at any corner of the world where you can communicate over email, text, various other platforms, as they say. So, international solidarity has never been more possible. The only question is, are we in a position to execute?

CS: I was really grateful for your research on digging into Sir Francis Drake and John Hawkins. A lot of times they're glanced over.

When I went through my K-12 education I actually didn't even learn about them. I think when I learned about Sir Francis Drake, it did not involve any of the history of showing him being the monster he was. I had heard about the truth of John Hawkins through RZA ironically, through listening to an old *Gravediggaz* song called "The Night the Earth Cried." In that song he says, "Separated to portions and tricked by John Haughty Hawkins," that was a bar in his song, which actually made me look into him in middle school.[10] Your work really broke open these two figures and showed them really for what they were as being pirates and thieves. I was wondering if you had anything to add?

GH: What's interesting is that Sir Francis Drake is considered a hero. I remember when I was doing research in San Francisco; in San Francisco, California, there's still a number of buildings and hotels named after Sir Francis Drake. I find it very interesting that understandably and justifiably there is an effort in the United States to remove the name of Columbus from various buildings and schools, etc. But Sir Francis Drake has gotten a pass so far, and I underline so far.

Sir Francis Drake and his comrade, John Hawkins, they are major reasons why we're sitting here in North America communicating in English, because basically, he was a parasite upon a parasite. What I mean is, a lot of the early wealth in London, under Queen Elizabeth was built by the piracy of Sir Francis Drake, who would raid Spanish ships, groaning with wealth looted from the Incas of today's Peru and the Aztecs of today's Mexico, and as the ships were crossing the Atlantic, Sir Francis Drake's ships would come out of nowhere and then board the Spanish ships, take all the wealth, kill all the people and then eventually transfer all that wealth to London. That's what I mean about being parasites upon parasites, the Spanish are the parasites, acting parasitically upon the Indigenous Incas and Aztecs. Then, Sir Francis Drake would then loot from them, speaking of the Spanish, and that's how London got in the passing lane by basically, being a parasite upon a parasite. Of course, I'll leave it to the political psychologists to wonder if the lineal descendants of Anglo culture still reflects that parasitical nature of being parasites upon parasites, which may be the worst parasites of all.

CS: That's well put. For my last question, I wanted to talk to you about some of the newer projects you're working on. I had read that you were working or toying with the new idea of US Black Americans

---

10. Gravediggaz, "The Night the Earth Cried," track 9 on *The Pick, the Sickle and the Shovel*, Gee Street/V2/BMG Records, 1997, CD.

in the 19th century wielding ancient history. I was wondering if that was in reference to David Walker?

GH: Yes, I have this project. It's going to deal with that. That is to say, the US negros in the 19th century, they were always being told that they were inferior. So, they would then point to ancient Egypt, and particularly the role of the Nubians in that part of Africa, not only in today's Sudan, but heading north into Egypt, which was an advanced civilization. Obviously, which bequeathed a lot of knowledge to ancient Greece, for example, which is thought to be the seedbed of a good deal of so-called European civilization. I was going to explore that historically and also look at US relations with Egypt and also looking at the whole phenomenon of Egyptology, which is this sort of archaeology and unearthing, ancient Egyptian civilization, which of course, was originally spearheaded by Napoleon in the late 18th century, and then the torch was passed to the English. That is to say, these countries that think that they're part of an advanced civilization, inevitably, they get involved in Egyptology, because of course, eventually the torch was passed to the United States. John D. Rockefeller became a devotee of Egyptology, for example, sponsoring mini digs in ancient Egypt. I'm going to deal with that and I'm going to deal with US diplomatic relations with Egypt during the 19th century. The political developments in Egypt, which then, you know, this Black American fascination with Egypt continues in the 20th century, with regard to these philosophies of Africentrism, Afrocentrism, and also a large expatriate Black American population in Egypt. And then this is why you do research, I just found out because I'm also doing this project on Texas, *The Counter-Revolution of 1836*, it's on 19th century Texas, which of course, secedes from Mexico. Part of the story involves during the US Civil War, France takes over Mexico. That's where the holiday Cinco de Mayo comes from if you'll recall.

CS: When Maximilian was ousted?

GH: Exactly, under Maximilian. So, what happens is that the French, who by that time have a foothold in Africa, they dispatch Sudanese troops to fight along French troops against the great Mexican national hero, Benito Juarez. Of course, you know about ciudad Juarez just across from El Paso, Texas. Or you may know of the movie from the 1930s about Juarez and where he's not played by a Mexican, he's played by Paul Muni, who is of Eastern European descent, but that's another story.

I'm finding out more and more. Here's another project I'm working on. It's always fun to talk about stuff you haven't done, and that is I started off wanting to do a project about Sir James Brooke. I write about him in my book *Race War* because he and his family take over a part of what is now Indonesia and rule it like an apartheid fiefdom for about 100 years until the Japanese invade in the 1940s.[11]

So, I still might do that, but you know, the archives are all locked down because of the pandemic. I've just been reading dissertations and I haven't been able to find enough dissertations and master's thesis about this. So now I'm sort of expanding to look at Southeast Asia and look at Malaya, because as you know, after World War II the British squash a communist led insurgency in what is now Malaysia then called Malaya and the United States and also the French when they're fighting in Vietnam, they look to the British effort in Malaya as sort of a template as to how you squash insurgencies.

What's interesting is that the insurgency in Malaya is spearheaded by the Communist Party, which is suddenly Chinese and the same holds true for the Communist Party in Indonesia, post-World War II, which is heavily Chinese. You may know that in 1965, the US allies with the Indonesian military execute a decapitation of the Indonesian Communist Party. I should also say that a decapitation of the business community, the national bourgeoisie of Indonesia, which is heavily Chinese, too. It's really a signal event of the 20th century.

I wrote a piece that you can now find in the journal *Diplomatic History*, where I talk about the insurgency in Malaya, the anti-Chinese element of that insurgency, the decapitation of the Indonesian Communist Party, and what impact that might have had on the People's Republic of China, because it's estimated that 500,000 people were killed. It was like Rwanda, I mean, there was 500,000 people killed in a matter of weeks, mostly of Chinese ancestry.[12] I speculate what impact that might have had upon the Chinese Communist Party. So, I'll just leave it aside.

CS: I must look up that piece.

GH: Thank you and good luck to you.

---

11. Gerald Horne, *Race War: White Supremacy and the Japanese Attack on the British Empire*, New York: New York University Press, 2004

12. Gerald Horne, "The North Atlantic Echo Chamber of 'Race Hatred.'" *Diplomatic History* 44, no. 3 900–903. doi:10.1093/dh/dhaa025

Chapter 4

Jazz and Anti-Fascism
July 17, 2021

CS: I know you're a fan of Keith Sweat so I don't want to don't get my questions twisted here. Dr. Horne, you're from St. Louis and your younger brother is a jazz musician. I believe Joseph Bowie, trumpeter, and Lester Bowie, trombonist, were from your area. I was wondering if you could paint the picture of when jazz first entered your world and psyche.

GH: Yes. Growing up on Brighton Avenue in the 4100 block of North St. Louis, we were blessed to have as neighbors, the Bowie family, the patriarch of the family was actually a music teacher. If I'm not mistaken, he taught music at Sumner high school. He had these sons, Joseph of course, played the trombone and he was about the same age as my younger brother Marvin, who played the guitar. Probably from about the time I was 12 or 13 years old, they had begun playing and they, of course, were younger than I was and then I shouldn't forget Byron Bowie, who was about my age. Lester Bowie is probably the most celebrated of the Bowie brothers, being a founder of The Art Ensemble of Chicago and being world renowned for his avant-garde compositions.

However, I think it's probably fair to say, I probably became aware of this music even before then, because my older brother who played the clarinet also collected albums. So, I recall growing up listening to Horace Silver, for example. Readers may know he was a pianist; you may be familiar with his signature composition "Song For My Father," "The Cape Verdean Blues." Of course, his roots were in Cape Verde, off the western coast of Africa, now a part of the independent nation of Guinea Bissau. People may know that for decades now, there has been a sizable migration of Cape Verdeans to New England. There's a sizable Cape Verdean population in Connecticut, Rhode Island, and Massachusetts, and Horace Silver comes out of that community. When you listen to his music, you not only hear the sounds and echoes of Black American music but the sounds and echoes of Cape Verdean music as well.

To return to the thread, I probably became aware of this music from the albums that my older brother was collecting. Of course, we were listening to these albums and also I should mention AM radio; there wasn't necessarily jazz on AM radio, but on a number of the Black stations in St. Louis. This may still be the case; I haven't visited there in a while.

There were blues. Blues was played on a regular basis. As I have suggested, and others have suggested, blues basically are the taproot of jazz. Blues flows organically out of jazz and as you know, blues music is this creation that stems from post slavery Black America with the lyrics oftentimes expressing the hopes, dreams, fears, tribulations aspirations of the Black people themselves. Blues, of course, comes out of the South. St. Louis, even though it's in the Midwest, was a recipient of various streams of migration from the south. If you look at your map, you'll see that St. Louis is right on the Mississippi River and due south is not only Memphis, which is another taproot of the blues, but also going further south to New Orleans, which oftentimes is given credit for being the home of this music we call jazz, which is developed in the late 19th century.

New Orleans, even though it was part of the Confederacy, had been captured by the Lincoln government forces early on during the Civil War between 1861 and 1865. There's this interesting tendency in the US military, even to this very day as a matter of fact, if I'm not mistaken, the Pentagon, the US military, your tax dollars, probably spend as much or more on music and instruments and musicians, as any other force in the United States. Now, I'm not sure if that's still the case, but certainly it was once the case and certainly what happened in New Orleans, in the 1860s is that there are military bands and with evacuation of New Orleans after the Civil War ends, many of the instruments are left behind and flow into the hands of many of the newly freed enslaved who then began to create this music, we call jazz. Which, as you know, is dependent upon expertise, not least with regard to horns, are trumpets, saxophones, trombones, French horns, bassoons, oboes, etc., or wind instruments, and strings, particularly the bass, but also the guitar.

Then of course, there's the anchor, which is the piano, or oftentimes the vibraphone. So, that along with the drums and the percussion, which predates New Orleans in the 1860s; you can trace the drums and the percussion, all the way back to Africa. In fact, you had anthropologists including Melville Herskovits, wrote this book some decades ago, *The Myth of the Negro Past*, where he's thought to draw a connection between African culture in Africa and African culture in North America. One of the "survivals" of the Middle Passage was obviously the music and was obviously his use of percussive instruments. So, there in a nutshell, you can espy the roots of the blues which then helps to create what is now this multi-billion dollar industry of US popular music, with offspring, including various forms of rock music, various forms of what is called R&B, or rhythm and blues, various forms of music that has taken the world by storm.

CS: Thank you for laying out those threads so nicely and I'm sure you include hip-hop in that genealogy as well with groups like *A Tribe Called Quest* and *Jazzmatazz* and so many others.

GH: Oh sure, particularly with regard to percussion. I mean, it's the beat that's at the heart, the throbbing hearts if you like, of all of these musical forms that we're talking about. There's this idea with regards to the origins of hip-hop, which you've mentioned that, in some ways, hip-hop comes out of this genealogy that I've just laid out, but in a unique fashion. That is to say that with the onset of neoliberal policies, people at the Reagan administration, beginning in 1980 in the United States where there is an attack on government programs, there's an attack on music programs in high schools, for example.

So, as a creative adaptation, you see this in places like the South Bronx, for example, in places like Los Angeles, for example, and other cities too numerous to mention, you see the youth react to having these musical instruments, figuratively if not literally stripped from their hands, by improvising with regard to beats with regard to pails. I remember growing up in St. Louis, there was this phenomenon known as hambone. I don't know if people are still familiar with that but basically, you created percussion, by having your hand slap your thighs basically, to create percussion and hambone even though I don't think the term was used. With regard to the rise of hip-hop, in some ways, can be seen as a root of hip-hop, insofar as you had youth who refused to say, or refused to accede to this decision that their music should be taken from their hands as these instruments were taken from their hands by creating these beats. Then of course that leads to what we call rapping which I'm sure I don't have to explain to your audience what that is and therein you see the flowering of another multi-billion dollar industry.

CS: Yes, and rest in peace to Biz Markie, too, on the news that just came out.

GH: Yes, I was singing his signature tune all night last night.

CS: That's awesome. So, more on the origins of jazz. You mention in your book *Jazz and Justice* the candelabra thesis. I really like how you mentioned some other origins or beginnings of jazz. You wrote, "when enslaved Africans in Barbados in 1675 were launching a revolt, the signal for launching was to be sent by trumpet. And by 1688, authorities on this Caribbean island had declared illegal the 'using or keeping of drums, horns or other loud instruments which may call together or give sign or notice to one another, for their wicked designs and purposes.'"[1] I was wondering if you had any comments on these ruminations and the candelabra thesis?

GH: Well, yeah. That's the idea. First of all, my friends in New Orleans get very upset when I try to suggest something other than the idea I just articulated a moment ago, that all of these musical tendencies flow from New Orleans in the way that I just described with the end of the Civil War, military bands, etc. There's another hypothesis, which I call the candelabra thesis, which is that the music was developing simultaneously in different communities, for example.

I think one of the reasons why we point to New Orleans as the sole legitimate source for the rise of this music, in some ways, it has to do with the uniqueness and peculiarities of archiving. What I mean is: Tulane University early on, which is in New Orleans, some archivists had the bright idea to begin to collect the oral histories of Black musicians. So, if you look at the early chapters of my book, I quote quite a bit from these oral histories of Black musicians, some of whom were born just after the Civil War, many of whom had come to maturity by the 1890s, for example.

That source, that rich protean source that these Tulane archivists had the foresight to create, has tipped the scale in favor of seeing New Orleans as the sole legitimate source, the flowering of this music. But if you had had a similarly inclined archivist in Memphis, for example, who had begun to collect oral histories from musicians, and of course, if you look at the history of musicians coming out of Memphis, there are quite a few, including the great Charles Lloyd, the saxophonist, who many people associate with California because *Forest Flowers* one of the better selling albums of these musicians we call jazz musicians, of all time, if I'm not mistaken was recorded in California. Charles Lloyd had that sort of, if I may, a sort of California aspect, so to speak, and then Jimmy Mumford, there's so many great musicians out of Memphis.

Then you could say the same thing for St. Louis. Actually, you could say the same thing for New York and Chicago. We all know about Kansas City and there's this unique story about the rise of the music in Kansas City. Oftentimes, the way it's told has a certain

---

1. Gerald Horne, *Jazz and Justice: Racism and the Political Economy of the Music*, New York: Monthly Review Press, 2019, 12

quirk to it. The way it's told is that about 105 years ago, in the aftermath, and during World War I, which was 1914 to 1918, you had a crackdown on the red light district of New Orleans, Storyville and many of the early musicians, Black musicians who created jazz have their roots in Storyville. So, with the crackdown, instead they begin to migrate, and they begin to migrate north. You would think that, okay, they're migrating north with New Orleans on the Mississippi River. St. Louis is on the Mississippi River, but Kansas City is 230 miles west of St. Louis; it's not along the Mississippi River. If you don't believe me look at your map. Then that raises questions about, well, how does this music migrate to Kansas City. Maybe there was a preexisting tradition in Kansas City? So, in any case, I think there's something to be said for this candelabra thesis and I'm sure as historians oftentimes say that further and future research will help to bear out that thesis.

CS: Thank you for explaining that. In one of your footnotes, I really liked the story about saxophonist Charles Lloyd, you wrote about the Indigenous roots of Sally Sunflower Whitecloud, who was Charles Lloyd's great grandmother, who refused to walk on the Trail of Tears when they took her land.[2]

GH: The Trail of Tears: first of all, I should mention that I have a long footnote in this book, which is meant to tease future research and future researchers. Because there's an extraordinary number of these musicians who are defined as Black who have Native American roots. Of course, this is up to and including Jimi Hendrix, for example. I think we need further and future research on the ties between the Indigenous population of North America and the African population.

Now, of course, we know quite a bit not only in terms of the music, but we know quite a bit about that history. In my book, *Negro Comrades of the Crown*, I talk about the close ties between the Indigenous of Florida and the Africans who basically merged.[3] That is to say that they united to fight against the settlers and fought what many ways was the longest war that the US military has ever been involved, Afghanistan notwithstanding. They fought the settlers and the US government, from the US takeover of Florida circa 1820, up until the

---

2. Gerald Horne, *Jazz and Justice: Racism and the Political Economy of the Music*, New York: Monthly Review Press, 2019, 353

3. Gerald Horne, *Negro Comrades of the Crown: African Americans and the British Empire Fight the US Before Emancipation*, New York: New York University Press, 2012

1850s, when many of them were forced to evacuate en masse. Now, they evacuated en masse to southern Texas and northern Mexico.

You mentioned the Trail of Tears, which is an interesting story in and of itself. We associate the Trail of Tears with the so-called, as they were called "civilized tribes," which included the Cherokee, the Choctaw, Creek, etc. The Cherokees in particular had sought to assimilate into US culture, up to and including converting to Christianity, to adopting the dress of the settlers, creating an alphabet, where they were publishing newspapers, which is still a major source for accounts of that time, but many of them were slave owners. They owned Africans.

So, we have the Trail of Tears, you had the US government, particularly Andrew Jackson, who was a favorite president of the 45th US president, Mr. Trump. In fact, he had this picture on his wall at the White House. Andrew Jackson said, you folks got to go from Georgia in particular, but also from parts of Carolina, parts of Alabama and they were supposed to go to Oklahoma, which is supposed to be the land of the Native Americans for as long as the rivers shall flow and the grass shall grow. But alas, that was just one more promise not kept by the settler government.

In any case, many of the Cherokees and the other so-called civilized tribes had enslaved Africans in tow, and so you had an enslaved African population in Oklahoma beginning in the 1830s and 1840s. That's a whole other story, I won't take up our time which is supposed to be a talk about the music. We'll talk about this story, but in any case, Charles Lloyd is just one of many of the musicians defined as Black who can fairly be said to have a Native American bloodline to use that phrase and as I said, it really should be researched further.

CS: Yes, and like you said, these threads all intersect. Thanks for bringing that together. For my next question, I'd like to step back and see if you could talk about some of these autonomous or DIY spaces that jazz artists started up? One example includes the Clef Club in Harlem that James Reese Europe opened. You wrote that it was "a combination gathering space for musicians, labor exchange, performance space, and a way to circumvent malign influence on the music."[4] I believe some musicians started a nightclub in the Canary Islands as well and this book focuses a lot on the mob and racketeering as well.

---

4. Gerald Horne, *Jazz and Justice: Racism and the Political Economy of the Music*, New York: Monthly Review Press, 2019, 16

GH: Well, a subtitle of this book includes the phrase "the political economy of the music." What I was trying to do in *Jazz and Justice* is tell a story about how early on these musicians were trying to claim more of the fruits of their labor that went into creating those fruits. In other words, even today, I'm sure you know, and I'm sure your audience knows, the political economy of the music is that the musicians and the artists create, but only a sliver of the musicians and artists are able to reap a significant percentage of the wealth that they have produced. Actually, of course, that's the nature of capitalism. I'm sure some of the readers are saying, "Hello Professor Horne," you must realize that. Yes, I do. But in any case, I think it takes a particularly obnoxious turn with regard to this music, because what happens is that these Black musicians were creating so much wealth, they were relatively unique in that circumstance, in terms of generating all of this wealth, and then not being able to appropriate a decent percentage of that wealth.

From early on they were trying to organize clubs as you mentioned in your question. They were trying to organize record companies. I spent quite a bit of time talking about the effort by the bassist, Charles Mingus and the drummer Max Roach, beginning post World War II, post 1945, to organize a record company, Debut Records. But it's very difficult to be a working musician on the one hand, and some of these working musicians, as you know, some of these folks practiced 15 to 16 hours a day. So, if you're practicing 15 to 16 hours a day, I don't know how you find the time to organize a club, organize a record company, even if you have a staff.

The other stumbling block is that it's not as if the vultures were willing to accept this competition, lying down. As I say in the book, one of the interesting aspects of popular culture in the United States, not least, the music business is the infiltration if not domination by organized crime types. These people are oftentimes thugs. I don't mean that in any positive sense, the way it has evolved today. I mean, that they were willing to use their fists and guns to enforce their diktat. Indeed, I tell a story about 1920s St. Louis, where there was a battle royal between organized crime types on the one hand, and the Ku Klux Klan on the other. At issue was that organized crime wanted to employ Black musicians in clubs that they controlled, and the Ku Klux Klan objected on racist grounds. So, they rumbled, and perhaps predictably, the organized crime faction prevailed. So Black musicians won the dubious right to be exploited, as opposed to being excluded. In microcosm, that sums up neatly, the often-desperate plight, not only of Black musicians, but Black people, whereas you're fighting to be exploited, as opposed to being excluded. Obviously, both options are unattractive to put it mildly, but I guess that being exploited means that you take a little money home, whereas being excluded means you take nothing home.

CS: The horrific margins of continued white supremacy.

GH: Oh sure, and it continues, as you know to this very day. Another thing is how this evolves. I tell the story of Ahmet Ertegun of Turkish descent. He was the son of a Turkish diplomat, posted to Washington, DC in the 1930s, a Jim Crow town. Like many, young Ahmet was captivated by the music. But what happens is that there was Jim Crow in Washington, which meant that it was difficult to have Black and white to use those two categories, cheek by jowl in clubs.

So, Ahmet begins to organize soirees at the Turkish embassy in Washington, DC, where he would invite musicians, Black musicians to play and other musicians to play and from that seed grows the mighty oak that is Atlantic Records. So that's the origin of Atlantic Records by these sons of Turkish diplomats. Of course, they make a major fortune from Atlantic Records. I can't say that Ahmet Ertegun was less exploitative than non-Turkish owners of music companies, and in any event, he became a kind of pillar of the US establishment. He opened his commodious estate in Turkey, to the likes of war criminal, Henry Kissinger, for example. He was close to the Rockefellers. If this were a different kind of interview, I would have a digression about the construction of whiteness, the construction of white supremacy, because interestingly enough, as I say, in my book on the 16th century, the construction of whiteness, comes out of religious conflicts, not only conflicts between Protestant versus Catholic, but also conflicts of Muslims, particularly Ottoman Turkey, which was the major power of the 1500s, versus Catholics. In some ways, many of the European Christians unite under this new identity politics of race and whiteness, which makes it even more ironic that by the 20th century you have this man of Turkish origin, becoming a major progenitor of this Black popular music.

CS: Yes, that does really tie into your book *The Dawning of the Apocalypse*. I'd like to talk about patriarchy and women in jazz who are often overlooked and not highlighted enough. Can you share some stories of resistance from your research? I'd like to name some of the women jazz artists in your book that you wrote about: Vi Redd, Mary Lou Williams, Clora Bryant, Dorothy Donegan, Betty Carter, Billie Holiday, Lena Horne, Dakota Staton, Myra Taylor, Shirley Horne, Marian McPartland, Dinah Washington, Abbey Lincoln, Annie Ross, Nancy Wilson, and many more in your book.

GH: That's right. Well, for whatever reason, as you were reciting that litany, my mind got stuck on Mary Lou Williams, perhaps, because she was such a talented musician, such a talented pianist, and she was also present at the creation of the Kansas City turn in the 1930s, which of course, gives rise to Charles Yardbird Parker whose roots are in fact in Kansas City, Kansas, as opposed to Kansas City, Missouri. Mary Lou Williams and many of those other women artists and musicians you mentioned had particular difficulties. They had particular difficulties in terms of being accepted by not only fellow musicians, but also by critics. I quote one critic who suggests that certain instruments should be barred from the hands of women, because supposedly, they were too dainty to deal with a big bass fiddle, for example. As you know, even today, with regard to jazz musicians, a lot of the organizing of gigs, that is to say employment opportunities, it's almost along the principle of a pickup basketball game. Whereas, for example, Chris Steele has the gig because he is a celebrated pianist and this club in Denver wants him to play. Chris Steele then calls other musicians, his bassist friend, his drummer friend, and his horn player. So, it's like a pickup basketball game, to an extent.

So, the women musicians oftentimes recounted stories of how if they had the gig, and they're calling a male horn player, that they would encounter difficulties, because perhaps the partner of the male horn player would get suspicious of this woman calling her "man." Then, of course, we haven't even talked about the rather difficult road conditions particularly early on in the 1920s, and 1930s, where musicians are traveling from town to town, oftentimes on buses, for example. Of course, there was a blanket Jim Crow that ensnared musicians of color across the board.

But then there's a particular negative aspect that the women musicians have to endure. Because oftentimes, there's the question, of boarding arrangements, sleeping arrangements, etc. That then opens up women to be harassed, sexually harassed, for example. It was a very difficult climb for these women musicians, and that litany of musicians you recited, all of them had stories along the lines of what I've just articulated.

CS: Thank you for sharing those stories and then what you were saying about the stereotype of women being too dainty to use an instrument reminds me of when bell hooks was talking about how when the computer first came out businessmen said that male fingers were too big to use computers and that only women would be able to use computers, which turned into quite a lie.[5]

5. bell hooks, "A Conversation with bell hooks," YouTube video, 58:34, March 23, 2020: https://www.youtube.com/watch?v=RqSVcnanjM8

GH: What's interesting, even on Wall Street today, I mean, if you go back and look at *The Wall Street Journal*, you'll see that there's this claim that you will have a fall in the stock market, a precipitous fall in the stock market, because of what I would call fat fingers. That is to say, some man, he meant to type this letter, he typed that letter or that numeral as opposed to this numeral and the stock market goes haywire. That story always struck me as being sort of an excuse, probably for fraud and profiteering. But it's still reported in the pages of *The Wall Street Journal* as matter of fact. We haven't had one of those fat finger stories in a long time. So, pick up *The Wall Street Journal* this week and don't be surprised if you read one.

CS: We may be due for one. I'd like to ask you about some examples of direct action with jazz artists. An example that comes to mind is Bessie Smith and when she ran off the KKK. I love that story. In *Jazz and Justice* there's a story about Rahsaan Roland Kirk and Lee Morgan interrupting the Merv Griffin Show, can you elaborate?

GH: Right, exactly. So, the musicians, you know, the artists, they reflect the times just like hip-hop artists reflect the times, reflect the reaction to neoliberalism, for example, and the denuding of public schools, of high school bands. The musicians reflect the times of the 1960s when there's this tumult, when there's the rise of what's called Black militancy, and that's reflected in the lives of the musicians who stormed the stages of these productions in New York.

You mentioned *The Merv Griffin Show*, there are other talk shows that are produced in New York where they stormed the stage. Interestingly enough, you have these house bands like. I'm sure you're familiar, if you look at Stephen Colbert, he has a house band led by Jon Batiste. If I'm not mistaken who has New Orleans roots. Questlove out of Philadelphia has a house band *The Roots* on one of the talk shows, but for the longest, these Black musicians were excluded from being part of house bands.

So, they decided to take direct action because these are good gigs. They're steady, you know, steady employment is probably the apex for the musician in terms of income, but they were generally excluded. They were excluded from the orchestras in Hollywood as well. From the studio orchestras, which were on contract to produce music scores. A person like Elmer Bernstein, who was an Oscar winner who conducted all these compositions for a score for music for a movie, well, then, there was Universal or Warner Brothers or MGM, they'd have a house band, who would then play the music? But then the Black musicians were excluded. They had to take direct action, basically.

Of course, you also had unionizing efforts. There hangs the tale, since we're talking about Jim Crow, we're talking about US apartheid. We're talking about so called colored unions and we're talking about so called white unions. As I've tried to explain when the colored unions were liquidated, that was not necessarily a step forward, to put it mildly, for the Black musicians because with the so-called colored unions, they had a certain kind of autonomy that they could wield. But with the liquidation of the colored unions, they would then fold it into the larger white unions where oftentimes they had difficulty attaining leadership positions. They had difficulty having any say, or any voice. Oftentimes, the club owners would not want to hire them, would oftentimes hire a non-Black musician who was not as competent or talented. If you had a colored union, there was autonomy to protest, but once they were folded, once these Black musicians were folded into the non-colored union, so to speak, they lost that autonomy. Oftentimes, there was a kind of class collaboration between the leaders of the white unions and the owners of the clubs to exclude Black musicians. So, it's a very complicated and torturous story and one more strand in the fabric of the political economy of the music.

CS: Thanks for breaking open those stories, to continue along with artists reflecting the times I was wondering if you had any stories on Charles Mingus, and how he had the song "Free Cell Block F, 'Tis Nazi U.S.A." He had a song about Attica, "Remember Rockefeller at Attica." You wrote how Mingus had a song dedicated to Emmett Till and Mingus said in an interview I was listening to, "I've often felt, no flag, no country, no love, or nothing."[6]

GH: It's interesting that you mention Charles. Just a few days ago, his grandson, Kevin Mingus called me. I think he said in Amsterdam, but he was visiting his grandparents in Texas. He had read my book. So, he wanted to call me and said that it had inspired him to continue some research he was doing on his grandfather, Charles Mingus, who, of course, had roots in Nogales, amongst the border of Arizona and Sonora, Mexico, but grew up in Southern California and Los Angeles and was not only a bassist; Mingus put out some very wonderful solo piano albums as well.

---

6. Charles Mingus, "Charles Mingus Interviewed by Nesuhi Ertegun," track 41 on *Passions Of A Man: The Complete Atlantic Recordings (1956-1961)*, Atlantic Records, 1997, CD.

You mentioned some of his rather politicized song titles. I work on this program on the Pacifica station in Los Angeles, KPFK, one of our signature tunes is "Haitian Fight Song" by Mingus. Of course, "Fables of Faubus" is still worth listening to, it deals with the school desegregation crisis in Arkansas in 1957, where President Eisenhower under international pressure was forced to call in federal troops to patrol the hallways of Central High School in Little Rock, Arkansas to make sure that these nine Black students who were desegregating this high school we're not mauled and subjected to mayhem. Mingus wrote about that. As I mentioned a moment ago, he was involved in Debut Records.

He wrote a fascinating memoir, *Beneath the Underdog*. There is also a fascinating documentary film about Mingus; there's a scene in this documentary, which is quite revealing and sort of microcosmic in terms of the travails of Black musicians, because the scene shows him being evicted from his New York residence, somehow cameras were there and rolling. As he's objecting, they're taking his stuff out and putting it in the streets. It's quite poignant.

Once again, it points up, and this allows me to mention something else that I should mention before our time expires, which is that because of these atrocious conditions that these Black musicians faced in North America, quite frequently they went into exile. Charles Yardbird Parker spent a good deal of time in Europe. So did Miles Davis. Dexter Gordon spent time in Copenhagen [mispronounces]. Copenhagen excuse me. Once I said, Copenhagen [mispronounces], which I thought was the correct pronunciation, and this critic corrected me and said, "That's how the German Nazis pronounced it. So, what are you a German Nazi?"

So, Copenhagen, Copenhagen, and Art Farmer went to Vienna. My brother spent a lot of time in Tokyo, because for the longest there have been more jazz clubs in Tokyo than in New York. Of course, you get a better welcome to put it mildly, in Tokyo. In fact, I start the book by talking about this Black musician in 1930, in Shanghai, who was about to be subjected to being roughhoused by these Euro-Americans, and he retaliates and as he says, he's treated like a conquering hero by the Chinese who apparently wanted to do the same thing from time to time.

So, what happens in the context of these musicians like Charles Mingus, who are these world class artists and creators, but being treated like trash? As LeBron James once said, they take their talents and instead of going to South Beach they wind up in—well, Yusef Lateef in Nigeria, Art Blakey in Japan, Miles Davis in Paris, Dexter Gordon in Copenhagen.

CS: Thank you for sharing that. Going back to Mingus' song, "Fables of Faubus," I love lyrics: "Boo! Nazi fascist supremacists! Boo! Ku Klux Klan with your Jim Crow plan."[7] Talking about artists having to go into exile it really reminded me of a lot of intersections with your book, *The Bittersweet Science*, about boxing.[8]

GH: Definitely. Well, particularly with regard to organized crime, organized crime plays a major—I mean, these are the two avenues for Black people, generally, and Black men in particular—who wanted to escape the mines, escape the custodial positions, escape the low wage havens. Music and sports, particularly boxing, were the avenues and the stumbling block in each was organized crime and, of course, in the boxing book, I talk about these profiteers in boxing. Who include the man I mentioned a moment or so ago, when Donald J. Trump was bequeathed to us a phrase akin to Richard M. Nixon's phrase, remember Richard Nixon, the US President? During the height of the scandals, he says, "I am not a crook." Trump has just been quoted after the tumult of January 6, 2021, saying, "I'm not into coups," but I think that both statements, both so-called denials, should be read as meaning the exact opposite of what is intended.

CS: Along with that and conjuring up what you said about Mingus being evicted at the time is this whole story of not only mobsters getting put onto publishing rights or the dubious Joe Glaser. You point out how Gershwin stole music from Eubie Blake and how *The Beatles* and *The Rolling Stones* were mimicking Black artists. You wrote about how Panama Francis, the drummer for Buddy Holly said, "Listen to Presley" and how he copied Otis Blackwell "note for note."[9]

GH: Well, yeah, and one of the most notorious cases involves the great Duke Ellington, the pianist, composer, conductor, orchestra leader, who was born in Washington, DC at the turn of the 20th century. Early on in his career, you had this guy named Irving Mills, who put his name on many of Duke Ellington's compositions. What that means today is that the rights to this music becomes very valuable. You see how Bob Dylan just sold his catalog for millions and millions of dollars. So, certain Duke Ellington tunes, if someone wants to buy the rights, they have to go to the estate of Irving Mills,

7. Charles Mingus, "Original Faubus Fables - Remastered," track 2 on *Charles Mingus Presents Charles Mingus (Remastered)*, Candid Productions, 2022, Digital.

8. Gerald Horne, *The Bittersweet Science: Racism, Racketeering and the Political Economy of Boxing*, New York: International Publishers, 2020

9. Gerald Horne, *Jazz and Justice: Racism and the Political Economy of the Music*, New York: Monthly Review Press, 2019, 305

not the estate of Duke Ellington. I understand that's now a common occurrence where these musicians sometimes through naivete, sometimes because they're just overwhelmed and out muscled by the other side, sign over all the rights to their creations. Once again, it's just another tell-tale story about the evolution and devolution of capitalism.

CS: Yes, and Irving Mills is the overarching villain of this book I saw going through it. You've mentioned that people for decades keep trying to bury jazz and declare it dead, but this declaration is a farce.[10] I was wondering what intersects do you see with newer jazz artists on the topic of jazz and justice, such as Terrace Martin, Robert Glasper, Kamasi Washington, Jason Moran, and others?

GH: Well, I'm glad you mentioned that: Kamasi Washington, for example, out of Los Angeles has gotten a lot of attention, justifiably and understandably, because he's not only a creative musician, but it's not easy keeping a band together. He's been able to do that. Then if you look at Houston and Washington and New York, and perhaps other cities, you have these high schools of the arts, it's a reversal in the sense of what I described from the rise of neoliberalism in the 1970s, where you had a denuding of arts and music and high schools, to the point now, where in recent years, you've had the development of high schools whose focus is on the arts.

Therein you begin to see the rise of this newer generation of musicians. Then you begin to see also, for example, to see a Thelonious Monk competition, which I think is headquartered in Washington, which has been the seedbed for the rising of many, many musicians of late. Then there's the old standby, you still have these musicians who make their mark abroad, and they establish a name overseas, and then are able to translate that into notoriety here in the United States of America. But it's still an uphill climb. I mean, you still have these vulture-like piratical managers and club owners and record label owners. We still have short sighted critics who do not appreciate turns in the music. For example, I'm sure you're familiar with the kinds of brickbats Miles Davis was subjected to during the course of his career of various critics who appreciated the older styles of Miles but didn't like the newer styles of Miles. So, the struggle continues.

10. Gerald Horne and New Economic Thinking, "Jazz and Social Justice with Gerald Horne," YouTube video, 45:53, August 22, 2020, https://www.youtube.com/watch?v=5H7qrJZhj24

Chapter 5

Claude Barnett and the Pan African Press
December 19, 2021

CS: I really love your book, *The Rise and Fall of the Associated Negro Press: Claude Barnett's Pan African News and the Jim Crow Paradox.* As always, the research is thorough, and it fills in serious gaps in the history of journalism. I was wondering if you could explain when you embarked on this project and what inspired you to go down this path?

GH: I have long known about the vast archives of Claude Barnett and the Associated Negro Press (ANP), with the originals being at the Chicago Historical Society, on the north side of Chicago, and a good deal of the collection being on microfilm. If you look at some of my past books, if you look at the book I did on Japan, *Facing the Rising Sun*, you'll notice that in the footnotes a lot of the references are to that particular collection, either the microfilm collection, or the original documents.[1]

It occurred to me that it would be useful to write *The Rise and Fall of the Associated Negro Press*, which seeks to focus on Barnett as an individual, and on his interaction with the world, that is to say with the world outside of the United States, and also the Associated Negro Presses' relationship with the world. For those who may not be familiar, the Associated Negro Press, as its name suggests, was a Black equivalent of the Associated Press (AP).

The Associated Press as you know is a wire service. If you look at your newspapers—particularly nowadays, newspapers are firing journalists left and right. A lot of what you read in your newspaper outside of say, Washington and New York, are basically from the Associated Press. Because they just publish articles for other newspapers to use the AP. Of course, the AP plays a role in US elections because the count and the analysis, and the prediction of who

---

1. Gerald Horne, *Facing the Rising Sun: African Americans, Japan, and the Rise of Afro-Asian Solidarity*, New York: New York University Press, 2018

prevails, such as in number 2020, basically comes from the AP. So, the AP has been a very powerful press organ and the ANP was a Black equivalent. It had stringers all over the world; by stringers I mean, not necessarily bureaus which were staffed with journalists and writers on the payroll, but stringers, meaning those who sent articles to the Associated Negro Press headquarters in Chicago, and then got paid in return.

Of course, the stringers not only were luminaries, such as Zora Neale Hurston, the anthropologist; novelist, intellectual, Langston Hughes; Richard Wright; Ernestine Anderson, etc. The vocalist for the Duke Ellington band was a stringer. That band toured all over the world. So, one of the points, amongst others, that I tried to make is that in the era before the internet, I think the ANP did a fair job of apprising global events. I think what happened is that in the era of Jim Crow and US apartheid, their readers had a felt need to reach out to the international community and to keep up with what's going on across the globe, because it was a matter of life and death. But with the erosion of Jim Crow post 1950s, that felt need, has tended to dissipate and I think our community is the poorer as a result.

CS: Thank you for opening that up. The ANP's influence was monumental. You write in the book that the ANP "at one time served 150 US Negro newspapers and 100 more in Africa in French and English."[2]

GH: Yes, it's an interesting story about the ANP's relationship to Africa and Claude Barnett's relationship to Africa. First of all, with regard to his relationship to Africa, one of the intriguing vignettes in the book takes place in the 1950s, when he is seeking information about what's happening in the sprawling nations, then known as the Belgian Congo, now, of course, the DRC, the Democratic Republic of the Congo, to be distinguished from its twin across the Congo River, which is the Republic of the Congo, or Congo Brazzaville. Barnett writes this colonial official, in a sense seeking information and also upbraiding him for the depredations perpetrated by the colonizers in the Congo, in the Belgian Congo, and then towards the end of the letter, he drops a bombshell which is that he's trying to improve his collection of African art. So, he's wondering if this colonial official can help him in that regard. Therein you begin to see the contradictions of Barnett, but not only Barnett—but having entrepreneurs like Barnett in this sensitive political position.

---

2. Gerald Horne, *The Rise and Fall of the Associated Negro Press: Claude Barnett's Pan-African News and the Jim Crow Paradox*, Urbana: University of Illinois, 2017, 5

You see the dialectic where on the one hand, because his enterprise, the Associated Negro Press depends upon ferreting out information about the Congo. He's engaged in a good faith effort to ferret out this information from this Belgian colonizer. But at the same time, he's an entrepreneur. So, he's looking to feather his own nest, getting Congolese art. That vignette illustrates the dilemma of not only having an entrepreneur and a sense of the political position, but also of Claude Barnett in particular.

I should say at this point, that Claude Barnett comes out of the Tuskegee School of Booker T. Washington. He patterned himself after Booker T. Washington. Washington, of course being the turn of the 20th century Black leader, who, I guess you could say charitably, stressed Black self-reliance and Black entrepreneurship. Of course, the problem there was that if you got to be too big of an entrepreneur, then Euro-American competitors could take a sledgehammer to your enterprise.

You still have this discussion today. When I'm on Black radio, I'm oftentimes peppered with inquiries about, should people sort of desert the political field, and concentrate on building businesses. Without an understanding, as I say, in my book on boxing, *The Bittersweet Science*, is that if you build a powerful enterprise, as a Black person, as the character of my boxing book, Truman Gibson did, but you don't have influence with the prosecutorial authorities and your opponents and antagonists do, what will happen is that you'll wind up in court facing prison time, which is basically what happened to Truman Gibson.[3]

In any case, Claude Barnett, he also illustrates the paradox of Jim Crow, in the sense that the paradox being that during the Jim Crow era of segregation, what happens is that *The New York Times*, *Washington Post*, et al, we're generally not hiring Black Journalists, for example, or any journalists not of European ancestry. That gave him sort of monopoly rights in the field and gave him tremendous bargaining power, which he wielded assiduously to drive down the payments he had to make to the stringers. What happens with the erosion of Jim Crow beginning in the 1950s is that *The New York Times* and other mainstream publications, they begin to hire Black journalists and that in a sense moons his enterprise.

At the same time, Africa is coming to independence and they're seeking to train their own corps of journalists. They are in less need

---

3. Gerald Horne, *The Bittersweet Science: Racism, Racketeering and the Political Economy of Boxing*, New York: International Publishers, 2020

of journalists, journalistic writings from the ANP, and so Claude Barnett's enterprise is getting it from all sides. Then there is his less than
adroit maneuvering on the international scene. That is to say, I begin
the book talking about his close relationship to Kwame Nkrumah
of Ghana, the founding father of this West African state, surging to
independence in 1957. But what happens is that Nkrumah won't
necessarily dance to the tune played by Uncle Sam, he won't necessarily adhere to the diktat of the United States.

Relations between Washington and Accra, Ghana's capital, become
ever more complex and complicated. Claude Barnett, being a US
national, but also being of African descent, once again, he's stuck
on the horns of a dilemma. It's like being an entrepreneur, while trying to ferret out information from the Belgian Congo. So, on the one
hand, he tries to maintain good relations with President Eisenhower,
with Vice President Nixon. But on the other hand, he tries to maintain relations of a sort with Kwame Nkrumah. At the end of the day,
there's no question that the former relationship with Washington
takes precedence over the latter, relationship with Nkrumah. Interestingly enough, when Nkrumah is overthrown, with CIA assistance
in 1966, rumors still persist, that the Black American Ambassador to
Ghana, Franklin Williams, a former NAACP official was complicit.

Now by that time, of course, Claude Barnett was on his last legs,
but certainly in the run up to the overthrow of Nkrumah his relations
with Ghana had deteriorated. I think that one of the points that this
book helps to illustrate is that there is a tension between this identity
we casually refer to as African American. That is to say, that African
refers to roots in a continent that's still bedeviled and besieged by the
North Atlantic bloc, led by the US and "American" refers to the country whose passport should carry and there is a tension between those
two identities that I'm not sure have been recognized altogether.

CS: Thanks for breaking open that dynamic. You cross so many
different nuances in this book, which is so well done like with the
anti-communism and the way you described Barnett. You refer to
Barnett once as "Janus-faced Barnett," giving intelligence to the
White House, but also then going for decolonization in Africa. Sometimes pro-union, sometimes anti-union; friends with Nixon, Hoover;
had tobacco ads with Chesterfields, and then also had investments
in Liberia with ties to the Republic Steel Corporation in Cleveland.[4]

4. Gerald Horne, *The Rise and Fall of the Associated Negro Press: Claude
Barnett's Pan-African News and the Jim Crow Paradox*, Urbana: University of
Illinois, 2017, 176

This dynamic, it Interplays so much throughout the book, which makes it such a good read and adds to the historiography.

GH: Well, it's interesting that you mention tobacco. I do these interviews for the Pacifica station in Los Angeles, KPFK. Just yesterday, I interviewed the historian Keith Wailoo about his book *Pushing Cool*, which deals precisely with this contradiction of Black American elites who consort with big tobacco.[5] That is to say that after the Surgeon General's report of 1964 comes out of questioning the health impact, shall we say, of smoking cigarettes, i.e., lung cancer, emphysema, etc., big tobacco panics, starts looking for new markets and so they began to engage in what Wailoo calls racial marketing, targeting the Black community, pushing menthol cigarettes in particular, such as Kools, and Salems, and Newports, for example, which has a devastating impact on the health outcomes of Black Americans. But what happens is that big tobacco then begins to make contributions to Black members of Congress, to the NAACP, to other organizations of that type.

When the NAACP leader is asked if that money is tainted, he says, "sure, the problem is there taint enough of that money." So basically, what happens is that the community is sold out, in a sense, and in some ways that process begins with Claude Barnett and his relationship to big tobacco, doing advertising for Chesterfield cigarettes, for example. Once again, here's the problem, on the one hand, he's a so-called Black leader. On the other hand, he's an entrepreneur and so there's a tension, if you like, between "race" and "class" and Claude Barnett, in a sense, personifies that kind of tension.

CS: Thanks for explaining that. Going on the other side of the line of these tensions you write much about how the ANP is a force for anti-fascism. There are many examples of articles talking about anti-Jim Crow to anti-fascism, like when Barnett went after *The Catholic Review* for being Franco supporters, and even calling out the contradictions. I think it was Gordon Hancock who said, "did the Communists inspire the Nat Turner [slave] rebellion" and these other contradictions between anti-communism and Jim Crow and all of these issues that the ANP really parses out.[6]

GH: What's interesting, I'll never forget, I was doing research in the original documents of the Associated Negro Press in Chicago.

5. Keith Wailoo, *Pushing Cool: Big Tobacco, Racial Marketing, and the Untold Story of the Menthol Cigarette*, Chicago: University of Chicago Press, 2021

6. Gerald Horne, *The Rise and Fall of the Associated Negro Press: Claude Barnett's Pan-African News and the Jim Crow Paradox*, Urbana: University of Illinois, 2017, 170

I'm going through a file, and I come across an ANP report written on the personal stationery of Adolf Hitler. So, what happens is that in May 1945, as fascism was crumbling in Berlin, an ANP reporter gets into the office of Hitler and begins writing reports that are then sent to Chicago, which then I look at, in the run up to taking notes. It was quite startling, and quite shocking.

But with regard to the ANP, and Barnett, and anti-fascism, what I'm sure you realize, and readers realize, is that during World War II, which in the US phase is from 1941 to 1945, the US ruling class is united, shall we say, generally speaking, with regard to the defeat of Hitlerite fascism, and to the defeat of Japanese militarism. That of course, leads them into this wartime alliance with the Soviet Union. It also creates favorable conditions for pushing back against Hitlerite cousins and relatives here in North America, speaking of the Dixiecrats, speaking of the advocates of Jim Crow.

So fertile soil is created between 1941 and 1945 for the erosion of Jim Crow in the succeeding decade. You'll see this unusual alliance portrayed in Hollywood cinema. If you go to YouTube, for example, you can find a Hollywood film released by Warner Brothers entitled *Mission to Moscow*, which is a pro Soviet film to put it mildly. But that was because the United States was in alliance with Moscow and it wanted to create, "propaganda" to erode anti-communism so this wartime alliance could thrive, and so it was FDR, President Roosevelt himself who encouraged Jack Warner to make this film, which Jack Warner did and of course after 1945 when the war is over and it's followed by the Red Scare and the Cold War, then Hollywood moguls like Warner are hauled before Congress and asked why did you make these sorts of films? Why did you produce this communist propaganda? The congressional members did not want to hear that it was at the behest of the White House. It would be as if Sylvester Stallone were hauled before Congress and asked why he made films some decades ago that saluted and touted the likes of Osama bin Laden. I'm thinking of his *Rambo* series, for example, I think it was *Rambo 3*, where you have a bin Laden figure.

So, Claude Barnett was surfing that wave of anti-fascism. That was probably the finest hour of the Associated Negro Press, not only because of its really great reporting on the war, with very detailed reports filed not only from Eastern Europe—in my book, I cite in some detail some of the stories that his reporters were filing—but also from places like Iran, for example, in the 1940s, where you have reporters. Because one of the major summits that involved Roosevelt, Stalin, and Churchill of Britain, too, if I'm not mistaken, that take place in Tehran in 1943. As noted, Barnett rides that wave, but then, as we all know, after the fascists and the militarists are defeated, the United States pivots and sponsors the Red Scare and the Cold War against not only the Soviet Union, but of course domestic communists as well, not only domestic communists, but any who happened to veer from the line and it's a very irrational kind of attack. It reminds me in some ways of the irrational attacks on critical race theory today, which objectively are a little nutty. I mean, if you think about it, it's really irrational. There's a precedent for that; that's not the first time that there's been an irrational attack on progressive forces. Many progressive forces oftentimes are taken aback because the attacks are irrational, and you wonder how they can gain traction. But somehow they do.

CS: You really elucidate this point when you're talking about how Paul Robeson was denied a hotel room in Chicago, not because he was Black, but because he was a "bad citizen" of this country.[7] You make the "wider point…that racism was acceptable, but radicalism was not."[8]

GH: Well, sure. That's part of the post 1945 dispensation. I think that we're reaping the bitter harvest, the bitter crop of that dispensation now, where once again, there was those who thought that okay, we'll toss Robeson and the so called pro-Soviet forces overboard and then that will allow liberalism to flourish and progressivism to flourish. But now, we see that was a false hope because with the attack on critical race theory, you see that it's anti-racism itself, that's under siege. It's really almost like a cliche, in the sense that so they came for the communists and people say, well, I'm not a communist, and they're tied to Moscow anyway, so bye-bye, toss them overboard, but then that wasn't enough. I mean tossing the communists off the dogsled into the jaws of the pursuing wolves did not sate and satisfy the pursuing wolves.

Now, they want the progressives, they want the liberals, and there are not as many forces around to defend the progressives and defend the liberals. Of course, Claude Barnett was able to navigate those cross currents to a degree because he was an entrepreneur, he was trying to make money. Albeit he was trying to inform his community as well, but above all he was trying to make money. He could have a marriage of convenience with people like Robeson during the war, World War II, 1941 to 1945, but would not necessarily stand by his

---

7. Gerald Horne, *The Rise and Fall of the Associated Negro Press: Claude Barnett's Pan-African News and the Jim Crow Paradox*, Urbana: University of Illinois, 2017, 133

8. Ibid., 83

side thereafter. As noted, when Jim Crow begins to retreat this has an impact upon his business and sooner rather than later, his business is default.

CS: Thank you, and going back and forth on this nuance again, Barnett and the ANP saw the value of internationalism and solidarity against global white supremacy. They used their contacts sometimes working with President Johnson to try to sway Jim Crow laws, but at the same time, they were also under surveillance, meaning the ANP as well. One thing along with that I found really interesting was the reporting that the ANP did, taking how Africa was seeing the violence in Alabama in the US and how they were really just disgusted by it. I never had learned about any of these reporting's such as Modibo Keïta from Mali, who talked about how there needs to be solidarity with Alabama and that Africans need to reach their hand overseas and all the talks on Jim Crow from Africa and how influential that reporting was.

GH: Well, yeah, that's part of the contradiction. I've talked about that in a number of books, for example, my book on Kenya—*Mau Mau in Harlem?: The US and Liberation of Kenya.* I talk about how the United States was once again on the horns of a dilemma, to coin a phrase,[9] because on the one hand, there was this felt need and desire to make an appeal to decolonizing Africa, as we noted with regard to Nkrumah. Therefore, you begin to see, as the Soviet Union and Eastern European countries begin to extend scholarships to African students, the United States does the same. That's how Barack Obama senior winds up at the University of Hawaii, for example, in the late 1950s, early 1960s.

Then the problem they have is that they're inviting these African students into a Jim Crow society, where you're not allowed to go into certain restaurants. You're not allowed to go into certain hotels. I mean, if you are sworn in as a witness in a courtroom, there is a separate Bible. There are separate graveyards, and of course, there's remnants of that separate graveyard system that still exists. They're even separate graveyards for pets, for example.

So, the question then becomes how do you make an appeal to these Africans, students, diplomats, etc., who are coming to the United States, who you're trying to woo in this Cold War battle, when they're being treated as if they're less than human? So, the United States responds fitfully. They try some sorts of work around. For example,

---

9. Gerald Horne, *Mau Mau in Harlem?: The US and the Liberation of Kenya,* New York: Palgrave Macmillan, 2009

in the Kenya book, I talked about how there's this idea of giving African diplomats a button lapel so that when a shopkeeper sees that button on their lapel it's okay to let them in the store. But then of course, the broader and wider approach is to pass the Civil Rights Act of 1964, which fundamentally seeks to desegregate racially as they say, the United States of America. That "benefits" many Black Americans but at the same time, as noted, there's a paradox because with desegregation, you have all of these businesses like Claude Barnett's ANP enterprise, that arose in order to serve a segregated Black community. But once segregation begins to decompose, the rationale for those businesses begins to decompose. Therein lies the paradox of Jim Crow that's embedded in the title of this book.

CS: One of my favorite side stories or ongoing stories through this book was Alice Dunnigan, who was one of the first women hired by the ANP and she started writing when she was 13. You wrote she acted as "a feminist prod" to Barnett talking about gender segregation.[10] I really liked the back and forth and the vitriol between her and Barnett. Could talk a little bit about some things you found on Dunnigan and her influence? She even said that she was jumping up so much at an Eisenhower press report that her "knees became weak" and her "legs ached." She said, we got to "put on our boxing gloves and come out fighting."[11]

GH: Once again, Dunnigan is an example of how Barnett and the ANP benefited from a segregated job market, that is to say, in the era of Jim Crow, Dunnigan did not have that many options. So, working with Claude Barnett's ANP in some ways, is one of the few jobs as a journalist that she could hold, because of course, she would not be hired in the *Washington Post* or *New York Times* or *Baltimore Sun*, etc. But then after Jim Crow begins to decompose, she gets more opportunities, and she can say bye-bye to Claude Barnett and get a better paying job.

It's also interesting as well, that with regard to the press conferences that she attends at the White House she oftentimes talks about how the officials from Eisenhower on down—Eisenhower being the US president at that time in the 1950s—they rarely call upon her. I've heard glimmers of something similar happening even in the 21st century, particularly during the Trump years, with Black reporters,

---

10. Gerald Horne, *The Rise and Fall of the Associated Negro Press: Claude Barnett's Pan-African News and the Jim Crow Paradox*, Urbana: University of Illinois, 2017, 113

11. Ibid., 152

not necessarily being called upon. Once again, I think one of the themes with this book is that the more things change, the more they remain the same.

In any case, as I recall in the book, I talk about how the Chinese regime begins to comment upon that unfortunate situation where you have this Black woman reporter who's routinely ignored by US officialdom. Then she wants to cover the meeting in 1955, in Bandung, Indonesia, a very important global gathering of emerging African and Asian countries, for the most part—although there was a representative from Tito's Yugoslavia there; Tito being the founding father of modern Yugoslavia, a state that no longer exists, as it broke up into its component parts, including Slovenia, Serbia, Bosnia, Herzegovina, what is now northern Macedonia in the 1990s.

What happens is that Barnett does not want to send her to Bandung. He worked out an arrangement with other journalists, and as any journalist could tell you, it's as if when Obama was in the White House and he would spend Christmas in Hawaii, and if you were a White House reporter, you would see it as a plum assignment to be sent to Hawaii from snowbound Denver. Then the boss decides not to send you and send somebody else, of course, you'd be steaming and that's what happened to Dunnigan. So that gives her more incentive as the walls of Jim Crow begin to crumble to finally take her leave and move on to greener pastures. Although, I think she is correct to suspect that there was more than a scintilla of male supremacy and male chauvinism embodied and embedded in her conflicts with Barnett and the Associated Negro Press.

CS: Yes, and as you point out that patriarchy is right there when she's saying she's getting paid $25 a week and men were getting offers for her job at $60 a week.

GH: Yes, sure. I mean, Claude Barnett, as they say in the United States, he operated by the laws of the marketplace. What that means is that the marketplace has embedded in it this kind of bigotry and discrimination. That's what allowed him to be able to corner the market with regard to Black journalists. But then the marketplace also devalues the work of Black women journalists or Black women workers generally and he took advantage of that by paying her less. He would say that I don't make the rules I'm just following them. There was a certain illogic to that particular phrasing.

But once again, I think the wider point is—and I have to keep hammering home this point because it's one of the reasons I wrote the book—it illustrates the dilemma that we face when we have entrepreneurs leading political movements. Because entrepreneurs will oftentimes pursue their class interests and those class interests do not necessarily dovetail with the interest, particularly of a wider Black community, which is overwhelmingly and predominantly not entrepreneurs. They're working class. They sell their labor for a wage.

Therefore, they would tend to benefit from the construction of a union, a strong union. Whereas Claude Barnett, being an entrepreneur, he would see the construction of a union the way the devil sees holy water or the way in the movies when the vampire sees the sign of the cross, I mean it would be horrifying. So that's the kind of tension that's still with us, I'm afraid to say.

CS: Thank you for that. I was wondering if you could speak on the genealogy, past and future of revolutionaries like Claude Barnett, you write in the book that "David Ruggles, James Horton, William C. Nell, Samuel Cornish, David Walker, Frederick Douglass—either came from the ranks of printers, editors, agents, or patrons in newspapers, or solidified their reputations there."[12] Looking at the past, I was wondering if you could dovetail that with what influence did Barnett have. Barnett died in 1967, the Panthers were just getting started. Is there any influence there? The ANP also reported on Malcolm X, sometimes with scrutiny, sometimes kindly, still inside of that paradox.

GH: Well, first of all, I think that obviously in the 21st century, wide vistas have been open for all manner of journalists, editors, to have influence through blogs, through vlogs, through the internet, which is sort of modern-day pamphleteering. I think that in a society like the United States, the written word becomes increasingly crucial and critical. I would also say, I would like to see more of these latter day Claude Barnett's and Frederick Douglass' report more in those two men's tradition, which involved a lot of international reporting. I think that despite the fact that the internet shrinks the world, it makes it possible for us to tune in to *Al Jazeera*, from Qatar, or to *Press TV* from Iran, or to *CCTV* from China, *Africa Digest* from South Africa, or even *Africa 54*, from the *Voice of America*, *African News Tonight* from the *Voice of America*, BBC *Focus on Africa*, *France 24*, *Deutsche Welle* from Germany, *Africa Link*.

All of this is at our fingertips, which is historically new and historically convenient. I don't necessarily see people taking advantage of that. It's necessary to take advantage of that because I think that

---

12. Gerald Horne, *The Rise and Fall of the Associated Negro Press: Claude Barnett's Pan-African News and the Jim Crow Paradox*, Urbana: University of Illinois, 2017, 3

particularly for oppressed people and given the strength of the right wing in the United States, which is flexing its muscles with every passing day—of course, the latest trend is for mainstream press to tell us to expect a coup in 2024. In other words, first they tell us that the United States is the paragon of democracy and now they're telling us to expect a coup in 2024. I mean, it's almost as if they were saying the United States is the paragon of free speech and if you don't accept that we're going to take your free speech. It's all sorts of contradictions.

This devolves, this increases the importance of our modern-day pamphleteers, those with podcasts and blogs and vlogs and YouTube channels to try to get the word out because there's a five-alarm fire. Claude Barnett—I think it's fair to say, even though as our remarks today and the book suggests—I am, shall we say, somewhat critical of many of his efforts. On the other hand, for about 50 years, intermittently, he did a fair job. For example, I focused on international affairs, but somebody could go into the Claude Barnett archive and do a similar book on public health, for example.

I would say that archive may be one of the most important in Black America. Perhaps more important than its major competitor, which is the NAACP archive at the Library of Congress in Washington, DC. So, there are many more stories that can emerge from that vast archive in Chicago, which of course, is on microfilm as well.

I think that the rise of the Black Panthers in 1967, the ascendancy of Malcolm X and the last months of his life in some ways, it reflects the more positive aspects of the Barnett legacy. Positive in particular, with regard to internationalism. Of course, we all know about Malcolm X's tour of Africa. We all know about the Black Panther Party and their relationship to Algeria, their relationship to socialist Cuba, for example. So, in some ways, they were taking the baton from Barnett and running faster, until they too were struck down.

So now what we have to do, those of us who are still in the land of the living, is to pick up that baton and just like Malcolm and the Panthers ran faster than Barnett. Now we have to run faster than Malcolm and the Panthers. I think we're capable because we have more tools. As noted, there was no Internet when Malcolm and the Panthers were around. It was a real chore to keep abreast of what's going on in the world and you have to keep abreast of what's going on in the world in order to develop a strategy.

As noted, it was no accident that Jim Crow began to crumble because Africa and the Caribbean were coming to independence. There was a connection between the two. Likewise, with US imperialism under siege, with regard to its relationship with China, which obviously has backfired, and the anti-imperialist contradictions, with regard to its relationship to Turkey and France, in particular, its inability thus far to dislodge the Cuban Communist Party from power and its inability thus far to stop the left wing tide in this hemisphere, which not only encompasses Cuba, but perhaps by the end of the day today, today's December 19, 2021, it will encompass Chile as well.

Chapter 6

Paul Robeson: Internationalist, Anti-Fascist
January 23, 2022

CS: My first question is when did you first hear Paul Robeson and become enthralled? Also, you had a friendship with Paul Robeson Jr. Is that correct?

GH: I'm not really sure when I first heard of Paul Robeson, certainly by the age of 17 when I left St. Louis for Princeton University, because of course, Paul Robeson spent a good deal of his childhood in Princeton University. That was made known to me almost from the day I arrived. I might have heard of him even before then, because I still have in my mind's eye, my mother telling me about the execution of Julius and Ethel Rosenberg in 1953. I was told at a very young age, and of course, Paul Robeson was one of the campaigners for Julius and Ethel Rosenberg. The purported so-called atomic spies who allegedly leaked the "secrets" to building atomic weapons to Moscow. Although you can go online now and find the designs for atomic weapons. As a matter of fact, I recall in the 1970s, The *Progressive Magazine* of Madison, Wisconsin, published a series of articles about how to design an atomic weapon, you can probably still find that article.

So, with regard to Paul Robeson Jr., I of course knew him in New York. I knew his daughter Susan Robeson, as well, who would be Paul's Sr.'s granddaughter. Paul Jr., if that's the correct designation, and I oftentimes appeared on WBAI FM 99.5 on your FM dial in New York City, the Pacifica radio station in various programs. I was acquainted with them and of course really enjoyed his two-volume biography of his father.

CS: Yes, and didn't he write a longer refute to one of his father's biographies, like as a refute of all the errors in it?

GH: Well, what it is, is that Martin Duberman, was tasked by Paul Jr. to write the so-called official biography of Paul Jr.'s father, and this very long book, Paul Jr. was dissatisfied with the book. I recall when I was working on my Robeson biography at NYU, New York University, I can't recall which collection but there is a lengthy point by point refutation of the Duberman biography by Paul Jr. As I recall, it's even longer than the Duberman biography, I think the Duberman biography was about 700-800 pages, this is probably longer. To put it mildly, Paul Jr. was displeased with this biography. Unlike many people who are displeased, he went and wrote his own biography, which as I said is very useful, very interesting; there are two volumes.

CS: That's awesome to have that documented. My next question is, can you lay a foundation of the importance of language for Paul Robeson and his dedication and obsession with his studies? You wrote how his father taught him Hebrew, he was a Greek scholar and Robeson would study language for up to 12 hours a day sometimes.[1]

GH: Robeson was obsessed and fascinated with languages. He said that if he had not taken the career path that he did take he would have been quite satisfied to be a professor of Philology, which is a professor who studies the structure, and comparative nature of languages. He also felt that it had a political purpose, insofar as he thought that it resonated with people if you could speak to them in their own tongue. I think in the book I talk about before he goes to do a concert in Norway, he picks up the study of Norwegian, so that he could speak to the Norwegians in their own language.

He, of course, was very fluent in Russian, which held him in good stead during his visits to the former Soviet Union. Paul Jr. also was fluent in Russian. Indeed, one of the ways in which Paul Jr. earned a living was by translating Russian scientific documents and other documents into English. Both Paul the elder and Paul the Jr. had a fascination with the Russian language in particular, which in some ways stems from their mutual fascination with Pushkin, who oftentimes is given credit for being the father of the modern Russian language and is still a writer who is continuously read, not only in Russia, but in translation all over the world. He's a 19th century writer, and of course, was of African descent.

Paul Sr. was fluent in most of the major European languages. He studied African languages. He studied Chinese and of course, sang in Chinese. I think you can still find online, Robeson Sr.'s rendition of the Chinese national anthem, which I believe was entitled "March of the Volunteers." Language was very important to Paul Robeson Sr.

---

1. Gerald Horne, *Paul Robeson: The Artist as Revolutionary*, London: Pluto Press, 2016

CS: You had a footnote in your book, you wrote that Robeson knew 25 languages and was "capable of singing in 24."[2] One thing I really found interesting was not only his internationalism but how he spoke of the solidarity and internationalism of music. You explain in your book how Paul felt a connection with the Welsh and Irish as well. He said that "Gaelic folk songs are [close] to our own."[3] One of his favorite movies was *The Proud Valley* filmed in Wales that he did, and I was wondering if you could talk about this notion of internationalism and music. As you mentioned, with knowing the language, it's just one amazing thing which made him so popular. He had talked about these similarities between Hebridean songs, Chinese, African and Hungarian folk songs which were part of the "pentatonic mode."[4]

GH: Well, yes. I think you've summed that up nicely. I think that Robeson Sr. was trying to not only build bridges between and amongst different ethnic groups and different peoples, but also was trying to suggest a commonality between and amongst different ethnic groups and different peoples. Oftentimes, in concerts, he would start off singing a so-called Negro spiritual and then flow from his voice ineluctably into a song from another group, for example, and then that would flow ineluctably into a song from another group. He was trying to show that there was an underlying commonality between and amongst all these different renditions, trying to show that humanity is one, which, in a sense, was undergirding his political project, particularly the political project insofar as it dovetails with socialism, because the idea then, and I daresay even now, is that all peoples are marching inevitably to a similar beat towards an end goal of socialism.

The way things stand now, many of us in North America will be late to the finish line, so to speak. In any case, it reminds me of the line from Martin Luther King Jr., the speech that he gives right before he's assassinated in Memphis in April 1968. He says, "I may not get there with you" but I know we'll all "get to the Promised Land."[5] Well, one way to translate that is in Robeson-like verbiage, in the sense that Robeson expired circa 1976, as I recall, and he obviously will not get there with us, but I would dare say that he would agree

2. Gerald Horne, *Paul Robeson: The Artist as Revolutionary*, London: Pluto Press, 2016, 201-202

3. Ibid., 8

4. Ibid., 8

5. *At the River I Stand*, directed by David Appleby, Alliston Graham, and Steven John Ross (California Newsreel, 1993), DVD.

that we will all reach that end point of socialism sooner rather than later, or, as used to be said, socialism or barbarism.

CS: The Mountaintop speech is so powerful by Dr. King. I was wondering if you could speak about the notion that Robeson found other places in other places like discovering "Africa in London," and the Soviet Union in Africa?[6] Your book seemed to have a focus on London as well, which was a really interesting perspective because it highlights the importance England has for Robeson.

GH: Well, Robeson spent about two decades in self-imposed exile in London. From London, he travelled, particularly throughout Europe. I recall when I first started going to London, to do research, and one of the things that struck me was how, on a mass level and elite level, in London, there was obvious discrimination against those of Nigerian origin, Jamaican origin, West African origin, East African origin, Caribbean origin, etc. But, as a person from the United States, one of the things that struck me was the nature of accent discrimination in the UK.

Of course, you have accent discrimination in the United States of America. It always strikes me how even in the south, newscasters generally don't speak with a southern accent, because it's seen as somehow regressive, or retrograde etc. That is a prelude to suggest that Robeson felt comfortable in London, although he was well aware of what I just made reference to, which is the rampant discrimination not only against those of Jamaican, Caribbean, African descent, but also against the Black British population, whose roots stretch back hundreds of years in England.

I've only personally traced it back to the 1500s but there are others who have traced it back further than that. I think that, generally speaking my own perceptions of how I was treated in London, compared to how I'm treated in the United States led me to write a book *The Counter Revolution of 1776* that tries to revise the traditional understanding of the revolt against British rule that led to the formation of United States, insofar as many historians had noted previously, by several orders of magnitude, Africans had not stood with the rebels.

Interestingly enough, that's where Robeson and I diverge because Robeson was quite proud and mentioned it frequently. He was quite proud of the fact that his ancestors actually did, were some of the minority who did stand with the so called patriots in 1776. Now,

6. Gerald Horne, *Paul Robeson: The Artist as Revolutionary*, London: Pluto Press, 2016, 6

of course, he was saying that in order to refute the idea, which is quite rampant in this country, and perhaps for good reason that Black Americans oftentimes side with the antagonists of the United States of America, such as during the War of 1812, when they helped the British sack Washington, D.C. in August 1814. Men fled on boats to Trinidad and Tobago where their descendants continue to reside. Robeson was also trying to refute the idea that his being pro-Moscow was somehow inconsistent with being a US patriot.

This shows how matters evolve, because I consider myself to be a lineal descendant of Paul Robeson but that does not necessarily mean that I accept every jot and tittle of what he espoused. Particularly with regard to the origins of the United States, because I think one of the things about history is that history has a certain fluidity, that is to say that certain facts are immutable, such as the Declaration of Independence July 4, 1776. But what changes is our interpretation of why it happened at that particular moment. Those interpretations change based upon new insight, based upon new documents, based upon new revelations, based upon our perception of contemporary reality.

So, I would say that I agree with Robeson with regard to his feeling more comfortable in London than he did in New York, for example, because I certainly feel more comfortable in London, and have felt more comfortable than in New York. But like Robeson, as a Black American, you feel more comfortable just about anywhere on planet Earth than in the place where you're born. Of course, I would say that this stems from the fact that the enslaved population in the 18th century, engaged in class struggle against the slave masters, they did not engage in class collaboration, that is to say, siding with their oppressors, who were rebelling against British rule for their own reasons, and for their own reasons, their own class interests, the enslaved population chose not to join, for the most part of that rebellion.

It's very interesting that even people on the left, who consider themselves to be driven by a class analysis, when it comes to analyzing Black people in the 18th century, they dropped class analysis to start talking about race, which is fine, I'm down with talking about race. But these same people, they oftentimes just miss race analysis as identity politics, except when it comes to the 18th century when they wallow in what they otherwise condemned as identity politics, but excuse this with the digression but I've been involved in these debates of various sorts on these matters. This issue has occupied a good deal of my mental space, I'm afraid.

CS: No, thank you for breaking that open. Going back to where you and Robeson diverge do you think this has to do with the strong hagiography or mythology of the US beginnings and how like Du Bois would say this propaganda of history has had more holes poked through it since Robeson's day and through scholarship and scholars like you as well?[7]

GH: Oh, sure. I mean, as I said, you mentioned Du Bois. I'm reviewing the latest edition of *Black Reconstruction*, where he talks about the propaganda of history.[8] One of the things that strikes me about *Black Reconstruction*, many things strike me, but to the point on the table right now, one of the things that strikes me, is the pessimism that Du Bois has about the United States of America. Now, of course, he's writing in the 1930s. I understand why there might be a certain amount of pessimism given the lynchings and almost casual oppression. But nowadays, for example, despite on the one hand, a lot of serious discussion about the rise of fascism in the United States, and a possible coup d'état that could take place within a few years with the next presidential election, more revelations are emerging about the attempted coup on January 6, 2021.

Yet, we have running parallel to that, a number of scholars who are much more, how should I put this, unlike Du Bois, they tend to view the past with rose colored glasses. They see the organizing of the Republican Party in the 1850s as leading almost inevitably to the abolition of slavery. Du Bois would beg to differ. There are even scholars who see the formulation of the US Constitution in the late 18th century, despite the idea of three-fifths of a human being, being affixed to the enslaved population of African descent. This document is seen as an anti-slavery document, despite the fugitive slave clauses, etc.

So, I think that fortunately history evolves. I mean, for example, I read the book decades ago. Now I'm reading it again. I'm only up to page 300. But as I recall, one of the areas where Du Bois lags is in integrating Indigenous history into his overall narrative. But that fault of Du Bois, which I think will be threaded throughout the text, as I said, I read it decades ago, and I'm just reading it again and haven't finished. That happens today, 2022, despite decades of scholarship and Indigenous history, despite the fact that we now know that Hitler—for example, per quotations that you'll find in the writings of scholars, like Claudio Saunt at the University of Georgia, has written

---

7. W.E.B. Du Bois, *Black Reconstruction in America 1860-1880*, New York: The Free Press, 1999

8. Gerald Horne, "Abolition Democracy: W.E.B. Du Bois and the making of Black Reconstruction," *The Nation*, May 3, 2022, https://www.thenation.com/article/society/web-du-bois-black-reconstruction/

about the Trail of Tears and the Cherokee expulsive and others—that Hitler felt that he could credibly replicate in the 1930s, what the US settlers and the US leaders replicated in the 1830s.[9]

Because as he saw things, there was hardly a flutter globally, with regard to the genocide against the Indigenous population, the expropriation. So why would there be a flutter in the 1930s when he trekked east from Berlin? So that is an illustration, it seems to me of how history does not stand still, history as some would have it is arguments without end, and our interpretations of the past, oftentimes change depending upon the temper of the moment. Because oftentimes, people feel they need a history that sheds light on the process. And if history is not shedding light on the present, will, I think you'll see the history is discarded.

I think that's one of the reasons right now, why so many students are not studying history, because they don't find it relevant. They don't feel that it's shedding light on the present. It's antiquarian as we used to call it and so once again, I don't think my divergence from either Robeson or Du Bois, on certain matters of history should be seen as detracting from their historic importance, or even necessarily critical of how they view things. It's more of a commentary upon where we are today, in 2022 and the revelations that have emerged since Du Bois' death in 1963, Robeson's death in 1976. It would be as if, you know, DNA is uncovered, if that's the correct verb, circa 1953. And so, Charles Darwin did not uncover DNA, although you can say that he laid the foundation per say, but in any case, it's not an insult to Charles Darwin. When people today speak of DNA, they're standing on his shoulders, new insights have emerged, revelations have emerged and only those who are inflexible intellectually and politically, would seek to argue otherwise.

CS: Yes, definitely different branches have the same roots or even like rhizomes and other things are all connected and feed from those foundations. I'd like to talk about Robeson as an anti-colonist and anti-fascist. You had a really good quote from Robeson in the book on internationalism speaking of Japan invading China, and Italy invading Abyssinia. Robeson said, "the time seems long past when people can afford to think exclusively in terms of national units...." I thought that was such a great quote from Robeson.[10] Can you talk

---

9. Claudio Saunt, *Unworthy Republic: The Dispossession of Native Americans and the Road to Indian Territory*, New York: W.W. Norton & Company, 2020

10. Gerald Horne, *Paul Robeson: The Artist as Revolutionary*, London: Pluto Press, 2016, 52

about the significance of the Civil Rights Congress and the Council on African Affairs and just how monumental these creations were?

GH: Well, first of all, the Council on African Affairs comes to existence circa 1937, under the aegis of Robeson. Even though he's in London, it's a US based organization. It comes as a direct result of his interaction with Africans in London, such as Jomo Kenyatta, the founding father of modern Kenya, to with whom he was close, and of course, he also interacted with C.L.R. James of Trinidad and Tobago, and Kwame Nkrumah of Ghana, etc. Now the Council of African Affairs was designed to seek to undermine colonialism. Note that as of the time of the Council on African Affairs founding, you had fundamentally only two "independent" African nations, one Liberia, which was in many ways a neo-colony of the United States, founded in the 19th century as a result of expulsions of free Negros and enticements of free Negros in the United States to leave the United States. Then there's Ethiopia, on the other side of the continent, in East Africa, which was at that point in the 1930s, under siege by Mussolini's fascist Italy, in an attempt to eliminate its sovereignty.

Just a footnote here, in current research that I'm doing on Northeast Africa, one of the points that I find intriguing is that in the 1890s, Italy, pre-fascist Italy, once again was trying to subdue Ethiopia, in the Horn of Africa. One of the reasons it was not able to accomplish that goal was because the Ethiopians or the Abyssinians, as they were then called, were armed to the teeth by Russia, interestingly enough for various reasons. That's caused me to think a bit more deeply about the pre 1917, pre–Bolshevik Revolution, in Russia and its role in the world and how that might help us to understand a Russia today in the 21st century.

In any case, the Council on African Affairs had as its chief executive officer for a good deal of its history, the former Howard University professor Alphaeus Hunton, who like so many was jailed because of a refusal to name names in the early 1950s. Interestingly enough, jailed alongside him was the mystery writer Dashiell Hammett. Some of your comrades may know from his work, such as *The Sandman*, which was turned into a movie series, *The Maltese Falcon*, one of the more popular writers of that time, who of course, was very close to the US left, as well as his partner, Lillian Hellman, who was a playwright and writer. You may be familiar with her play *Watch on the Rhine*, which was turned into a movie and other works of note.

In any event, the Council on African Affairs, founded by Robeson, as an expression of his interest in Africa was also assisted mightily by his spouse Eslanda Robeson, who was not only his spouse, but his business manager and she was really the person who sort of lit a fire under Robeson, who might have been content to just study languages, and perhaps become a professor of Philology as he thought he might become, but for her pushing him into various arenas. I mean, he basically becomes a singer and an actor as a result of her influence. She too, was an anti-colonial crusader, visiting South Africa with her son, their son, Paul Jr., in the late 1930s. Traveling throughout the continent, as well, her books on that journey are still available, certainly in libraries. I'm not sure if they're still in print. But alas, what happens in 1956, is that as a result of the Red Scare and McCarthyism, anti-communism, in short, the Council on African Affairs is run out of business.

The same holds true for the Civil Rights Congress, which comes into existence in circa 1946 as a result of a merger of different organizations, including the National Negro Congress, which had come into existence in the 1930s. This also included the International Labor Defense, which had come into existence in 1930, spearheading the fight to save the lives of the Scottsboro Nine, the nine black youth in Alabama accused falsely of sexual molestation of two Euro-American woman. They were headed to execution before the International Labor Defense, which as the name suggested was global in scope. They launched a global campaign against US Jim Crow, not unlike the global campaign against apartheid South Africa, involving demonstrations at US legations globally, US corporations globally, leading to their lives being saved, leading to a change in the law, as promulgated by the US Supreme Court in the 1930s.

It was really the prelude and the precursor to the anti-Jim Crow push of the 1950s. The third group that merges to form the Civil Rights Congress in 1946 is the National Federation for Constitutional Liberties. These organizations came together and they formed the Civil Rights Congress. They focused on cases like the Scottsboro case that is to say cases of racist repression, the case of Willie McGee, for example, a Black man in Mississippi who's accused of raping a Euro-American woman, a woman with whom he was having an affair but when the affair was uncovered, she accused him of rape, and he was executed. Actually, executed outside, rather ghoulishly. Many Euro-Americans gathered to cheer. It was like a state sanctioned lynching and instead of a rope, they had an electric chair they were able to set up outside and of course, other cases, I won't go into the details.

The Trenton Six, for example, the Martinsville Seven out of Virginia, the case of all the Communist Party defendants who were perpetually on trial. The Civil Rights Congress was led by one of Robeson's closest comrades speaking of the Black lawyer from San

Francisco, William L. Patterson, who also was jailed during their time. For our purposes here, one of the most important contributions of the Civil Rights Congress, and Robeson was their filing a petition at the United Nations charging the United States with genocide against Black people. A very important intervention. It put the US ruling class in the dock. It put enormous pressure on the United States to get its house in order. It was a gigantic step forward, and of course, Robeson paid a very heavy price as a result, because up until that time, up until the advent of the Red Scare, the post-1945 Red Scare, he may have been the best known so-called US Negro in the world. But after the Red Scare attained liftoff, his income plummeted from the high six figures to the low four figures. It was difficult for him to find a hall that would be rented to him to have a concert. His passport was taken so he could not leave the United States to pursue a living. He was hauled before congressional committees and grilled. Fortunately, unlike Patterson, he was not jailed, although he came mightily close, as did W.E.B. Du Bois, who was put on trial during the same time for being a purported agent of Moscow; Du Bois was campaigning against nuclear weapons. If you were against nuclear weapons that meant that you were pro-communist, apparently. So, in sum, those are the stories of the Council on African Affairs and the Civil Rights Congress.

CS: Thank you for breaking those topics open and just to give a timeline that was 1951 when he presented the petition to the UN, accusing the US of genocide against African Americans?

GH: Yes, that was 1951 and it caused quite a stir. Quite a stir.

CS: Yes, and before the formation of the Civil Rights Congress, Robeson visited Dachau in 1945 as he explained in his essay "Genocide Stalks the U.S.A."[11] Then he spoke at the Joint Anti-Fascist Refugee Committee, as you wrote, he spoke about the hypocriticalness of the Nuremberg trials.[12]

GH: Oh, yes. I mean, that was part of the internationalism of Robeson. Of course, I guess some who are reading now may wonder, why did he leave London, where he left in the late 1930s, to return to United States, given what I've said thus far? A lot of it has to do with the eruption of World War II in Europe, August-September 1939, and the fear that he and his family would be trapped because London, I'm sure many realized, was bombarded relentlessly by neighboring

---

11. Paul Robeson, "Genocide Stalks the U.S.A.," *New World Review*, 20, no. 2 (February 1952): 26-29

12. Gerald Horne, *Paul Robeson: The Artist as Revolutionary*, London: Pluto Press, 2016

Germany. Many people were sleeping in subways. One of the things that strikes me about London during my visits in recent years, is the violent anti-German sentiment in Britain, which I think in some ways undergirded Brexit, the British exit from the European Union, in so far as Germany, in many ways is dominating the EU and that anti-Berlin sentiment, a lot of it stems from not only from World War II, but World War I as well, where German troops killed a many a Britisher.

So, he left Britain, returns to the United States and for a while he was on the same page as many in this country because he was anti-fascist. There was growing concern in the United States about the rise of fascism. He was a movie star. He was a singer. That said he was probably the best known Black American. He had a stellar athletic career as an All-American football player at Rutgers University, his alma mater. He was also a baseball catcher of some note and played professional football for a while. Indeed, that's how he met Eslanda his wife because he suffered an injury, and she was working at the hospital where he was hospitalized. That's how they encountered each other. So, in some ways, Robeson was a combination of Michael Jordan and Denzel Washington, and pick your singer of note, be it John Legend of Lil Nas X, whatever? He had a certain kind of notoriety based upon those stellar credentials.

CS: And a lawyer on top of all that.

GH: And, of course, a lawyer on top of all that but then things began to change, circa 1945-1946.

CS: Going back to when they left England, do you think this was also informed from them being on the frontlines of the Spanish Civil War and knowing that bombings were coming? Can you talk a little bit about the amazing work he did during the Spanish Civil War, singing on the front lines and the Negro Committee to Aid Spain?

GH: Well, yes. I mean, it's very interesting that the Spanish Civil War was taken up by many in this country, and not least Black people as their struggle. You had the Abraham Lincoln Brigade, which were volunteers from this country who went to fight in Spain. Many die in Spain. One of the few times where you had Black Americans commanding Euro-American troops was in Spain, certainly not in the United States or under the aegis of the US military.

Robeson was in the forefront of that struggle. As he saw it, one had to stop fascism in Spain with the war erupting circa 1936-1937. Otherwise, the flames of fascism would spread throughout Europe and the world, and of course, he had the gift of prophecy, because that proved to be accurate. So, he donated his talents to raise money for the combatants in the Spanish Civil War, the Republicans as they were called, small 'r,' and as I'm sure many know, the Republicans were defeated, the left was defeated, which inaugurated decades of proto fascist rule under the Spanish dictator, Francisco Franco, who was a comrade, of Mussolini, and Hitler.

Although wisely, he tried to cloak his assistance to them, which allows him to survive post-1945 before expiring circa 1975, which inaugurated a new era in Spanish politics. Some readers may want to look at the book by Richard Wright, the Black American writer, on Spain. He visits there, I believe in the 1950s and has a very useful dissection of Spain at that particular historical moment.[13]

But in any case, Robeson oftentimes said that the way he defined himself politically, was as an anti-fascist. Now, this comes up repeatedly, because when he's hauled before congressional committees in the 1950s, they try to argue that he is a member of the US Communist Party under an alias, which is something that Robeson denies. I suggest in my book, that his interrogators were not sufficiently flexible. What I mean by that is that it was probably more likely, even speaking from the vantage point of 2022 that he was a member of the British Communist Party, more so than the US Communist Party. Although it would not surprise me and once again, this is how history works if new information is dug up that suggests that he was in fact, a member of the US Communist Party under an alias but saw no reason to share that information with those who would seek to punish him as a result, but once again Robeson defined himself as an anti-fascist above all.

CS: Thank you, in any of your research did you see Paul Robeson have any interactions or writings about anarchists or anarchism? I know you wrote about his friendship with Emma Goldman.[14]

GH: Well, I don't recall that, but this is how history works. I mean, let me give tips to someone who would like to pursue that course. For example, we know that anarchists were very prominent in 1930s Spain. We know that Robeson was in Spain in the 1930s. So, it could be a matter of going through anarchist documents in Spain in the 1930s and see what comes up. We haven't received all the US government documents about Robeson. US government documents can be misleading, but in other ways they can be helpful to the researcher. One of the reasons we know so much about Martin Luther King is because the FBI was surveilling him relentlessly. We

---

13. Richard Wright, *Pagan Spain*, New York: HarperPerennial, 1995

14. Gerald Horne, *Paul Robeson: The Artist as Revolutionary*, London: Pluto Press, 2016

have tapes of his conversations, for example. So that may arise with regard to Robeson, but as of today, as I jog my memory, I can't come up with any clear connections between Robeson and anarchists, but I would not rule it out.

CS: Thank you for those tips. You have written about the detailed intense surveillance and even assassination attempts on Robeson's life, as well as burglaries Robeson dealt with and how his car was tampered with.[15] Just horrific stories in your book.

GH: Well, sure, especially the car. He was driving in the late 1940s or was being driven from St. Louis to Jefferson City, the Missouri capitol, and some miscreants loosened the lugs on the tire, so that the car would go off the road. He barely escaped death. Then there are the concerts in Peekskill, New York, where I know some years ago, there was a filmmaker doing a film about it. The film never arose but somebody really needs to revisit that and also writing, it's very important.

This is August-September 1949, Peekskill, New York about an hour north of New York City. Concerts where Robeson was performing for the Civil Rights Congress, a benefit. The left is assembled, so are anticommunists and neo-fascists. They begin to give a shellacking to the progressive forces. This is in August and so then they flee, the progressive forces flee and then they say, well, we can't let that happen. So, they come back in September, and it happens again, and Robeson barely escapes with his life.

These are real turning points in US history because one of the reasons why the United States is so right-wing is that the right-wing organized and just like they organized to commit genocide against the Indigenous population that claimed the land, the right-wing organized to bludgeon the left into submission and to intimidate the left. As a matter of fact, I still find it quite intriguing how today, despite all the blather and bluster about free speech and liberty, how so many people are intimidated by the right-wing? Now, you could argue that that's with good reason because they are willing to shed your blood, but it seems rather incongruous to make that common-sense observation that they're willing to shed your blood and at the same time talk about the United States as this cradle of liberty. I mean, the two do not go together.

CS: Yes, the hypocrisy. It's just baffling.

GH: Yes, I do interviews for KPFK in Los Angeles and since it's a bare bones operation, I not only do the interviews, I book the guests

---

15. Ibid.

too and it's really shocking to me how so many people were afraid to go on Pacifica, because it's associated with the left. I mean even if they're given an opportunity to promote their book, or whatever, promote themselves, but I guess they feel it would compromise their ability to be called by MSNBC or CNN. So, this is the country in which we now live.

CS: The incidents in Peekskill that you wrote about were horrific, one instance was where the crowd wanted to "scalp" Robeson.[16] You wrote how "'a police helicopter which circled noisily and low, directly over Robeson's head while he was singing, drowning him out....'"[17] The hospitals, you wrote, were "jammed with the injured" and how the white mob was chanting "'We're Hitler's Boys' and 'God Bless Hitler.'"[18]

GH: Yes, it was quite something. I mean, and that was not unusual and that's what's intriguing about Peekskill. It was reflective of the temper of the times.

CS: That really reminded me of Charlottesville as well.

GH: Well, that's for sure. Charlottesville, August 2017, when Heather Heyer is killed by a right-wing driver. This is part of this ongoing intimidation of people on the left, which makes people very reluctant to oppose the right-wing. Because they want to survive, understandably.

CS: I was wondering if you could talk about Robeson's solidarity with Indigenous communities. I know towards the end of his life he went to Australia. You wrote, "Robeson vowed he would return to the continent within six months to campaign for the Indigenous because he said, 'You have a serious problem here in Australia'" and he also showed solidarity with Guatemala after the coup d'état by the US.[19]

GH: Well, in Australia, and you know, I talk about this in my book, *The White Pacific: US imperialism and Black Slavery in the South Seas after the Civil War.*[20] The jaunts across the Pacific of many Black Americans and also many Black people in the Caribbean as well, there's probably more from the Caribbean, insofar as Jamaica and Australia are all part of the British Commonwealth. But more needs

---

16. Gerald Horne, *Paul Robeson: The Artist as Revolutionary*, London: Pluto Press, 2016, 121

17. Ibid., 123

18. Ibid., 123

19. Ibid., 184

20. Gerald Horne, *The White Pacific: U.S. Imperialism and Black Slavery in the South Seas After the Civil War*, Honolulu: University of Hawai'i Press, 2007

to be said not only about Robeson's solidarity with the Indigenous of Australia and New Zealand as well but Black America.

Then it goes the other way, because one of the top labor leaders in the United States, Harry Bridges, who founded the West Coast Longshore Union headquartered in San Francisco, led the general strike of 1934, one of the most important chapters in US labor history, helped to organize the sugar workers and the workers of Hawaii turning that archipelago from a redoubt of white supremacy and to what's the closest thing we have on the US flag to a social democracy. He of course, was born in West Melbourne, Australia and the United States tried to deport him repeatedly, from the 1930s up until the time he died, which I recall was in the 1970s. He and Robeson, of course, were very close. He and Robeson and William Paterson who, of course, was born in San Francisco, we're very close. Robeson is a person who we all need to know more about. We all need to study his example. We all need to try to emulate Robeson in terms of his industry, in terms of his willingness to study, in terms of his multilingualism, in terms of his anti-fascism, in terms of his forming organizations like the Council on African Affairs, in terms of his struggle for socialism. Robeson still carries lessons for the 21st century.

7

W.E.B. Du Bois: Sociologist, Scholar, Revolutionary
February 20, 2022

CS: Can you describe when you first encountered W.E.B. Du Bois and what effect his writing and thought had on you initially?

GH: Well, with regard to the first question, I'm not really sure. It may have been in high school. It may have been at university, but I cannot recall. But I don't think it's accidental that my first book dealt with Du Bois and I have continued to deal with him over the decades. This is because when I first began research on Du Bois, this was in the 1970s. I was living in New York and I was acquainted with Herbert Aptheker, who was then in the process of publishing a number of volumes about Du Bois and his work.

He had an office, as I recall, on East 30th Street in Manhattan. It was the office of the entity he then headed called the American Institute for Marxist Studies. I used to visit there to use the library, and by then, I had enrolled in graduate school in New York, after, of course, finishing this law degree at Berkeley. It was with my acquaintance with Aptheker that I became aware of the immense nature of the Du Bois archive, which, of course, is now sited at the University of Massachusetts, at Amherst.

One of the questions that struck me was how was it that W.E.B. Du Bois who had founded the NAACP, circa 1909, and had returned to that organization in 1944, during the height of the anti-fascist struggle, somehow was jettisoned by the organization, tossed overboard by 1948 as the Red Scare was being launched, and then coincidentally enough, as he was being tossed overboard, you had an erosion of the Jim Crow that he had been battling for most of his adult life. So, this seemed rather anomalous to me. That is to say, a lurch to the right with the Red Scare that ensnared Du Bois but then, a move at least on the surface away from the right with regard to the erosion of Jim Crow. It's those sorts of disjunctures that tend to attract the scrutiny of historians. That's what attracted my attention and led me to write this master's thesis first and then a doctoral thesis on Du Bois that then was published as my first book.[1]

CS: Thank you for breaking that down. I learned so much about Du Bois in all of your works and I really loved *Facing the Rising Sun* and *Race War*, too, and the things you brought out from Du Bois' work and archive.[2] I'd like to go back to your childhood, you mentioned when you were growing up, you had to move to North St. Louis, where you said you had experienced more racism. When Du Bois talked about double consciousness, he described a pivotal moment where he gave a white girl a card, maybe a Valentine's card in school, and she rejected it because of his race.[3] This is when he had a realization similar to Frantz Fanon's experience when he was yelled at by a white child on a train, or James Baldwin's experience when he was watching those racist cowboys in western films, where he was rooting for the cowboys and then realized he was seen as an enemy like the Indians in these films.[4] I was wondering if you could share a similar experience of when you had this moment that Du Bois describes?

GH: Well, it's sort of difficult to recollect in retrospect, not only because of the decades that have passed since I first began living in North St. Louis, but also because the racism was in the atmosphere. It was like the air you breathe. So, it's not as if there were toxic particulates in the air. The entire atmosphere was comprised of toxic particulates. It becomes difficult to single out any particular incident. Still, having said that, I do recall myself and some friends as being literally chased out of certain neighborhoods and vicinities. I do recall that Howard Johnson's, which was then a popular restaurant chain, and if I'm not mistaken also, kind of a motel launching site that Jim Crow obtained.

Therefore, it was difficult, shall we say, to eat there, because of the Jim Crow regulations. I do recall as a student, I'm not sure if this is

---

1. Gerald Horne, *Black and Red: W.E.B. Du Bois and the Afro-American Response to the Cold War, 1944-1963*, New York: State University of New York Press, 1986

2. Gerald Horne, *Facing the Rising Sun: African Americans, Japan, and the Rise of Afro-Asian Solidarity*, New York: New York University Press, 2018; Gerald Horne, *Race War: White Supremacy and the Japanese Attack on the British Empire*, New York: New York University Press, 2004

3. W.E.B. Du Bois, *The Souls of Black Folk*, New York: Bedford Books, 1997

4. Frantz Fanon, *Black Skin, White Masks*, New York: Grove Press, 1967; *I Am Not Your Negro*, directed by Raoul Peck (Magnolia Home Entertainment, 2017), DVD

before moving to North St. Louis or after, but even to this day one of the major tourist attractions in St. Louis, downtown St. Louis, and not far distant from the Mississippi River is the Old Courthouse as it's called, where the case of Dred Scott, that he was the party in the important Supreme Court case of 1857. Whereby the High Court and Justice Roger Taney, made the now infamous remark that Black people had no rights that those defined as white were bound to respect.

So, I recall visiting the Old Courthouse and receiving instruction about the importance of that case, although I can't recall what I was told. Although I do recall visiting there and the memory of the Dred Scott case has stayed with me obviously ever since. Also growing up in St. Louis, I recall, maybe not at the time because it was 1955 but certainly, I recall the repercussions of the Emmett Till slaying. That's the Black youth from Chicago who visits his relatives in Mississippi, and he is snatched from his bed by racists and executed, lynched. I do recall that particular case, especially. So those are some of my memories of Jim Crow.

CS: Thank you for sharing those stories. I wanted to talk about Du Bois' work, *The Philadelphia Negro: A Social Study*, which he was one of the first to do Urban Sociology, he created American Urban Ethnography. When Sociology 101 syllabi rollout it's always focused on Durkheim, Weber, and Marx.[5] I was wondering if you could speak to this, why this is, and just the sheer importance of Du Bois' work on the Philadelphia study?

GH: Well, subsequent scholars have argued that the downplaying of Du Bois' work in sociology and indeed in ethnography is a result of the racist blinders that tend to obscure vision, even today. That is to say that there is difficulty in elevating this person of African ancestry into the pantheon of scholarship, because it conflicts with the foundational ethos of settler colonialism, which has involved the denigration and downplaying of the attainments and accomplishments of people of African descent. But it's well past time to move beyond that time, the primitivism. It's well past time to recognize the historic importance of *The Philadelphia Negro* and the other works that Du Bois executed in that vein, because they have continuing relevance.

CS: Thank you, it's really apparent how visionary Du Bois was by reading your biography on him. He spoke about how he was inspired by Ethiopia when they defeated Italy in 1896 and when

---

5. W.E.B. Du Bois, *The Philadelphia Negro*, New York: Kraus-Thomson Organization, 1973

Japan defeated Russia in 1905.[6] Can you talk about this early anti-colonialism that Du Bois had, continued to have, and he got more and more radical as he aged. Du Bois said that Japan's victory over Russia was the "beginning of the end of 'white supremacy.'"[7]

GH: Yeah, it's interesting that you mention that because I've been talking about that a lot lately in the context of the current crisis between Russia and Ukraine. That is to say, what I've been telling audiences is that if you look at your map, you'll see that a good deal of European territory is Russian territory and that Russia's population even today is about twice the size of the number two country, the Federal Republic of Germany. But there's been a disjuncture in global politics because, as the Western European nations as I talk about in my 16th century book, were moving west across the Atlantic onto the Americas in the south, to plunder Africa, Russia was moving east establishing its window on the Pacific, speaking of Vladivostok in 1860.[8]

So, what that has led to is that first London in 1905 was trying to restrain Russia, because it helped to finance the Japanese attack on Russia in 1905, which Du Bois, Nehru, Ho Chi Minh and others worldwide were struck by, in a way that Du Bois was struck and then that of course led to Japan upending the entire British Empire in 1941 by its attack on Hong Kong and Singapore. The attack on Singapore in particular, was seen by Du Bois and many others, this is February 1942, as another withering blow against the pretensions of white supremacy.

Even before then, in the 1850s, you have the Crimean War, where Britain, France and the sick man of Europe, as it was then defined, speaking of Ottoman Turkey, again, gang up on Russia and what helps to unite this skein of events is the other important landmark that you mentioned, which is the 1890s defeat of the Italian invaders by the Ethiopians. Now, what's striking about that epochal event, and it's something I've uncovered for preliminary research I'm doing on a project concerning Northeast Africa, including Egypt and Ethiopia, is that the Ethiopians or the Abyssinians, as they were then called, were armed to the teeth by Russia.

---

6. Gerald Horne, *W.E.B. Du Bois: A Biography*, Santa Barbara: Greenwood Press, 2010

7. Ibid., 50

8. Gerald Horne, *The Dawning of the Apocalypse: The Roots of Slavery, White Supremacy, Settler Colonialism, and Capitalism in the Long Sixteenth Century*, New York: Monthly Review Press

So, even before 1917, you had this dynamic that Du Bois espied subsequently, with the formation of the Soviet Union post 1917 with the Bolshevik Revolution. Even before then, however, you had Russia in its own interests, Czarist Russia, seeking to foil its antagonists on the European continent. Because as I said, you had this anomaly of these global powers, France and Britain in the first instance, not necessarily having unrivaled untrammeled hegemony on their home continent. Of course, after 1917, as Du Bois and others pointed out, this becomes a dominant trend in global politics. This then leads us to the early 1970s after Du Bois' death, when once again, in order to foil Moscow, Washington does a maneuver eerily reminiscent of 1905 with the British financing of the Japanese attack on Russia, when the anti-Soviet entente between Washington and Beijing is effectuated. Which, in the short term seemed to "work" but in the long term, because of the massive foreign direct investment that China received as a result, has created this juggernaut. Which bids fair to leave US imperialism spiraling in the dust and of course has now led to this de facto alliance between Russia and China, which now may mark a Copernican shift in the global correlation of forces.

So, in this context, Du Bois was not able to live to see what we may be witnessing, which is how these maneuvers around Abyssinia in the 1890s, 1905, and of course, the early 1970s, has now led us perhaps to this tectonic shift in the global correlation of forces. Now I know this is veering well beyond the discussion of Du Bois but it's something that I've been talking about quite a bit to mass audiences, at least what I perceive to be mass audiences on the radio.

It may not be too soon to suggest that in this context subsequent historians like Du Bois will see the Cold War as a catastrophic success for US imperialism. Success in so far as the collapse of the Soviet Union did for a while create unipolarity and this pretension of the sole remaining superpower headquartered in Washington. But in the long term, it helped to assist the rise of China. It helped to turbocharge religious zealotry, vis a vis Afghanistan in the 1980s, which was part of the undermining of Moscow. Even with regard to the Soviet Union collapse, that then freed Moscow from sending subsidies to Moldova to Georgia to Turkistan and the other republics of the then Soviet Union, allowing it to husband its resources and now create not only a nuclear power that has hypersonic missiles, which I'm not sure Washington has in its arsenal. Also, it allows Moscow to then help to create divisions in the North Atlantic camp, that is to say, President Macron of France calling NATO braindead some months ago, the obvious reluctance of Germany to sign on altogether with regard to this latest adventure in Ukraine. So, in some ways, to come back to the thread of our conversation, events today are validating and vindicating Du Bois' insights at the onset of the Cold War, which he staunchly opposed.

CS: Thank you for tying all those threads together and I had heard that you said the chancellor in Germany is trying to moonwalk away from Washington.

GH: Yes, he certainly is and still is for that matter.

CS: My next question is about Du Bois and his prolific writing. He was first published in *The Globe*, as you wrote when he was 15. He wrote 27 articles in two years.[9] He launched *The Horizon: A Journal of the Color Line*. He edited the journal *Moon*. He started a scholarly journal called *Phylon*. I was wondering if you could talk about the significance of the journals and newspapers that Du Bois started, such as *Freedom* with Paul Robeson and *The Crisis*, which ran from 1910 to 1934.

GH: Well, *Phylon*, is a scholarly journal that he started after he left the NAACP in the 1930s and moved on to Atlanta University; it is a social science journal of some prominence, at least historically. *The Crisis* is a news journal that also featured poetry and contributions to the arts, founded more or less the same time that the NAACP was founded, and Du Bois was the top editor. He funded children's publications. You mentioned *Freedom*, and this is in addition to writing for the Black press. All of this, all of this writing, by the way, was subjected to an annotated bibliography by Aptheker, which was published some years ago. It's a rather thick volume, but it bespeaks the busyness of Du Bois from 1868 until his passing in 1963.

CS: *The Crisis* was one of the few periodicals that highlighted the anti-apartheid struggle. *Freedom* was as well. You wrote that *Freedom* had Nelson Mandela on the cover in 1952.[10]

GH: Yes, *Freedom* also has been getting subsequent prominence because of the fact that Lorraine Hansberry, the prize-winning playwright—*Raisin In the Sun* is her signature work—worked at the *Freedom* office and wrote for *Freedom*, and then she took courses with Du Bois at the institution then known as the Jefferson School for Social Science. *Freedom* was a very important publication. It's still being used as a reference for those who are seeking to understand the early Red Scare, the early Cold War. Also within the ranks of

9. Gerald Horne, *W.E.B. Du Bois: A Biography*, Santa Barbara: Greenwood Press, 2010

10. Gerald Horne, *Paul Robeson: The Artist as Revolutionary*, London: Pluto Press, 2016

Freedom were Alice Childress, the playwright—*Trouble in Mind* is one of her signature works. Beah Richard went on to stardom. She was in *Guess Who's Coming to Dinner* with Sidney Poitier, amongst other movies. So, *Freedom* was a very important publication, I think it's fair to say.

CS: Thank you. Speaking of Du Bois and him being a visionary, I was wondering if you could talk about his influence on the prison abolition movement and him foreseeing the devil in the details in the 13th amendment. You wrote, "Du Bois was a pioneer in exposing the grimy underbelly of the convict lease system, which led to mass arrests of African American men in particular, then turning them over to plantations and other employers for brutal labor. In a prescient comment, Du Bois concluded that by referring to 'that sort of social protest and revolt, which we call crime,' we elide the wider point that 'we must look for remedy in the same form of these long social conditions and not in intimidation, savagery, or the legalized slavery of men.'"[11]

GH: That's an important point. It reminds me that even bourgeois politicians—at least in passing, not necessarily consistently—have suggested that it's important not only to look at "crime" but "the causes of crime." Once you begin to look at the latter, as Du Bois' work suggested, you open up Pandora's box of capitalism, because it's obvious that people do not want to be imprisoned. People do not want to run the risk of being imprisoned. Therefore, it's appropriate to look for deeper causes with regard to these skyrocketing rates of incarceration in the United States. That not only leads to the conclusion that the United States is a superpower, in terms of incarcerating a higher percentage of its own citizenry, than any other nation, on planet Earth, but also a superpower in terms of executing Black people, and in terms of incarcerating Black people.

I'm editing this book on Texas. I recall that one of the lines I was just looking at from this book, which among other things, examines the post-Civil War era in Texas. A line in that text says that what happens post 1865, post US Civil War, is that there is a shift from the plantation to the penitentiary, the plantation to the prison, as a major site of exploitation.[12] Not only that, but the parallel is even more eerie given your astute reference to the convict lease system,

---

11. Gerald Horne, *W.E.B. Du Bois: A Biography*, Santa Barbara: Greenwood Press, 2010, 36-37

12. Gerald Horne, *The Counter-Revolution of 1836: Texas Slavery & Jim Crow and the Roots of U.S. Fascism*, New York: International Publishers, 2022

whereby the imprisoned could then be "leased" to employers. Not far from where I'm sitting in Texas is the city of Sugar Land. As the title suggests, it was once the site of sugar plantations. Only recently, I'm speaking of the last few years how the bones and fragments of dead Black prisoners have been excavated, who had been victimized post 1865 by the convict lease system in Sugar Land. Now I believe a memorial is being constructed to their memory. So, Du Bois, per usual was quite prescient in espying, that the post-Civil War dispensation would have these hidden time bombs or not so hidden time bombs in terms of these explosions that have now as noted lead to this carceral state, as it's oftentimes referred to, speaking of the United States of America.

CS: Thank you, can you talk about Du Bois and the vastness of his writing, just his amazing work of fiction that he produced, and his embedding of history, his persuasion in his fiction, such as the novel *Dark Princess*, which talks about Black and Japanese solidarity, or *The Ordeal of Mansart*.[13]

GH: *Dark Princess* is probably Du Bois' work of fiction that's received the most attention. I think it's because of the theme that you just outlined. That is to say, the theme of Afro-Asian solidarity, which is a theme that's of even more relevance today, as much relevance as it might have had over a century ago, or about a century ago, when Du Bois first wrote this novel. Then there's the theme, not only of Black-Japanese solidarity, but Black-South Asian, or Indian solidarity, as well.

Then there are the other novels that he wrote in the 1950s that have a lot to do with the 19th century in particular and the plight of Black people in the 19th century. Then, of course, Du Bois also committed poetry to paper as well. In fact, there have been entire studies on what's been called the art and imagination of Du Bois, which once again, speaks to the protean character of his intellect.

CS: Speaking of Afro-Asian solidarity, Du Bois signed an open letter condemning Roosevelt for the internment camps.[14]

GH: In my book *Facing the Rising Sun*, I deal in part with Black reaction to the Japanese-American internment.[15] I think I deal with

---

13. W.E.B. Du Bois, *Dark Princess: A Romance*, Jackson: Banner Books, 1995; W.E.B. Du Bois, *The Ordeal of Mansart*, New York: Mainstream Publishers, 1957

14. Gerald Horne, *Race War: White Supremacy and the Japanese Attack on the British Empire*, New York: New York University Press, 2004

15. Gerald Horne, *Facing the Rising Sun: African Americans, Japan, and the Rise of Afro-Asian Solidarity*, New York: New York University Press, 2018

it in the book *Race War* too, but it's obviously a subject that I think deserves a standalone study. One could start with looking at it through the lens of Du Bois, because as noted, he was a student of Asia, and Asian History, had visited Japan and China in the 1930s, returned to China, as you know, in the late 1950s, as I recall, after he had received his passport back from the US authorities, after it had been taken from him during the height of the Red Scare. Then, once again, with prescience I wrote quite a bit about the rise of Asia, which will probably be the major story of the 21st century.

CS: My next question deals with *The Souls of Black Folk*. You wrote how it has Black nationalist consciousness. You wrote, "The book also reflects a keen awareness of Du Bois' realization that African Americans were tied inexorably to darker peoples worldwide...."[16] I'm wondering if you could talk more about Du Bois and this international solidarity that he possessed and always sought to transmit. He raised money for anti-colonial movements in Africa, especially Kenya and South Africa.[17]

GH: Du Bois was not only an observer, he was a participant. What I mean is that as your citation from *The Souls of Black Folk* suggests, he was an observer. He, like some others, tended to place the struggle of Black people in North America in the wider context of the struggle of Black people in the Caribbean, and in Africa, and indeed in the struggle of what he would call darker peoples, globally as well. But he was a participant insofar as when the United States, under unremitting global pressure during the onset of the Cold War and the Red Scare in the 1940s and early 1950s, makes the profound decision to move away from the more egregious aspects of Jim Crow.

Du Bois was a participant insofar as he was one of the early targets, because US authorities felt, perhaps correctly, that leaving him unmolested would be dangerous to their interests. So, he was placed on trial circa 1951, was handcuffed at the age of 83, and unlike many of his comrades was able to beat the charges. This was as a result of his supposedly being an agent of a foreign power because he advocated banning nuclear weapons.

Du Bois at that time, was also a leader of the Council on African Affairs, which had been initiated by Paul Robeson in the 1930s but took off like a rocket post 1945 with the rise of the anti-colonial movements in Africa. You've mentioned the struggles in Kenya and

---

16. Gerald Horne, *W.E.B. Du Bois: A Biography*, Santa Barbara: Greenwood Press, 2010, 39
17. Ibid.

South Africa in particular, which had a particular resonance on this side of the Atlantic, insofar as both Kenya and South Africa were settler regimes, that is to say Europeans à la North America invading. Of course, unlike North America, they did not to the same extent, at least, liquidate the Indigenous population of Kenya and South Africa because they were needed to work, unlike North America, where the Indigenous population was generally also not wholly liquidated.

Then a subsequent labor force was brought across the Atlantic, speaking of the African population. Although, of course, we now know that a significant percentage of the Indigenous population was also enslaved. Not only in North America, but we're sold into slave markets across the world, including slave markets in North Africa and Ottoman Turkey, for example. So, *The Souls of Black Folk*, in some ways it outlines a political agenda that Du Bois proceeded to follow until his dying days.

CS: Thank you for breaking that down. In your research did you ever read about Du Bois' reaction to the genocide of the Herero and Nama?

GH: You mean in Namibia?

CS: Yes, in Namibia, which was so-called German Southwest Africa at the time.

GH: I can't retrieve that off the top of my head. Although, the best way to ascertain that is—I don't think I have it nearby—to look at the aforementioned annotated bibliography of Du Bois' work, which Aptheker published some years ago, which has a very good index. You could just look into the index and see if he wrote anything about that.[18] Of course, nowadays, if you were going to be thorough, you would also want to consult with the sound archives because of course, Du Bois' speeches are captured on sound, some of which can be found on YouTube, SoundCloud to Pacifica radio archives in North Hollywood. Other such archives can be found at the *BBC* archives, outside of London and perhaps even, although I'm not sure if they exist, but perhaps even in Ghana, as well, where of course, he spent his last years.

CS: Thank you for the breadcrumbs on that. My next question is about Du Bois who died in 1963 in Ghana. He was working on the *Encyclopedia Africana*. Can you talk about his legacy of Pan-Africanism and what it lent to the Black Panther Party and his influence today

---

18. Herbert Aptheker, *Annotated Bibliography of the Published Writings of W.E.B. Du Bois*, New York: Kraus-Thomson Organization, 1973

to the continued struggle as we were mentioning on prison abolition and the continued fight against global white supremacy?

GH: Well, I'm in the process as we speak of writing a review of a new edition of his magnum opus, speaking of *Black Reconstruction* published in 1935.[19] A revisionary examination of the period following the US Civil War 1865 to roughly 1876, where the newly emancipated Africans and their allies sought to construct a kind of social democracy prematurely. I think that one of the contributions of *Black Reconstruction*, amongst others, is not only its overthrowing of the then historical consensus as represented in the cinematic defamations, known as *The Birth of a Nation*, released in Hollywood 1915 or *Gone With the Wind* released in 1939.

Du Bois leads the charge to set the record straight and of course that path breaking work is now viewed as the new consensus. In this review of *Black Reconstruction*, I praise the work but also remind readers that another contradiction of reconstruction that Du Bois did not point out was the anomaly of Black voters being routed in East Texas by the Ku Klux Klan as Black soldiers in West Texas, we're routing Indigenous populations under the guise of the Buffalo Soldiers. That is to say that the demand that came from Reconstruction, 40 acres and a mule in some ways it represents the fruit of a poisonous tree because you're asking the Indigenous to give up their land claims as opposed to it being subjected to roundtable negotiations.

Not unlike the Lancaster House talks in the 1970s that led to the independence of Zimbabwe, then known as Rhodesia, where these land claims had to be settled sense the Europeans had seized a good deal of the land. But I think in terms of the theoretical contribution of *Black Reconstruction*, that still stands tall because it's one of the early and still too infrequent attempts to look at US history and Black history through the lens of Marxism, through the lens of the floodlight of social science.

Du Bois in this book speaks of the abolition democracy, for example, that's the term he uses repeatedly. Which of course, you hear echoes of that in terms of the idea of prison abolition today, or even abolition feminism, which is the title of a new book.[20] He speaks of the general strike of the enslaved that turns the tide against the slave owners during the US Civil War. Of course, I issue a friendly

19. Gerald Horne, "Abolition Democracy: W.E.B. Du Bois and the making of Black Reconstruction," *The Nation*, May 3, 2022, https://www.thenation.com/article/society/web-du-bois-black-reconstruction/

20. Angela Davis, Gina Dent, Erica Meiners, and Beth Richie, *Abolition. Feminism. Now.*, Chicago: Haymarket Books, 2022

amendment and rephrase that as a wildcat strike insofar as general strikes oftentimes presuppose a certain kind of coordination at the top, which was not necessarily present. It was more at the spontaneity of a wildcat strike.

I think that *Black Reconstruction* in many ways is the capstone of Du Bois' entire writing career. Now of course he engages in self-criticism when he says that the book would have been improved if he had access to archives. It's oftentimes forgotten that Black scholars as a result of Jim Crow were barred from archives for a good deal of the 20th century and certainly in the 1930s when Du Bois was finishing this work. So even that self-criticism is in a sense misplaced because if he wanted to go to archives it would have been difficult for him to do so, although not necessarily impossible, but certainly difficult. So those are my reflections on that topic.

CS: Thank you. I look forward to reading that review as well. When you're talking about the access to archives and racism in the history profession and just the US as a whole, it reminds me of Eric Foner who had brought up that Du Bois was published in 1910 in the *American Historical Review* and it wasn't until 70 years later, in 1980, when another Black person was published in this review, and that was John Hope Franklin.[21]

GH: That is true. That is true and things have hardly improved since then.

CS: I was wondering if you saw similarities between Du Bois' term "American Assumption" and what you had talked about in your books on the 1600 and 1700s on Bacon's Rebellion, if you saw a similarity between these two points? Du Bois' "American Assumption" to paraphrase was an iteration of I'd rather be white and poor and have race alliance instead of class collaboration, which goes against their own class interests.[22]

GH: Yes, he talks about that quite a bit in *Black Reconstruction* because in *Black Reconstruction* he posits that there was this alliance across class lines between and amongst European settlers. In fact, one of the points I make in this review is that we need to re-envision the United States and settler colonialism, in fact, as constituting a prison house of nations, with only the settler's allowed self-determination, which they executed by establishing a headquarters in Washington

---

21. Eric Foner, "Black Reconstruction: An Introduction," *South Atlantic Quarterly* July 1, 2013; 112 (3): 409–418. doi: https://doi.org/10.1215/0038 2876-2146368

22. W.E.B. Du Bois, *Black Reconstruction in America 1860-1880*, New York: The Free Press, 1999, 277

DC. But with Indigenous policies generally excluded from self-determination unless you consider their being placed on reservations and given a kind of sovereignty there as a form of self-determination. Certainly, the African population and the population of Mexican origin have been systematically deprived of self-determination. As noted, this inheres in settler colonialism because in my 16th century book I talk about the first English forays across the Atlantic to what is now called North Carolina in the 1580s where you have settlers of varying class backgrounds all sponsored by the 1 percent. So, it's that kind of class collaboration that explains the Trump phenomenon. It explains the ascendancy of US imperialism. It even sheds light on the remarkable events of the past week in Ottawa Canada to cite one example amongst many.[23]

CS: This is my last question which you already kind of touched on. I was going to ask you about Du Bois' "The Propaganda of History," how it relates to today, what gaps still need to be filled in with this racist narrative of history that is so often taught and written, and what hope you see in the work being done to fight against the propaganda of history?[24]

GH: Well, I think we need a knitting together. For example, there's been enormous progress with regard to Indigenous history in this country. But other than say, Roxanne Dunbar-Ortiz's *Indigenous Peoples' History of the United States* or something like that, it hasn't worked its way into an overall narrative of the history of the United States. You did have a cinematic attempt with the marvelous documentary by the Haitian filmmaker Raoul Peck, *Exterminate All the Brutes*, which I highly recommend. But to the extent that we can rewrite this history is, is dependent upon the balance of forces politically. And if you look at the balance of forces politically, today, what you see is a demagogic attack on so called critical race theory, an attempt to penalize teachers for teaching accurate and adequate history of this country, that brings to the fore, genocide, mass enslavement, etc. However, I think we still have to keep pushing because we know that the struggle that Du Bois faced when he was pushing, in a sense was much more formidable than anything we've encountered or

---

23. "Ottawa Declares Emergency as Trucker-Led Anti-Government Protests Spread," *Democracy Now!*, February 7, 2022, https://www.democracy now.org/2022/2/7/headlines/ottawa_declares_emergency_as_trucker _led_anti_government_protests_spread

24. W.E.B. Du Bois, *Black Reconstruction in America 1860-1880*, New York: The Free Press, 1999

even contemplated thus far. So, I think that that recollection gives us both optimism and emphasis for the future.

CS: Thank you very much and I salute you for all the work you've done for history and opening my mind extensively and I'm sure so many others around the world feel the same way.

GH: Right on.

Chapter **8**

Shirley Graham Du Bois: Anti-Colonist, Scholar, Revolutionary
March 27, 2022

CS: This interview is about Shirley Graham Du Bois and your wonderful book *Race Woman*.[1] Can you describe the moment in your life when you were introduced to the writings and thought of Shirley Graham Du Bois?

GH: That's difficult to say, but as I do mention in the book, the genesis of the book begins in midtown Manhattan. I had just left the Pacifica radio outlet set, that then had an office on 8th Avenue and 35th. I bumped into David Du Bois, her son. I had known him previously, although I can't remember the circumstances and he told me as we were chatting, that he had all of her papers at this flat in Cairo, Egypt. Of course, being a researcher, I decided then, that I would arrange to go to Cairo to examine these papers, which I proceeded to do. I spent, I think it was about 10 to 12 days there, in the study, where the papers were cited, they're now in Cambridge, at an affiliate of Harvard University. The Schlesinger Library, I believe, is the name which specializes in collections on women's history. I accumulated enough notes, of course, I had my laptop with me taking notes, I accumulated enough notes that eventually formed the core of the book that eventuated about 20 odd years ago.

CS: That was 1993 when you bumped into her son, David Du Bois?

GH: That sounds about right.

CS: So, I wanted to go back to some of the formative years of Shirley when she was growing up. You tell this horrifying story about her brother, Lorenz, who was hit in the head by "a white eighteen-year-old" who threw a rock and he wasn't able to get help from any of his neighbors.[2] I feel like this is a really formative story and then

---

1. Gerald Horne, *Race Woman: The Lives of Shirley Graham Du Bois*, New York: New York University Press, 2000

2. Ibid., 8

also on the other side of it is the strength that she got from her father. I really liked the story when you said the mob approached her dad's church and he was saying that he was ready to fight back and hit. "Her 'father fired one shot in the air...They were afraid of one man who had a gun—and who was not afraid!'"[3] I thought that was such a powerful story.

GH: Well, in reminding me of those vignettes it reminds me of a recent vignette involving the former New York City mayoral candidate, Maya Wiley. When she was about 11 years old—she's a black woman, by the way—she was on a boat with her younger brother and her father, George Wiley, who you may recall was a welfare rights campaigner, and he somehow drowned. The two kids somehow managed to get to shore and begin knocking on the doors seeking help in this Euro-American neighborhood. This was in *The New York Times* some months ago and these folks, they all turned their backs, they wouldn't, they wouldn't talk to these two kids who just lost their father.

I'm still—I guess the reason why I'm recounting that story, is that I'm still somewhat stunned by it. Just the insensitivity, the inhumanity displayed towards children. It's, in some ways, an embryo and embryonic vignette that goes a long way to explaining the history of the United States. It's almost like an X-ray and that, of course, is a vignette that I recount because it shows that what happened to Shirley Graham, Lola Graham, as she was sometimes known, was not necessarily unusual. That's what makes it so horrifying. That this was part of the warp and woof of Black life in North America. It's quite a commentary, but it's no less tragic.

CS: This story also reminded me of 2013, of Renisha McBride, a 19 year old woman who had crashed her car. She knocked on a door for help in Dearborn, Michigan, and the person shot her when she was asking for help in the middle of the night.[4]

GH: Yes, there was another case like that in North Carolina. That's, that's really remarkable. I mean, it's a saddening commentary on the nature of this society. Not a surprising commentary. Not necessarily a shocking commentary, but certainly a disappointing commentary.

CS: Can you speak about Black feminism in Shirley Graham Du Bois' work and how this intertwined with patriarchy? I also think

---

3. Ibid., 41

4. "Charges Filed Against Homeowner in Shooting of Renisha McBride," *Democracy Now!*, November 18, 2013, https://www.democracynow.org /2013/11/18/headlines/charges_filed_against_homeowner_in_shoo ting_of_renisha_mcbride

it's why her story hasn't been told broadly until you really embarked on this project. As you wrote, she "was more resolute in resisting the snares of white supremacy and less successful in resisting male supremacy." This is a dynamic you bring up throughout the book.[5]

GH: I know, even though I feel that that thesis is documented in the book, it's—I have to say—it's met with some resistance, but I don't find it particularly shocking.

What I mean is, that if you look at the position of a Black woman in the first half of the 20th century, you will find that many of them were understandably and justifiably moved by lynchings which disproportionately targeted Black men and that then led many women to oppose this kind of terror. It helped to forge a bond across gender lines between Black men and Black women.

The patriarchy that at times infested the Black community, notwithstanding the male supremacist attitudes, that infected some Black men notwithstanding. Now, if you look at the gender question, what you'll find as many scholars have documented is that Euro-American women, oftentimes, shouldered aside Blank women. You might be familiar with the book, by Stephanie Jones-Rogers of Berkeley, it's about Euro-American women slave owners. She puts forth the provocative thesis, which I guess should not be shocking, that during the heyday of slavery, a significant percentage of slave owners were Euro-American women, and it's not as if they were sympathetic to their sisters.[6]

Then during the high tide of the suffragette movement, about 100 odd years ago, you found that there were many Euro-American women who did not want to march shoulder to shoulder with Black women. Look at the works on Mary Church Terrell, for example, a Black woman of affluence, who was also a suffragette, of course, an early graduate of Oberlin College in Ohio. So, this made it difficult for many intelligent politicized women, such as Shirley Graham, eventually Shirley Graham Du Bois, to bond with their melanin deficient sisters, because the melanin deficient sisters we're not necessarily interested in bonding with them.

The confluence of those circumstances that I just referenced, that is to say, the horror at the terror inflicted on Black men, the reluctance of Euro-American women to bond with their sisters across the color

5. Gerald Horne, *Race Woman: The Lives of Shirley Graham Du Bois*, New York: New York University Press, 2000, 10

6. Stephanie Jones-Rogers, *They Were Her Property: White Women as Slave Owners in the American South*, New Haven: Yale University Press, 2019

line, it helps to create a Shirley Graham, which I think then gives resonance to that sentence you just quoted from the book. I was at a conference at Oberlin College in Ohio, which was also Shirley Graham's alma mater, right before the lockdown of the pandemic, so this must have been late February 2020.

The conference of course focused on Shirley Graham Du Bois, and I encouraged any of those assembled to write a new biography. I take seriously the admonition with regard to history, that it's an argument without end, and that history is not frozen in time. I think that's one of the problems we face in this country right now, whereby, you have lawyers and constitutional lawyers trying to freeze the Constitution in time in the late 18th century. You'd have to be locked into whatever the interpretation was in 1788-89, which is obviously ridiculous on its face. That's the way they roll as the saying goes.

I welcome a different interpretation, because as I said at Oberlin, when I was writing and researching that book, I was critical of her later infatuation with Maoism, now times change, currents change, and a later historian might take a different point of view, which is fine. Or maybe they won't take a different point of view. But in any case, I think that we should encourage new examinations, new scrutiny of important trends, important personalities, because history should be useful to explain the present. It's like these interpretations of 18th century US history, which posits that this grand democratic experiment and the men who crafted it walked on water, we haven't seen the likes of them before.

It's not very helpful in terms of explaining police terror, war, US violations of international law. I mean, it's rather hopeless in that regard, and I think that we need history that helps to shed light on the present so that we can build a better future. Therefore, that's my interpretation of historiography, and therefore that's why I welcome a fresh look at Shirley Graham Du Bois.

CS: Thank you for breaking that open and it really seems akin to what you've talked about before, that it's each generation's duty to rewrite history. I think that you may have been talking about that at the Oberlin talk.

GH: Oh yeah, definitely, that's my credo, but it's not just my credo. It used to be a credo to many historians, but as an emblem of how conservative the country has become, I don't hear that credo as often as I used to. Now, you know that after the collapse of the Soviet Union, this thesis arose about the end of history, that the point was, according to those who made this analysis, so-called, that history was evolving towards what you basically have in the United States of America, and that's it, end of story.

It seems to me as I've argued before that complementing the end of history viewpoint was the end of historiography viewpoint. Historiography being these changing interpretations of history over time. So, if there's an end of history, there's also an end of historiography. It seems logical that we don't really need new interpretations. We just need the sort of buffing and polishing of the interpretations that we have. That has been a dominant viewpoint. Although, in light of recent events, not least the crisis in Eastern Europe, that particular viewpoint may also wither away.

CS: Yes, I could see that as just polishing erasure, if that was to remain the dominant thesis, which would be very dangerous.

GH: Oh, sure. I mean, of course, I've been involved in this because of my work on early North American history. The book I wrote on the 16th century, for example, and, of course, the book I wrote on 1776, the book I wrote on the 17th century. So, I've been involved in these debates. Obviously, in those books, I was trying to craft a new interpretation.

I was also trying to do something else because I wrote a review essay in *The Nation*, the left leaning weekly out of New York City, about the book by Eric Williams, *Capitalism and Slavery*, and in that review essay, I use an analogy of the jury in the Rodney King case, over 30 years ago.[7] Recall that Rodney King was the Black motorist captured on tape being pummeled and beaten by officers of the law. When the case goes to court and to the jury, the officers charged with roughhousing, and manhandling him, the defense lawyers do not show the tape continuously. They would show a frame or two from the tape and then suggest to the jury that there was no crime and show another frame or two, and then put a similar spin.

The analogy I drew in *The Nation* was that is what historians do. Many of our historians specialize on 1850 to 1865, or they specialized on 1750 to 1790. So, there's no, there's little from before 1750, little after 1790. Little before 1850, little after their circumscribed history 1865. So, it becomes easier to dodge continuities of oppression. It becomes easier to write a misleading history. One of the things I tried to do in my work is to write a continuous story from the origins of settler colonialism in North America, in the 1500s, up into the present day, so that you can get a better understanding of the trends of the continuities, of the discontinuities, which I would hope would put our strugglers in a better position to struggle.

---

7. Gerald Horne, "The Politician-Scholar: Eric Williams and the Tangled History of Capitalism and Slavery", *The Nation*, October 5, 2021, https://www.thenation.com/article/society/eric-williams-capitalism-slavery/

CS: Yes, it's invaluable, the work and the research you've done, from *Black and Red* to *Race Woman* and beyond, they all fit into these larger narratives you've done of larger timelines, which is awesome. I love that whole thesis.

GS: Yes, I mean, back to historiography, I also have just written, a review essay on the latest edition of the Du Bois' *Black Reconstruction*, which as you know, comes out in the 1930s.[8] Looking at the period from, technically, the post-Civil War period up to 1877, but actually, it's fair to say it's probably going from about 1854. It revises the then current interpretation of that period. It's an example of a fresh look at a historical period that then revises the contemporary understanding. The contemporary understanding before Du Bois, was that this was a tragic era of Negro incompetence and Negro misrule, and Du Bois says, "no. It's a heroic era that's overcome by terror, spearheaded by the Ku Klux Klan, by unreliable allies in the Republican Party, etc."

It underscores why it's useful to have fresh looks at the past because now, Du Bois' history is the dominant interpretation. In the review essay, I take issue with one point that Du Bois mentions, which I think reflects an updated upgrading of the history. That is to say that, like many Du Bois posits that the land question is central. I'm sure you're familiar with the slogan 40 acres and a mule. The point that I bring up is that in almost 800 pages of text in that book, Du Bois hardly grapples with the Indigenous question.

The fact that the Indigenous had some claim and have some claim to the land, and that it's perhaps inevitable that the Reconstruction experiment would not end well, particularly since, as I say in my Texas book, in East Texas, you had Black people being routed by the Klan and terrorists, and in West Texas, you had Black soldiers as an emblem of their newly crafted citizenship, rousing the Indigenous. It seems to me that that was an unsustainable proposition, and I think that future examinations will bear that out. The larger, wider point being that we should not seek to squash these attempts to gain a deeper understanding of the past by examining the past with fresh eyes, which, of course, was one of the points that I made at this conference on Shirley Graham Du Bois at Oberlin College in late February 2020.

---

8. Gerald Horne, "Abolition Democracy: W.E.B. Du Bois and the making of Black Reconstruction," *The Nation*, May 3, 2022, https://www.thenation.com/article/society/web-du-bois-black-reconstruction/

CS: Yes, I wholeheartedly agree. Speaking of feminism and patriarchy, I wanted to talk about *Freedomways*, a publication that first came out in 1961. It seemed that was really spurred when she was in China. A woman explained to her that she should hire a housekeeper and how she shouldn't be "spending her days doing housework and waiting on her husband."[9] This conversation led to *Freedomways*, which was just an amazing, influential publication. I was wondering if you could talk more about that?

GH: Well, it's interesting, you know, a founder of *Freedomways*, Esther Cooper-Jackson, is still in the land of the living. She was born in 1917, she'll be 105 in August. Her colleague, Dorothy Burnham, is 107. Dorothy Burnham is the mother of Margaret Burnham, who is a well-known lawyer, former judge in Boston and of course was a defense counsel in the case of Angela Davis in the early 1970s.

So, *Freedomways* was—I have to say, I wrote many, many articles and reviews for *Freedomways* when it was in existence. If you look at my Civil Rights Congress book, you'll see in the introduction I thank Dorothy Burnham because she had the files of the Southern Negro Youth Congress, which was like a predecessor of SNCC, the Student Nonviolent Coordinating Committee, the shock troops of the anti-Jim Crow movement in the South, in the 1960s.[10] I'm sure she must have deposited them in the library by now, but I don't really know. I thank Esther Cooper-Jackson, her papers are at NYU. I thank Louise Thompson Patterson's papers are at Emory University in Atlanta, Georgia. These were three Black women stalwarts of the left, they all helped me. In fact, with my Shirley Graham Du Bois book, because of course, Esther Cooper-Jackson worked closely with Shirley Graham Du Bois on *Freedomways*, which was a quarterly review. Alice Walker, the novelist wrote for *Freedomways*.

Jack O'Dell, you may recall, was a former trade unionist with the National Maritime Union and had been a member of the Communist Party. In fact, he began to work with Dr. King and in the early 1960s President Kennedy calls Martin Luther King into the Rose Garden of the White House because he wants to talk without being surveilled by the FBI. He tells Dr. King to get rid of Jack and Dr. King says sure. Then of course, he tries to continue a subterranean relationship with Jack, which then of course is uncovered by the FBI, which is one of

---

9. Gerald Horne, *Race Woman: The Lives of Shirley Graham Du Bois*, New York: New York University Press, 2000, 160

10. Gerald Horne, *Communist Front?: The Civil Rights Congress, 1946-1956*, Rutherford: Fairleign University Press, 1988

the reasons they call him the most notorious liar in the United States of America.

So, I worked with Jack on *Freedomways*. I worked with him on Pacifica radio, where he was chairman of the board. As matter of fact, I'll be honest, Jack once convinced me to do something I regret. when he was chairman of the board of Pacifica, I was living in Southern California—I still regret this, I probably shouldn't even talk about it, but I'll talk about it. So, Jack, he was chairman of the board of Pacifica as noted, KPFK in Los Angeles, which I'm now doing weekly shows for. They had a number of "Black nationalists" on the air, who were oftentimes baiting the Jewish community and it was causing problems. So, Jack asked me to intervene, which I did, because I respected him. But I must say, it won me no friends and in retrospect, I shouldn't have done it. I should have told Jack to do it, you know? If you think they're a problem, you know, you take care of this problem. Why do I got to take care of this problem? But anyway, Jack has passed on now.

There's been a documentary film about him and of course, a book, if not books, detailing his central role. He also was an adviser to Jesse Jackson during his presidential runs in the 1980s. He was quite a figure. He wound up in self-imposed exile in British Columbia, Vancouver. That's where he spent his last years.

But in any case, also part of the *Freedomways* crew was John Henrik Clark, who has been become a sort of leading figure, if you like, for many of our Black nationalist friends. I got involved in the controversy there too, I must confess because I think when I was doing the Shirley Graham Du Bois book, Clark's papers are at the Schomburg, the library in Harlem, where my papers are by the way. So, I was going through Clark's papers and I ran across these articles that Clark had caught and had kept. They were from the Sun Myung Moon newspaper, that was this Korean evangelist who had a fortune, and he made a big foray into Harlem, during that time—this is in the 1990s. They had a newspaper and so the clippings were about Clark's relationship with this anticommunist faction in Angola in Southwest Africa. Now that was a big issue then. I write about it in my *White Supremacy Confronted* book, the confrontation between UNITA, the sort of Maoist Black nationalist force in Angola and the MPLA which was tied to the Cubans and the Soviets.[11]

---

11. Gerald Horne, *White Supremacy Confronted: U.S. Imperialism and Anti-Communism vs. the Liberation of Southern Africa, from Rhodes to Mandela*, New York: International Publishers, 2019

So, when I saw these articles I told Esther Cooper-Jackson's spouse, James Jackson, about it, who was a leader of the US Communist Party. He and Clark had crossed swords. Perhaps I shouldn't have told Jackson about it, but I mean, Jackson might have known about it anyway, but anyway, that's another episode that I'm not sure if I did the right thing. Although it was a matter of public record, it's not like you know, it's not like I was revealing secrets, I mean, it was in the newspaper.

Anyway, *Freedomways* was quite a publication. It's interesting, it went out of business in part, because it took a pro-Palestinian position, a very strong pro-Palestinian position which outraged a number of people. I'll never forget visiting their office in lower Manhattan, I still remember the address because it had two addresses, 80 East 11th St and 799 Broadway, because it had two entrances. I used to visit there all the time and as I said, you know, if you go back and look at the issues, you'll find many of my articles. As a matter of fact, I remember one book review I wrote the comes up in my Southern Africa book, this Soviet analyst writes a book about Southern Africa that I review. In the book, he makes allegations about the American Committee on Africa, which by that time, this is the 1990s was a leading anti-apartheid organization. He makes allegations about one of the leaders having curious ties to US intelligence and being a diligent reviewer, I mentioned that in the *Freedomways* review that caused consternation. In fact, if I'm not mistaken, I deal with the subsequent consternation in my Southern Africa book. I'm almost sure I deal with that in that book.

So, *Freedomways* is a very important publication and Shirley Graham Du Bois deserves kudos for working with Esther Cooper-Jackson and Dorothy Burnham who just passed her 107th birthday.

CS: That's amazing. Thank you for sharing those stories. Speaking of Esther Cooper-Jackson, wasn't she also part of the Sojourners for Truth and Justice that Shirley was part of too? Can you talk about that group and the story you wrote about when they fought for Rosa Lee Ingram, a Black woman "who fought back when she was assaulted by her landlord"?[12]

GH: Yes, this is getting a lot of play now fortunately. The historian Dayo Gore, now at Georgetown, formerly UC San Diego, has

---

12. Gerald Horne, *Race Woman: The Lives of Shirley Graham Du Bois*, New York: New York University Press, 2000, 144

written a book dealing with this.[13] Erik McDuffie at University of Illinois has written a book dealing with this.[14] I just read a book by another Georgetown historian, Soyica Diggs Colbert, she's written the biography of Lorraine Hansberry.[15] In fact, I just interviewed her for my KPFK show, and it'll probably be broadcast in a week or two.

Lorraine Hansberry also was part of Sojourners for Truth and Justice. You may recall that she was the prize-winning playwright and writer, *Raisin in the Sun*, which helped to burnish the reputation of the young Sidney Poitier on Broadway, it was one of her signature works. She was also very political. She worked with Paul Robeson's newspaper. She worked with Sojourners. She was quite friendly with Shirley Graham Du Bois, quite friendly with that whole left-wing crew, which included of course Claudia Jones, who, according to Diggs Colbert's biography of Hansberry, Claudia Jones and Lorraine Hansberry once shared a flat in Harlem.[16] Shirley Graham Du Bois of course, was part of Sojourners. Rosa Lee Ingram, she's the Black woman in Georgia who was assaulted by her landlord in the agricultural sense. He receives retaliation and comes out on the short end of the stick, shall we say? So that was a major political campaign to free her to make sure that she received justice.

Louise Thompson Patterson, who I mentioned a moment or so ago, also was part of Sojourners and you know, Louise, I'll never forget right before she died, I visited her in a nursing home on 112th and Broadway, right across from St. John the Divine church. It was a very sad circumstance because she hardly recognized me. As I said, you know, we knew each other. She had been very helpful to me. She was helpful to me in the Civil Rights Congress book. She was helpful to me in the Shirley Graham Du Bois book, helpful to me just generally. She barely recognized me, and she was drooling. She was in her 90s then. I remember thinking that if I'm lucky, I'll get to live as long as she did. She was born in 1901, passed away in New York in 1999.

---

13. Dayo Gore, *Radicalism at the Crossroads: African American Women Activists in the Cold War*, New York: New York University Press, 2011

14. Erik McDuffie, *Sojourning for Freedom: Black Women, American Communism, and the Making of Black Left Feminism*, Durham: Duke University Press, 2011

15. Soyica Diggs Colbert, *Radical Vision: A Biography of Lorraine Hansberry*, New Haven: Yale University Press, 2021

16. Ibid.

She got to 98 or so, but in any case, there's a biography of her too by Duke University Press.[17]

CS: By Keith Gilyard?

GH: Yes, exactly. So, she's received her due to that extent. Of course, she comes up in my William Paterson book because she was his spouse.[18] I'll never forget, I once visited, this is years before, he died in 1980, so this must have been before 1980. I visited them in their Harlem apartment, maybe I was already working on the Civil Rights Congress book, it's possible. I recall looking at his papers, in their Harlem flat and running across the *Honolulu Record*, which was this left-wing newspaper in Hawaii. Looking at that newspaper, of course, leads me to the book that I essentially wrote on the Hawaii left.

CS: Was that *Fighting in Paradise*?[19]

GH: Yes, which I must say, it sounds self-serving, but it's quite a story about how the left established this foothold in this far-flung archipelago, on the Hawaii islands. In any event, what led me to that project was this visit to the Harlem apartment, Esplanade Gardens 147th and Lenox Avenue in Harlem, high rise complex. That's what led me to that book.

CS: Oh, wow. I love that book, which talks about the longshoremen and the different unions and all the organizing.

GH: That union, they received their due from the historians, especially Harry Bridges, the union leader for decades, you know, well born in Melbourne, Australia, who the United States tried to deport for decades but were unsuccessful in doing so.

CS: Thank you for sharing that. My next question is on Shirley Graham Du Bois and anti-colonialism. She also had these differences, probably due to Maoism as well, where she did stand for Palestinian rights but then you also tell the story of how "in Accra she took" down the flag of Taiwan and put up "the banner of the Communist regime in Beijing."[20] I was wondering if you could talk about her anti-colonialism?

---

17. Keith Gilyard, *Louise Thompson Patterson: A Life of Struggle for Justice*, Durham: Duke University Press, 2017

18. Gerald Horne, *Black Revolutionary: William Patterson and the Globalization of the African American Freedom Struggle*, Urbana: University of Illinois Press, 2013

19. Gerald Horne, *Fighting in Paradise: Labor Unions, Racism, and Communists in the Making of Modern Hawai'i*, Honolulu: University of Hawai'i Press, 2011

20. Gerald Horne, *Race Woman: The Lives of Shirley Graham Du Bois*, New York: New York University Press, 2000, 156

GH: Yes, that was a signature, it must be said of the communist left, in particular, the Black communist left of that period. That's reflected in the Council on African Affairs, which Paul Robeson helps to initiate in the late 1930s and it's run out of business by the US government by 1956. Of course, W.E.B. Du Bois was a living symbol of that anti-colonialism as well as Shirley Graham Du Bois. Who after the coup against Nkrumah in Ghana, winds up in Cairo, Egypt. Matter of fact, the apartment that I visited there in 1993, I guess, was the same apartment that she had secured after fleeing Ghana, and Cairo at that time was a hotbed of anti-colonialism.

Recall that it was a place where many of the liberation movements in southern Africa had offices. In fact, in my Kenya book, I talk about how Cairo, the radio broadcasts from Cairo, were very informative in terms of galvanizing anti-colonial sentiments in Kenya, in the run up to independence in December 1963.[21]

So, Shirley Graham Du Bois, being in Cairo was sort of a logical confluence of circumstance, as was her embracing of Palestinians, which was an emblem of the government of GA Nasser, who is still viewed as an anti-colonial hero by many, including myself. She also was an anti-colonial campaigner, which then of course brought her into hot water with the United States because recall that, at a certain point she wanted to return to the United States for various reasons. The US authorities were reluctant to accede to her requests, much of it having to do with her anti-colonial stance and not to mention her putative membership in the US Communist Party. Finally, of course, the US authorities bent, and she was able to visit.

That led to her developing a relationship with the University of Massachusetts at Amherst, where then David, her son began to teach subsequently. Which of course, was a boon to him because David could make enough teaching at Amherst for four to five or six months to support his life in Cairo, because he would commute, Cairo to Amherst. David also became close to the Black Panther Party, as well. I think I mentioned that in the book. David was also a novelist.

CS: My next question is about Shirley and the Black Panther Party, Malcolm X, and how she had met with Malcolm X in Ghana and influenced him. She wrote her friend in 1967 about how she was inspired by the Black Panther Party, and she really embraced Black

---

21. Gerald Horne, *Mau Mau in Harlem?: The US and the Liberation of Kenya*, New York: Palgrave Macmillan, 2009

Power and also armed struggle.[22] Can you explain how influential this was compared to how many different generations she had been through?

GH: Well, the story of the Black Panther Party—I'm now exploring. I think this is something, this is a project I might have taken on since the last time we spoke. It's really sort of overwhelmed the other projects that I'm working on. I'm doing this project on the Black Panther Party in Southern California. Of course, the party itself was headquartered in Oakland.

Although I posit that a number of the leading figures that come out of the party including Eldridge Cleaver, the Minister of Education; Masai Hewitt; Angela Davis was chairperson of the Bobby Seale Committee in Southern California. George Jackson, the political prisoner, whose death helps to inspire the Attica revolt. Many of the leading figures and a lot of the money is raised too in Southern California through the good offices of the family of Donald Sutherland, the Canadian born actor and his spouse Shirley Sutherland; Marlon Brando, of course, the actor, in *The Godfather*, amongst other works *On the Waterfront*.

So, the Black Panther Party had a lot of influence. It's not just David Du Bois and Shirley Graham Du Bois. It was sort of a halfway house between the kind of Black nationalism reflected in the life and latter career of Malcolm X and the socialist option. The Black Panther Party was toggling between these two ideological structures and of course, unlike many organizations they tried to have an internationalist outlook. They had an outpost in Algeria. They sent delegations frequently to Asia, not least Vietnam. They were trying to politicize soldiers in Southern California at Camp Pendleton, Oceanside, just south of Los Angeles, just north of San Diego.

It's not surprising that Shirley Graham Du Bois and David Du Bois would be attracted to them because many in the Communist Party orbit were close to the Black Panther Party up to a point. In fact, when the Black Panthers had their Anti-Fascist conference in Oakland, Herbert Aptheker, the Communist historian, was the keynote speaker. William Paterson, who I mentioned a moment or so ago, oftentimes wrote with a Black Panther newspaper, and I talked in my biography of Patterson about his relationship with the party.

So, it was a very important moment. Although the moment—I say moment because it was like a meteor that flashes across the sky.

---

22. Gerald Horne, *Race Woman: The Lives of Shirley Graham Du Bois*, New York: New York University Press, 2000

I mean, the Black Panther Party's heyday was from about 1967 till about 1972, basically, and then they were subjected to murderous repression reflected in the movie *Judas and the Black Messiah*, which is just a thumbnail sketch of the kinds of murderous attacks upon them by the authorities. But it was a very important political phenomena and will probably arise again given current circumstances, and hopefully will arise with a deeper understanding of the conditions that we're now facing.

CS: Thank you for sharing that and I really look forward to that new project. My next question goes back to when you went to Cairo initially and then when you went deeper into other papers. What did you find most interesting or surprising digging through the archives that you didn't expect? You even wrote in the book that you opened some letters that Shirley Graham Du Bois hadn't, or in the footnotes, you said maybe it resealed itself?[23] What do you hope future researchers will dig and uncover?

GH: Well, it's interesting that you mentioned that. I didn't recall that I had said that. I was probably thinking about the time when I was doing the research in Cairo and David was going out for the day and he said, okay, you know, just go to it but please do not look at this file right here. Naturally, I looked at it. There were these very intimate letters between her and Kwame Nkrumah, the leader of Ghana. Of course, I didn't write about it and then subsequently, I've asked researchers who visited the Schlesinger Library in Massachusetts where her papers are cited and they say there's nothing there concerning that, so I assumed David got rid of those letters. But with that sort of episode, there's probably evidence in it elsewhere, basically, that's the way these things work with high profile personalities.

Then of course, other than the salacious aspects, it also has political overtones, insofar as she was older than he was and so to what extent did she influence him politically, for example, is a question for future scholars. That's why I welcomed at that Oberlin conference, further exploration and excavation of her life and legacy, because hopefully it'll deepen our understanding of the past.

In that biography, I didn't look at files in China, for example. Somebody needs to do that. As you know, in the United States, because of the 30-year rule, that is to say, in 2022 you'll have files released from 1992 and before. By 2032 there'll be files released from 2002. In other words, in the United States, the way things go is that new records are always being opened. That's one of the reasons why you need fresh

---

23. Ibid.

eyes because new evidence comes to the fore. We should not ignore new evidence. We should not be so wedded to past interpretations that we ignore new evidence. I mean that seems obvious to me. So that's what I was hinting at, for example.

CS: My last question is about just how good of an organizer Shirley Graham Du Bois was, not just with writing but in one sense, in her opera *Tom Tom* she was overseeing over "500 actors."[24] Then she ran programs for science and engineering on TV in Ghana with 600 people working under her.[25] I was interested in the Open Door Community Center of Brooklyn and the Brooklyn Inter-Racial Assembly, where she campaigned against police violence and then finally, I really liked the solidarity that her and W.E.B. Du Bois showed when they would have parties for kids whose parents were jailed or indicted by McCarthy, as well as raising the children of the Rosenbergs.

GH: Right, and also, since we're winding down, I should have mentioned this as I was wandering off into these highways and byways, that when the NAACP had a membership of 40,000 in 1940, 400,000 by 1944, obviously, that has a lot to do with the changing material conditions, the Anti-Fascist war and the fact that that puts the right wing on the defensive. It must be said that at that propitious moment Shirley Graham Du Bois and Ella Baker were two women who were largely responsible for that quantum leap. I should also mention her novel, *Zulu Heart*, which is a story about heart transplants in South Africa, you may know the story of heart transplants and how they were pioneered in South Africa where, according to this novel, at least, and to the best of my knowledge, it reflects reality that the hearts were taken from Africans and put into the bodies of Europeans. So, she takes that and then creates a whole fictional story about it. It's a very worthwhile novel for various reasons. Then her biographies for young readers. It's the genre that I've tried to contribute to, not as much as I would like, but you know I did a youthful biography of the Scottsboro Case, for example.[26] She did biographies for young people on various stories, mostly biographies. So that's one of the reasons why she still deserves attention.

---

24. Ibid., 17

25. Ibid.

26. Gerald Horne, *Powell v. Alabama: The Scottsboro Boys and American Justice*, New York: Franklin Watts, 1997

Chapter 9

The Liberation of Kenya, the Labor Movement, and Influencing Black Power
April 24, 2022

CS: This interview is based on your work *Mau Mau in Harlem: The US and the Liberation of Kenya*.[1] I was wondering if you could describe the situation in Kenya in the 1930s when Ralph Bunche arrived? You wrote about "Kenya's variety of Jim Crow" with toilets for Europeans and Asians but none for Africans from Kenya?[2]

GH: Well, first of all, Ralph Bunche, may be known to readers as a former Howard University professor in the 1930s, a man of the left, then, who in the 1940s leapfrogs into the US government bureaucracy, and then to the United Nations from 1945, where he wins a Nobel Prize. Although as I've indicated elsewhere, that was a very curious turn of events because what happens is that as Israel was being born, circa 1947, 48, 49, you see that the Chief UN Negotiator, Count Folke Bernadotte of Sweden, is assassinated by ultra-Zionist forces. Then Mr. Bunche takes his place and I think it's fair to say that Mr. Bunche was more pliable and manipulable than his late predecessors.

In any case, in the 1950s, Ralph Bunche came under fire from the US authorities because of alleged reported communist connections during his left wing period in the 1940s. He was already sour on Washington, one of the reasons he said he wanted to leave the US government bureaucracy for the United Nations was because of Jim Crow in Washington, DC. Speaking of Jim Crow in Washington DC, when he arrived in Kenya it was not unfamiliar to him in terms of the degradation of Black people. In terms of the hovels in which they were forced to reside. In terms of this racialized hierarchy, wherein you have European mostly British nationals living high on the hog

---

1. Gerald Horne, *Mau Mau in Harlem?: The US and the Liberation of Kenya*, New York: Palgrave Macmillan, 2009
   2. Ibid., 2

owning most of the land and certainly controlling the commanding heights of the economy.

Although, as I point out in the book, Kenya represents another trait of the British Empire, which is that at some point because of their desire to have a racialized hierarchy they began to rely more on Euro-American nationals and Euro-American nationals played a significant role in the Kenyan economy. Just as I start the book by talking about Euro-American whites who arrived subsequently in Kenya to help to prop up the tottering colonial regimes in the 1950s. It's also fair to say that there was a kind of relationship between people of African descent in North America and in East Africa, which began to blossom at the latter stages of the so-called Mau Mau revolt in the 1950s which of course leads to Barack Obama senior getting a scholarship to study at the University of Hawaii and I'm sure readers know the rest of the story.

CS: Yes. Thanks for breaking that open and giving that foundation and speaking about the collaboration between Kenyans and African Americans. I also wanted to ask about how people were memorizing Marcus Garvey's articles in Kenya and in 1925 there was an "anticolonial revolt" in Kenya, inspired by Garvey.[3]

GH: Well, the Garvey organization, the Universal Negro Improvement Association (UNIA), started by this Jamaican around the time of World War I, circa 1915, was inspired in part by the example presented by Booker T. Washington. It's very interesting about Booker T. Washington, I also say in *White Supremacy Confronted* that Walter Sisulu, who was probably Nelson Mandela's closest comrade in the African National Congress, he too, was inspired by Booker T. Washington.[4] Now, I should say that I hold no grief for Booker T. Washington in the context of US politics where, understandably and justifiably he's been juxtaposed against the example of W.E.B. Du Bois. Certainly, Booker T. Washington in the US context was willing to accommodate to Jim Crow. Of course, he did help to build what is now Tuskegee University, which is or was an institution of higher learning that not only educated many Black Americans, but it educated many Africans as well.

I think that therein you begin to see the attractiveness of Booker T. Washington because at that particular moment you saw a systematic

---

3. Ibid., 6

4. Gerald Horne, *White Supremacy Confronted: U.S. Imperialism and Anti-Communism vs. the Liberation of Southern Africa, from Rhodes to Mandela*, New York: International Publishers, 2019

effort by colonizing powers, be they in Jamaica or Southern Africa or Kenya, to deprive Africans of higher education. These same Africans could come to Alabama to Tuskegee and receive higher education. I think that many of them found that to be both attractive and inspiring. I think that that helps to explain how and why it is that a Marcus Garvey could be attracted to come to the United States about 105 years ago or so, in order to learn more about the example of Booker T, Washington.

As your comment suggested and as the book suggests the Marcus Garvey organization, the UNIA, enjoys astronomical growth. Not only in the United States and eventually having tens of thousands of members, developing a newspaper, *The Negro World*, which was sold throughout the Pan-African world, had strong branches not only in New York and Louisiana, but also in Cuba, Jamaica of course, the eastern coast of the Central American peninsula, particularly the Central American region, particularly of Costa Rica, and Nicaragua. Of course, in Southern Africa, South Africa and Namibia, many of the newspapers were delivered by Black sailors.

A Forgotten aspect of historic political economy is that oftentimes sailors, at least in the anglosphere, were of African descent. Many of them of course are of South Asian descent. The Garvey organization had influence in Kenya, and I think that it was perceived justifiably in the African context and the Caribbean context as being anti-colonial. Therefore, it was seen as providing a mortal threat and a mortal danger to colonialism, which was one of the reasons why there was an attempt to ban the newspaper, to jail those who were somehow connected with the Garvey organization, but ultimately that proved to be unavailing.

CS: Thanks for breaking down that history. I was wondering if you could talk about the influence that Japan had in the region in Kenya. You have also spoke about how Mussolini had sought to stir "up discord in Kenya."[5] This also ties into your other work on Tokyo. You said that "Tokyo's forces also expressed reluctance to shoot at askaris or East African forces."[6]

GH: Well, the influence of Japan on the Pan-African world before 1945 has been a particular interest of mine, reflected in a number of articles that you can find online. Certainly, in books. The book

5. Gerald Horne, *Mau Mau in Harlem?: The US and the Liberation of Kenya*, New York: Palgrave Macmillan, 2009, 7

6. Ibid., 68

I wrote, *Race War,* that came out, as I recall, in 2003.[7] Then there is the book that I wrote a few years ago, *Facing the Rising Sun.*[8] So basically, the story is that circa 1853, the US sails into Japan, and Japan is fearing that what had befallen Hong Kong in the previous decades, that is to say British colonialism, circa 1841-1842, was about to befall Japan. So, Japan goes through a rapid transformation, and is reflected in what's called the Meiji Restoration, whereby there is a battle between feudal forces and proto-capitalist forces. With the latter prevailing interestingly enough, Hollywood tackled that subject in the movie, *The Last Samurai,* which is very interesting, starring Tom Cruise. For whatever reason, Hollywood sympathizes with the feudal forces, not the capitalist forces, even though they're capitalist. I think it's because these capitalist forces in Japan, proved to be all too competitive.

I should also mention that I've talked about Japan in my books on the South Seas and Hawaii. The book, *The White Pacific,* which deals specifically with how and why it is that even today in the Hawaiian archipelago a disproportionate percentage of the US nationals there are of Japanese origin.[9] Because what happens is you have the independent Hawaii Kingdom before the US takeover in the 1890s and like Japan in the 1850s, the Hawaii Kingdom as it surveys the landscape it sees that it too could fall victim to a US takeover so it tried to work out a deal with Japan. But alas, it doesn't work, they're overthrown in any case.

Then you have the rise of Japan, which is resentful of the way Japanese nationals or Japanese Americans, in fact, are treated in Hawaii. I argue that that's a factor in the attack on Pearl Harbor, Hawaii on December 7, 1941. I've noticed that some of my critics, they didn't like me saying that. I think that sometimes the historians and the critics they prefer morality tales. So, you can't suggest that there might have been resentment in Japan towards racism directed at people of Japanese ancestry in Hawaii because then that might provide a rationale of Japan attacking Pearl Harbor. You have to make it seem as if this was just evil personified, there was no reason for it.

I say in the book *Facing the Rising Sun* that I carried no grief for Japanese imperialism, but I feel compelled to explain to audiences why

---

7. Gerald Horne, *Race War: White Supremacy and the Japanese Attack on the British Empire,* New York: New York University Press, 2004

8. Gerald Horne, *Facing the Rising Sun: African Americans, Japan, and the Rise of Afro-Asian Solidarity,* New York: New York University Press, 2018

9. Gerald Horne, *The White Pacific: U.S. Imperialism and Black Slavery in the South Seas After the Civil War,* Honolulu: University of Hawai'i Press, 2007

events happen, as opposed to just descending and devolving into simple minded morality tales.[10] In any case, another turning point comes with Japan's defeat of Russia, 1904-1905. A turning point in the struggle against white supremacy is revealed in the words and analyses not only of W.E.B. Du Bois but Ho Chi Minh, Sun Yat-sen of China, Nehru of India. At this point Japan is rising. It's flexing its muscles after World War I at the negotiation at Versailles to effectuate a peace treaty. Japan wanted written into international law, or some sorts of prohibitions against racism, which does not go down very well in Australia, an officially racist nation until maybe 1967, when under pressure from its US paymaster, it's forced to make wholesome steps away from the more egregious aspects of white supremacy.

What this leads to is that Japan feels that it can obtain leverage over its European and Euro-American antagonists by making an appeal to those who are subjugated within the British Empire and within the US state. Of course, this leads to many Black nationalists in the 1930s, for example, devising the concept of the Asiatic Black man, this was at a time when Africa was colonized and so these Black Americans, they looked at themselves as walking in the footsteps of Japan.

Then you see a similar appeal of Japan and Africa, not only in Kenya but also in southern Africa. I talked about the latter, in my book, *White Supremacy Confronted* on the liberation struggle in southern Africa.[11] So, this reaches a real fever pitch in the 1930s when imperial Japan and imperial Ethiopia basically bruit the idea of a merger of the royal family, just like that was quite common in Europe. As you know, say the royal family of Greece was to marry into the royal family of London, for example, or for the royal family in Germany to marry into the royal family of London, for example. It does not take off, but the fact that it was bruited obviously gives Japan an advantage in terms of its competition for hearts and minds in the Pan-African world. Because of course, you could be lynched in Dixie for reckless eyeballing, for looking at some woman of European descent, innocently.

Here you had Japan and Ethiopia talking about a merger of royal families. This becomes a major factor after World War II begins. I would argue as well that it's a major factor in loosening the bonds

---

10. Gerald Horne, *Facing the Rising Sun: African Americans, Japan, and the Rise of Afro-Asian Solidarity*, New York: New York University Press, 2018

11. Gerald Horne, *White Supremacy Confronted: U.S. Imperialism and Anti-Communism vs. the Liberation of Southern Africa, from Rhodes to Mandela*, New York: International Publishers, 2019

of colonialism, not only in Kenya, but I would say throughout Africa because the US basically dodges a bullet with regard to World War II, the Pacific War more specifically. My own estimation is—and this is obviously difficult to prove, because what I'm about to say is counterfactual—is that before the atomic bombings of Hiroshima and Nagasaki, August 6, August 9, 1945, it would have been very difficult to defeat the Japanese in Indonesian.

As a matter of fact, wherever you had European colonial empires, those were the places where Tokyo had dug deep roots. That is to say, Indonesia, India—Subhash Chandra Bose, an Indian national hero, of course, died fighting shoulder to shoulder with Japanese forces. In the places where Japan itself was the colonial occupier Japan was not greeted, shall we say, as conquering heroes. That would include China, in the first instance, and the Korean peninsula in the second instance, not least because of the depredations inflicted by the Japanese colonial occupiers during that time.

Now, Africa of course is a different story because there was no Japanese colonial occupation of Africa. Just as the United States looked to the now demonized Soviet Union to pull its chestnuts out of the fire, between 1941 to 1945, and that's hardly controversial. The only people I know who criticize the US alliance with Moscow during that time are the late President Herbert Hoover and the contemporary analyst Pat Buchanan. Otherwise, it's really not seen as that controversial and so likewise, for Africans to get the European boot off their neck they were looking to Tokyo and the colonial occupiers recognized that, and I've argued, this is a factor in the agonizing retreat from the more horrible aspects of colonialism and of its cousin, US Jim Crow, post 1945.

CS: Thank you so much for that history. Going back and building on the solidarity between African Americans and Kenyans, you wrote about how African Americans had shared stories of the Haitian Revolution and marched alongside Kenyans against Britain. Then Britain later forbade any meetings between these two groups. Later African Americans and Kenyans marched together "in demands for higher pay."[12] I was wondering if you could talk more about that?

GH: This was in Kenya in the in the 1950s?

CS: I have a note about 1942, a "battalion of the 812th engineers" came to Kenya and "'opened fired on the Police Station.'"[13]

---

12. Gerald Horne, *Mau Mau in Harlem?: The US and the Liberation of Kenya*, New York: Palgrave Macmillan, 2009, 8

13. Ibid., 8

GH: Right, right. What's interesting and there's been some writing about that, I think I've probably written about it, too, which is that the Black American soldiers are viewed suspiciously and skeptically in Australia by the Canberra authority, and certainly in Nairobi, because here you have these Black American soldiers, oftentimes they're carrying guns. Oftentimes, they're getting into scraps with Euro-Americans or Europeans, for example, this is seen as destabilizing to the colonial order. Many of the Black Americans are sympathetic to the African in Kenya.

This is not only with regard to the soldiers, as I've suggested a few moments ago. You also have Black sailors sailing into Mombasa, the major Kenya port, they too are viewed suspiciously. What's interesting as well is that this also goes back to the slavery period in the United States where South Carolina, one of the major slave states, tries to pass laws to keep Black sailors in ships where the Union Jack flies—that is to say under the British flag—try to keep them out of Charleston, for example. For similar reasons, reasons similar to why the British were seeking to keep Black American sailors out of Mombasa, it's a very interesting historical parallel and from a narrow authoritarian point of view their suspicions were justifiable because, as suggested, these Black outsiders if you like did sympathize with the enslaved in South Carolina, or with the colonized in Mombasa.

CS: I was wondering if you could break open more the Council on African Affairs (CAA) and the solidarity they showed with Kenya. You wrote about how Eslanda Robeson was in East Africa around World War II and she was appalled at the treatment of Kenyans and then I believe the CAA was formed shortly after.[14]

GH: The Council on African Affairs was initiated by her spouse Paul Robeson. He of course was the great socialist, singer, actor, activist, athlete, the tallest tree in our forest. He spent a good deal of the 1920s and the 1930s in self-imposed exile in London where he was exposed directly to the horrors of colonialism. He was associated with Jomo Kenyatta, who goes on to become a founding father of modern Kenya. The Council on African Affairs is initiated in circa 1937. It's driven out of business by the US authorities circa 1956, which was part of a full-scale onslaught against various wings that were perceived to be too close to the US Communist Party and that would include not only the Council on African Affairs, but also the Civil Rights Congress (CRC), which was led by Robeson's good friend William Paterson.

---

14. Ibid.

Together they filed a petition at the United Nations 1950-1951, charging the United States with genocide against Black people in the United States. The CRC were the subject of a book that I published some decades ago that's just came out in paperback a few months ago.[15] In any case, Eslanda Robeson, the spouse of Paul Robeson, traveled throughout Africa; she wrote about her adventure; it's a very enlightening book. She also traveled to Southern Africa as well. Like Ralph Bunche, she too was horrified and outraged with how the Africans were maltreated and mistreated in that part of Africa, and Kenya becomes a solemn cause for the Council on African Affairs.

Interestingly enough, although the council focused on colonialism generally, they seemed to devote special attention to the settler colonial regime—be they Kenya or Rhodesia, South Africa—and that's understandable because the United States itself is a settler colonial regime. Although interestingly enough, even though folks on the left could easily espy settler colonialism when looking overseas, they did not necessarily apply that same descriptor to North America, for whatever reason. The only explanations I can come up with are inadequate, explanations being the propaganda for the 1776 war has been so powerful that it has overwhelmed any sort of analysis of this process whereby Europeans invaded North America and seized the land from the Indigenous and then dragooned Africans to come across the Atlantic to work for free. I'm going to have to think about that a bit further because the saying that the propaganda is powerful, is insufficient and, of course it's going to be powerful propaganda for any state. So, I'll have to think about that a bit more deeply.

CS: Yes, and the propaganda was so powerful it became like this mythology that's still growing out today as you've written about.

GH: It certainly is, that's for sure.

CS: I was wondering if you could talk more about the role of the labor movement in Kenya, you wrote about the 1947 massive and organized strike that hit Mombasa and then Tom Mboya was for trade unionists and how this led into the 1952 state of emergency?[16]

GH: Yes, well, the labor movement in the United States, its finest hour was in the 1930s, when you have the organizing of the CIO, the Congress of Industrial Organizations, which unlike its predecessor, the AFL, the CIO organized plantwide, whereas the AFL would

15. Gerald Horne, *Communist Front?: The Civil Rights Congress, 1946-1956*, Rutherford: Fairleign University Press, 1988

16. Gerald Horne, *Mau Mau in Harlem?: The US and the Liberation of Kenya*, New York: Palgrave Macmillan, 2009

just say organize skilled workers. It would be as if you go into a university and you organize just the professors and don't organize the janitors and the cafeteria workers. So, it was the CIO that broke the mold and organized across the board, all workers in a particular worksite. They oftentimes, were led by communist organizers, which then leads to a rift internally. It leads to an attempt to put pressure on the CIO to ditch certain unions and of course these were big unions who would have reach into, say Kenya, for example.

I'm thinking of the National Maritime Union, which, as suggested, had sailors that sailed into Mombasa, Kenya on a regular basis, many of whom were Black. In fact, the number two leader of the National Maritime Union, Ferdinand Smith, the subject of a biography I wrote some years ago was of Jamaican origin and was deeply concerned about colonialism and racism and white supremacy.[17] So, unsurprisingly, you had an attempt by US labor to assist Kenyan labor as part of a kind of worker's internationalism, the likes of which is not as prominent today as it should be.

In any case, what happens is perhaps predictable. That is to say that Ferdinand Smith is deported from the United States, circa 1950-1951, as part of the anti-Communist Red Scare, and his union the National Maritime Union is weakened as a direct result. To the point now, where the union is a shadow of its former self and US vessels that are responsible for imports and exports to this very day are little more than floating slugs with terrible exploitation of the sailors. In any case, what happens is that as the anti-Communists become more prominent in the US labor movement they too begin to reach out to Kenyan labor.

Therein lies the story of Tom Mboya, of Luo ancestry, as is his compatriot, Barack Obama senior. Mboya has very close connections with these anti-Communist forces in the US labor movement. Recall that the AFL and CIO merge, more like a shotgun wedding in the mid-1950s. The CIO was weakened because of anticommunist purges and is swallowed by the AFL. They develop a relationship, that is to say the AFL-CIO with Tom Mboya, he visits the United States more than once, even after the state of emergency, circa 1952, and the onset of what's called the Mau Mau revolt, which we now know, was a bloody reign of terror, inflicted by the British.

In fact, some readers may know the story of how it was only about a decade or so ago that records of the reign of terror were somehow

---

17. Gerald Horne, *Red Seas: Ferdinand Smith and Radical Black Sailors in the United States and Jamaica*, New York: New York University Press, 2005

uncovered in a warehouse in England, where they had been shipped surreptitiously, not stored in the National Archives of the UK, in Kew Gardens, London, but gathering dust. Then that led to a lawsuit whereby some of the uglier stories of British depredation in Kenya came to light. Of course, the Africans who were the victims of these depredations, it came as no surprise or secret to them. But it came as a surprise to many others, particularly outsiders.

So, what's interesting is that you've had a basic flip of the script whereby Mau Mau has come to be a phrase that symbolizes, at least in the minds of some, a kind of bloody terror, when actually it was the British who administered bloody terror, including summary executions, torture, all manner of gruesome tortures. In some ways, exceeding the kinds of tortures masterminded by their bastard spawn now headquartered in Washington.

This is quite a story, and it also points out too why history continues to face the need to be rewritten because these records were only discovered about a decade ago. So, those such as myself—my book came out in 2009—so those records had not seen the light of day when I was doing my research, or when I visited Kenya to do my research. By the way, let me recommend to future researchers the Kenyan archives, which are in downtown Nairobi right across the street from a hotel, which means you can just cross the street. All you have to do is cross the street from the hotel to get to the archive. It's very convenient.

CS: Oh, that's awesome. Thank you. Speaking of just the sheer violence, you wrote about Operation Anvil and then you mentioned the Manyani prison camp, which held 18,000 Kenyan prisoners. It was "'one of the world's largest detention camps'" at the time.[18]

GH: Yeah, I mean, there's been an attempt by some, whose names will go unmentioned, to sanitize and criticize the ugliness and the smelliness of British colonialism. We're oftentimes told that British colonialism was a net plus. People learned how to speak English as a result of British colonialism, etc. When actually it was really just organized violence. It was organized terror from the barrel of a gun. I mean, certainly the power of the British Empire flowed from the barrel of a gun.

The story of how that evolved, I would point readers to my book on the 16th century, where I suggest that internal war in the British

---

18. Gerald Horne, *Mau Mau in Harlem?: The US and the Liberation of Kenya*, New York: Palgrave Macmillan, 2009, 129

Isles, particularly English wars against the Irish and the Welsh and the Scots, helps London to develop the framework for what becomes a powerful military industrial complex.[19] Then those weapons and those tactics used internally are then exported abroad to the Americas, to Africa, and to Asia. Having said that, it's no exaggeration to say that for various reasons, perhaps the worst excesses of the British Empire come in colonial Kenya.

I think it may have something to do with the fact that it was a settler regime, but it was a settler regime where the settlers were grossly outnumbered.[20] I don't recall the figures off the top of my head, but it's in the book and I think that because the settlers felt challenged and felt that their regime rested on an unsteady foundation, which is true—it did rest on an unsteady foundation—that as a result, they have to go overboard in administering all manner of ghastly torture and that is precisely what happened.

CS: My next question has to do with the effect of the laws mandating separate schools in Little Rock, the effect that this had on Kenya. You wrote about how people were talking about this in Egypt, and Uganda, and that coupled with the meeting of Africans and Asians in Bandung, Indonesia, in 1955, you write, "which made clear its unfiltered distaste for the kind of white supremacy that then obtained from Mombasa in Mississippi."[21]

GH: Those are major landmarks on the road to independence for Kenya and independence for Africa. Just to step back for a second and to return to a previous thread, I think it's fair to say that the British Empire was terribly weakened as a result of the pulverizing blows that proceed, both from Berlin and Tokyo. The British Empire tries to recover, that leads to the war in Malaya, now Malaysia, beginning in the late 1940s. That leads to the conflict over historic Palestine, but what you can see is that the British Empire is both weakened and is overstretched fighting all around the world to maintain its empire, mass demonstrations in Jamaica, for example.

So, this energizes those who have historically been victimized by colonialism, which leads to this important meeting in Indonesia in the mid-1950s at Bandung. Interestingly enough, you had a number

19. Gerald Horne, *The Dawning of the Apocalypse: The Roots of Slavery, White Supremacy, Settler Colonialism, and Capitalism in the Long Sixteenth Century*, New York: Monthly Review Press

20. Gerald Horne, *Mau Mau in Harlem?: The US and the Liberation of Kenya*, New York: Palgrave Macmillan, 2009

21. Ibid., 140

of Black Americans who traveled there, although not necessarily for positive purposes. That is to say, Congressman Adam Clayton Powell of Harlem who was trying to get in the good graces of Washington, which was busily trying to either expel him from Congress or jail him. He traveled there on behalf of the United States; the novelist Richard Wright, you may know his novel, *Native Son*; he wrote a book about his travel to Indonesia, it's called *The Color Curtain*.[22]

This was a meeting mostly of colonized countries and newly independent countries. Zhou Enlai of China was there, he was the number two leader in China. If I'm not mistaken, there was an attempt that barely failed to blow up his plane as he was traveling from China to Indonesia. You also had presence there, if I'm not mistaken, of representatives from Yugoslavia, which of course, it has constituent elements being Serbia, Croatia, Montenegro, Slovenia, etc, in southeastern Europe, but was pivotal in developing Bandung because of its role in trying to develop a so-called non-aligned movement, which would try to not be perceived to be in the camp of the socialist countries or capitalist countries. Although of course, as matters evolved many of the non-aligned countries wound up being perceived as being part of the socialist camp anyway, because the socialist countries supported them against the exploitation of the capitalist countries.

Bandung was a very important landmark. As noted, it gave a loud signal that imperialism and colonialism were to receive ever stiffer challenge. That was followed by the Suez Crisis in 1956, whereby Britain, France, and Israel fought to prevent Egypt from claiming the Suez Canal, which, during the 1860s—when Egypt was subject to colonial occupation, not only by Ottoman Turkey, but by Britain and France as well—the Suez Canal was built then, but Egypt had become independent subsequently. Gamal Abdel Nasser, the leader, wanted to claim the Suez Canal. Britain, France, and Israel objected. They waged war against Egypt but had to stand down because the Soviet Union, per my previous remarks about Bandung refused to go along with this and in fact, even the United States felt compelled to issue statements critical of this brigandage.

That was a turning point in world history because Britain drew the conclusion that the jig was up for the Empire. It had to draw closer to Uncle Sam. France, the opposite conclusion, that it had to develop itself independently. Even today you hear President Macron speak, and I underline speak about strategic autonomy of France. In

---

22. Richard Wright, *The Color Curtain: A Report on the Bandung Conference*, Jackson: University Press of Mississippi, 1994

any case, that was a signal to colonized countries that you did not necessarily have to bend the knee to the imperialist forces. Egypt showed them.

Then the next year in 1957, you had the segregation crisis in Little Rock, Arkansas, whereby President Eisenhower had to call in troops to protect Black kids from being mauled and beaten by their Euro-American classmates, as they seek to desegregate Central High School. It's a black eye for the United States, which is trying to portray itself as the paragon of human rights virtue. Earlier that year, this is the fall of 1957, you had Ghana independence. So that chain reaction—Bandung, Suez, Little Rock—was setting the table for the imminent demise and the imminent retreat of British colonialism, not least in Kenya.

CS: Thank you for breaking open that era so well. My next question is what really surprised you about the archives in Nairobi, Kenya that you weren't expecting to find?

GH: Well one I wrote about. It was a Hollywood movie made in Kenya.

CS: Was this the movie with Grace Kelly?

GH: Yes, but what struck me was the detailed notes in the archives about the filming of that movie, and of course, the same with exploitation. That's a given of the Africans who are employed as extras in the movie. But also, the opportunities that the movie production presented for advance by the liberation forces. Of course, Kenya, it's been a staple of Hollywood cinema. You might recall *Out of Africa* with Meryl Streep and Robert Redford.

Of course, Kenya, it exposes I should say of how Hollywood views Black people, or how Hollywood views Africa, because like many of these movies Africa is just the backdrop, it's just scenery, so the Euro-Americans can strut their stuff, like Meryl Streep and Robert Redford. I mean, you see that all the time. It has become almost a bad joke about Hollywood movies.

I mean, think of all the anti-apartheid dramas. Now, of course, there would be reasons to have Euro-American actors in anti-apartheid dramas because after all, we're talking about a nation South Africa that has about five million people of European descent and has exported to these shores, Elon Musk, Roelof Botha. I'm sure your audience doesn't have to be acquainted with Elon Musk, but Roelof Botha is of course perhaps the leading venture capitalist in Silicon Valley. He of course is the direct descendant of apartheid's last Foreign Minister, Pik Botha.

So, you understand why it would be the anti-apartheid dramas, you have these Euro-American actors like Kevin Kline, for example.

Or Marlon Brando, for example. But still, South Africa is in Africa, about 85 percent of the people were Black but you would never get that if you were to do a short survey of films about South Africa and the same holds true for Kenya too, as well. With regard to the archives, once again I recommend the archives. I think more work could be done on the role of the United States in Kenya. I think my book opens the subject, but more can be done.

CS: Thank you. I think the movie you wrote about was called *Mogambo*.

GH: Yes, that's it.

CS: My last question is about Kenya and the influence on Black Power movements, such as the title of your book suggests of Malcolm X. You've also written about the influence it had on Medgar Evers and Charles Evers, Kwame Toure, H. Rap Brown, and Robert F. Williams.[23]

GH: Yes, I think if I'm not mistaken, Medgar Evers gave one or more of his children Kenyan names. The title of the book comes from Malcolm X, from Malcolm X finding inspiration in that liberation struggle. I think the parallels of settler colonialism are clear, that is to say that the Africans in East Africa were subjected to settler colonialism like the Africans and the Indigenous in North America, were subjected to settler colonialism. Kenya was seen as an exemplar of how you weaken settler colonialism. I think also, paradoxically, the fact that Mau Mau had such a fearsome reputation, even though as I tried to suggest some of that's overblown and what was really fearsome was the reign of terror by the colonizers.

In any case, that fearfulness, I think, inspired many strugglers on this side of the Atlantic to deepen their own commitment to the struggle, and to heighten their own militancy with regard to the struggle. I think that's part of the lasting legacy of the liberation movement in Kenya. Now, of course since that time, Kenya has become a kind of pillar of neo-colonialism, but I think that that's due in no small measure to the changing global correlation of forces, whereby worldwide, the forces of socialism in recent decades, have been on the backfoot, have been on the retreat, and as the French elections today, April 24, 2022, suggest, oftentimes leaving an electorate with a choice between neoliberalism and neofascism. Now, if that happens to an advanced capitalist country like France, one of

---

23. Gerald Horne, *Mau Mau in Harlem?: The US and the Liberation of Kenya*, New York: Palgrave Macmillan, 2009

the top ten economies on planet Earth, well, one can only imagine what the choices will be for a relatively small country in East Africa, which suggests that perhaps we need a new stage of a liberation movement, this time directed at neocolonialism with the same fire and fury that was directed previously at colonialism.

Chapter 10

Solidarity, Mercenaries, and the Liberation of Zimbabwe
May 29, 2022

CS: This interview is going to be focused on your book *From The Barrel Of A Gun: The United States and the War Against Zimbabwe, 1965-1980*.[1] Dr. Horne while you were living in NYC in the 1970s, you organized numerous rallies in support of majority rule in Zimbabwe. I was wondering if you could talk a little bit more about this experience and organizing?

GH: Yes, in the 1970s, I was mostly living in Manhattan, mostly living in Harlem. There was residing in New York City at that time a compliment of students and exiles from Southern Africa, as well as Black Americans who had either been involved in relationships with or marriages with people from Southern Africa. Of course, New York City historically had been a lodestar with regard to Pan-Africanism. Insofar as the Black population is diverse, it's not only the descendants of mainland enslaved Africans but also folks from the Caribbean, and as noted folks from Africa as well.

At the time, the crisis in Southern Africa was receiving inordinate attention in the mainstream press and the Black press. Speaking of *The New York Amsterdam News*, based in Harlem, *The City Sun* based in Brooklyn, then you had a Black talk radio station, WLIB, which happened to be located in the same building on Second Avenue near 42nd Street in Manhattan. That radio station was housed in the same building as a number of liberation movements that had representation at the United Nations around the corner, at First Avenue and 42nd Street.

So that meant that we oftentimes were able to command the airways, speaking of WLIB, AM radio Black talk radio, a station that had been initiated by Percy Sutton, who had been a leading Black

---

1. Gerald Horne, *From The Barrel Of A Gun: The United States and the War Against Zimbabwe, 1965-1980*, Chapel Hill: University of North Carolina, 2001

politician. He had been borough president of Manhattan, had been a representative in the state legislature, as I recall, and had been an attorney for the family of the late Malcolm X, who of course had roots in New York City. So, it was a very convenient and comfortable relationship for those of us involved in Southern African solidarity, to command the airway by way of our relationship with WLIB and their station at Second Avenue near 42nd street.

We organized different rallies and different manifestations throughout the 1970s. It was—as they say in the United States—it was a racially integrated group, although heavily comprised of Black Americans, and of course, as noted with a compliment of folks with roots in the Southern Cone of Africa. Probably the highlight of our activity was the concert that we held at St. John the Divine Church, which is on Amsterdam Avenue and 112th Street in Manhattan. I used to live very close to that church, which is quite a formidable edifice, you may even want to look at it online. It has some unique characteristics that I cannot recall.

In any case, in the spring of 1980 we organized a fundraising concert for the two competing liberation movements in Zimbabwe, once Rhodesia, speaking of ZANU, the Zimbabwe African National Union and ZAPU the Zimbabwe African People's Union. We raised quite a sum it was either $10,000 or $20,000, I can't recall. The entertainment was provided, if I'm not mistaken, by Hugh Masekela, who was a popular South African recording artist and exile in the United States. His sister Barbara Masekela was a professor at Rutgers University in New Brunswick, New Jersey. Eventually, she became the chief of staff of Nelson Mandela, in South Africa, eventually, the South African ambassador to France after South African independence in 1994. The thousands of dollars we raised at that concert, were then turned over to the aforementioned organizations from Zimbabwe who then used the funds for their political campaigns. As you know the ZANU force wound up emerging triumphant during the election and that is a synopsis of the activities that I was involved in from the 1970s up until Zimbabwean independence in 1980.

CS: Thank you very much for the history on that and that was the Zimbabwe Emergency Concert that you were chairing a committee on? Then, it was after much discussion on which party the funds should go to it was just decided to split it and give it equally between the two parties?[2]

GH: Right. I can go into that if you're interested.

---

2. Ibid.

CS: Yes, if you'd like to.

GH: I talk about this in part in my book *White Supremacy Confronted*, which deals with the entire region.[3] *From The Barrel Of A Gun* just deals mostly with Zimbabwe, Rhodesia. So, there was a split in the liberation forces ranks, in Zimbabwe, once Rhodesia. There was one group that was perceived to be pro-Moscow, that's ZAPU, another group that was perceived to be pro-China, that was ZANU, and that cleavage manifested itself in the ranks in New York City.

There were similar cleavages there and what's interesting is that as time evolves, and as ZANU deepened its hold on the country, and of course what happened ultimately was that some years after independence, ZANU swallowed ZAPU. The emergent party is known as ZANU-PF, PF meaning Patriotic Front. What happened is that for a while the two forces were aligned in a so-called Patriotic Front. What's striking, looking retrospectively, is that ZANU ultimately engaged in a land reform, that is to say, taking land from the European minority, many of whom, whose roots in the country are rather shallow. That is to say, post-1945 as opposed to South Africa where the European minority, some have roots going back to 1652. Whereas the European minority in South Africa was about five million, in Zimbabwe, at its height, it was probably 200,000 in a population that today is about 12 million.

In any case, after the land reform, the ZANU-PF government was slapped with sanctions by the US authorities and the British authorities. ZANU argued that the agreement that led to elections in 1980, the so-called Lancaster House Agreement, mandated that London would assist with land reform in various ways and ZANU-PF said that London reneged on its obligation. ZANU-PF argued that it did not engage in land reform immediately upon coming to independence in 1980 because of the storm across the border in South Africa. They felt that land reform would complicate that particular struggle. So, they waited up to independence in South Africa in 1994. What's striking in my estimation, is that a number of the Black Americans who were most staunch in their support for China and most staunch in their support for ZANU basically flipped in reverse course after land reform and sanctions and the heat that came down.

I wrote an article in *Black Scholar* during the height of this controversy in the 1990s, if I'm not mistaken, entitled "Why Zimbabwe?"

---

3. Gerald Horne, *White Supremacy Confronted: U.S. Imperialism and Anti-Communism vs. the Liberation of Southern Africa, from Rhodes to Mandela*, New York: International Publishers, 2019

I start the article with a kind of curveball, writing that this small Southern African nation is a human rights disaster and then I site a litany of misdeeds by the ruling elite.[4] Then I conclude that paragraph by saying yes, Swaziland needs to be sanctioned, Swaziland of course, the neighbor of South Africa, now called Eswatini, a true human rights disaster. The point of the article was saying why are we spending so much time on Zimbabwe, which has an opposition press, opposition party, whereas Swaziland, its neighbor as well, is a royal autocracy and dictatorship.

Of course, it has a lot to do with the fact that ZANU, engaged in land reform, was perceived as reversing the fruits of settler colonialism, a process that is also embedded in North America, by the way, speaking of settler colonialism. There was an identification by the US ruling class with those who were being expropriated in Zimbabwe, as I point out in the book, the spouse of Henry Kissinger, former Secretary of State, had familial ties in Rhodesia.[5] Lyndon Baines Johnson, the former US president, had familial ties in Rhodesia. Ian Smith the leader of the Rhodesian Front, which fought independence and fought majority rule by Africans, had relatives in the United States. That helped to distinguish to a degree, Zimbabwe from some of its neighbors.

For example, in Namibia, which had been initially colonized by Germany before being swallowed by South Africa—post-World War I, post-1918—and South Africa itself, which, as noted, had settlers with roots in the Netherlands and in a French Protestant community, who as you know had been expelled. On more than one occasion, many of them flocked to South Africa, whereas Rhodesia was a British colony, not unlike North America and that led to a closer identification in my estimation with the settlers on that side of the Atlantic.

Now, this issue of China was quite intriguing because China's record at the time with regard to Southern Africa was nothing to brag about. But once again there's been a reversal because as time has passed, now China is in the crosshairs of US imperialism. I recall a time when China argued that the lines being pushed by the then Soviet Union—of peaceful coexistence between the socialist camp and the capitalist camp—was a sellout. Now of course, what they ignored at the time was that peaceful coexistence did not mean

4. Gerald Horne, "Why Zimbabwe?," *The Black Scholar*, 37, NO. 1 (March 22, 2007): 12: https://search-ebscohost-com.dml.regis.edu/login.aspx?direct=true&db=edsbro&AN=edsbro.A168083468&site=eds-live&scope=site

5. Gerald Horne, *From The Barrel Of A Gun: The United States and the War against Zimbabwe, 1965-1980*, Chapel Hill: University of North Carolina, 2001

peaceful coexistence with apartheid or peaceful coexistence with colonialism in Zimbabwe.

Interestingly enough, in my book *White Supremacy Confronted*, I point out how China at the time despite that line, finds itself on the same side in Angola with US imperialism of South African apartheid, but now times have changed.[6] Now the line from Beijing is peaceful coexistence because they recognize that they're dealing with these wild men in Washington who would have no hesitation to drop nuclear weapons on Beijing if they felt they could get away with it. As a footnote we just lived through in the last few days what may have been a very telling sign. You may recall that in Northeast Asia, US President Joseph R. Biden suggested that the United States could intervene militarily if China sought to reclaim Taiwan, the rebel province that China claims as its own. At the time that Mr. Biden was speaking you had a joint military exercise being carried out in the vicinity by Russian and Chinese bombers. They said it was coincidence, that it had long been planned. Others were not so sure. But what it reflects, of course, are the Copernican changes that have taken place in the world since the storm over Rhodesia Zimbabwe, culminating in Independence in 1980.

This 180-degree reversal, or I should just say reversal of field whereby some and I underline some who were quite critical of the Soviet Union, quite critical of liberation movements supported by the Soviet Union, have reversed field and have joined in the crusade against the ZANU-PF government they once supported. I have to believe that many of these folks were not able to withstand defeat that came down after land reform, but that's just an editorial opinion.

CS: Thank you very much for that background, and those links to right now. Speaking of settler colonialism, you wrote about Rhodesia and the comparisons between the so-called frontier in the US and the genocide and stealing of Indigenous land in North America. You pointed out how Peter Godwin had referred to sections of this war-torn nation as "Apache country," which was very reminiscent of what Roxanne Dunbar Ortiz had pointed out of Iraq be referred to as "Indian Country."[7] Of course, Teddy Roosevelt had said that Rho-

---

6. Gerald Horne, *White Supremacy Confronted: U.S. Imperialism and Anti-Communism vs. the Liberation of Southern Africa, from Rhodes to Mandela*, New York: International Publishers, 2019

7. Gerald Horne, *From The Barrel Of A Gun: The United States and the War against Zimbabwe, 1965-1980*, Chapel Hill: University of North Carolina, 2001, 36; Roxanne Dunbar-Ortiz, *An Indigenous Peoples' History of the United States*, Boston: Beacon Press, 2015, 56

desia "represented a great and striking conquest for civilization."[8] I was wondering if you could go into more of these comparisons that you found?

GH: Yes. I go into that in the book on Zimbabwe and go into it also in the larger book on Southern Africa. What's interesting is that in both books, I trace the route of certain settlers who moved west across North America, battling the Indigenous population of North America before winding up in Southern Africa, where they battled the Africans. Some of them even wound up in East Africa and Kenya, where they battled Africans. This was part of what could be called a white Atlantic or even a white Pacific insofar as many of them battled across North America wound up in Southern California and then took ships headed westward.

Some of them even wound up in Australia battling the Indigenous there. Interestingly enough, in my recently published book on Texas, *The Counter-Revolution of 1836,* I talk about a similar phenomenon. I talk about Lüderitz. If you look at your map, you'll find that a major city to this day in Namibia is Lüderitz, who was a European settler in Texas before he and or his descendants wind up in Southwest Africa, just north of Cape Town, South Africa. So, this is part of the process whereby settler colonialism was constructed. It was a transcontinental phenomenon. It was a Pan-European phenomenon, insofar as it involved not only those with roots in the British Isles but as in the case of Lüderitz, those with roots in Germany.

In the Texas Book I talk about many of the settlers having roots in Switzerland, for example, settlers having roots in France for example, and I referenced a moment or two ago the French Protestants or Huguenots, who played a role in the colonizing of South Africa, they also played a role in the colonizing South Carolina.[9] In fact, if you go to Charleston, South Carolina, to this very day you can stumble across a cemetery, a French Huguenot cemetery and read the headstones with the French names on them.

This is the process whereby settler colonialism was constructed. It was constructed as the title of the book at hand suggests, *From the Barrel of a Gun.* Because particularly in Africa, the Europeans oftentimes or the settlers were oftentimes outnumbered but they were able to level the playing field—as they say—by out gunning those they were fighting by having Gatling guns and machine guns and

8. Gerald Horne, *From the Barrel of a Gun...,* Ibid., 55

9. Gerald Horne, *The Counter-Revolution of 1836: Texas Slavery & Jim Crow and the Roots of U.S. Fascism,* New York: International Publishers, 2022

cannons and the other products of the nation's military industrial complex, which has now ballooned to a size that may have been difficult to imagine in the 1890s, when you first had settler incursions into what becomes a Rhodesia.

Of course, Cecil Rhodes was a British chap, who made a sizable fortune in South Africa in particular. Although the renaming process has been proceeding apace in that part of Africa, there are still entities named after Cecil Rhodes. You may recall the struggle in South Africa and in England by the way—Rhodes Must Fall—statues of him headed for the garbage heap of history. Rhodesia—Southern Rhodesia, Northern Rhodesia, speaking of Zambia—once carried the name, likewise, of Cecil Rhodes. When I was living in Zimbabwe, circa 1995, I recall visiting the grave of Cecil Rhodes in Zimbabwe, where I must say I treated the grave with utter disrespect, stamping on it and spitting on it.

CS: Thank you for sharing that. A similar grave that's in Denver that is hard to walk by without the same feelings is General Chivington's at Fairmount Cemetery. I was wondering if you could talk about the timeframe of 1965 when Ian Smith declared independence from Britain and the US supported the decision to the turning point in 1974, when you wrote "armed struggle was most intense," and then when tensions were heightening when Cuban troops were dispatched to Angola in the late fall in 1975.[10] As you mentioned, this is when the US, South Africa, and China were more aligned at this point.

GH: Yeah, that was quite a time. I mean, first of all, 1974 is the turning point. This is also a lesson that people in the United States need to understand, which is that when you interpret the history of Southern Africa, you interpret it not only by way of looking at internal dynamics—what's happening on the battlefield in that part of Africa—but you have to look at it globally. What I mean is that we know, for example, that you cannot understand the abolition of slavery in the United States without understanding the Haitian Revolution. I won't digress on that point. You can't understand the retreat of Jim Crow without understanding Caribbean and African liberation taking place simultaneously in the 1950s and 1960s and Washington seeking to compete for hearts and minds, in these newly emergent nations and the contestation with a socialist camp

10. Gerald Horne, *From The Barrel Of A Gun: The United States and the War against Zimbabwe, 1965-1980*, Chapel Hill: University of North Carolina, 2001, 6

but finding it difficult when Black people in particular are treated so atrociously here.

Likewise, we must try to analyze what's happening in the United States domestically, not only by debt of analyzing internal dynamics but looking at the situation globally and trying to figure out how we can leverage global currents on behalf of domestic concerns.

Which brings us to April 25, 1974. You had the culmination of a revolutionary process with the overthrow of Portuguese fascism, which then had knock-on effects in Angola and Mozambique. Mozambique coming to independence, circa June 1975. Angola, circa November 1975, although Angola's quickly swept up in a covert operation of the Central Intelligence Agency in league with South African apartheid to destabilize Angolan independence, which then leads to the dispatching of Cuban troops to Angola, which vouchsafed independence.

These events have impact of course in South Africa, leading to the Soweto Uprisings. Soweto being the township in Johannesburg— the African neighborhood in Johannesburg and the revolt there that has catalytic impact in terms of bringing an added spotlight to the conflict in South Africa. Of course, it has impact across the border in Zimbabwe because with Mozambique surging to independence and Angola surging to independence you have the possibility of the fighters in Zimbabwe having a rear base to go along with their rear base, preexisting rear bases in Zambia due north and Tanzania due east. So, you saw the noose tightening around the racist minority regime in Zimbabwe, then Rhodesia.

For years you had many African liberation fighters who had been trained in Algeria. Algeria, thousands of miles to the north on the Mediterranean Sea coming to independence in 1962. We're obviously marking the 60th anniversary of Algerian independence. We know that subsequently, you had—or actually contemporaneously—with Algeria supporting African liberation fighters, the Black Panther Party had its international headquarters in Algeria. Nelson Mandela received military training in Algeria as well. So once again, in order to understand the independence of this relatively small Southern African nation known as Zimbabwe you have to understand not only the internal dynamics but the external dynamics, what is going on in Portugal, Angola, Mozambique, Algeria.

Likewise, to try to understand the United States of America as powerful as it appears to be without understanding the wider and larger context, it seems to me is difficult at best. I mean, I don't think it's possible to understand the United States without understanding the wider context. That is a lesson that should be imparted, as well as imparting the lesson that the right wing was aware of this connection between the internal and the external.

That's one of the reasons why it has been estimated—and you can find that in the pages of the book on Zimbabwe—that after the war accelerated in Zimbabwe in the mid-1970s, that embittered US military veterans recently defeated in Indochina—from Vietnam, particularly by 1975—they then flock to the battlefield of Zimbabwe as mercenaries. Of course, there is official US complicity with regard to this illegal dispatching of mercenaries. Many of these Euro-American mercenaries wind up being killed on the battlefield, are buried in that part of Africa. Once again, to draw a contemporary parallel, I'm surprised that neither the US press, US corporate press, or the left press has focused on this remarkable trend that you see in the United States, whereby what I refer to as the treatise of apartheid or of Southern Africa.

Speaking of Elon Musk, supposedly the world's richest man; speaking of Peter Thiel, a major funder of the right wing, including Donald J. Trump, who is quite close to Blake Masters, who is running for the Senate in Arizona and JD Vance running for the Senate in Ohio. Of course, Peter Thiel spent a good deal of his childhood in Namibia. Botha might be the leading venture capitalist in Silicon Valley. He of course, is the grandson of Pik Botha, who was the final foreign minister of the apartheid regime. Just recently, Glencore—which is a major commodities trader and a blood sucking vampire when it comes to the commodities coming out of Africa— recently, it got into hot water legally. But a significant number of the leaders of that firm also have roots in apartheid South Africa. So, we're still living with the aftereffects of neo-colonialism and colonialism in that part of Africa. I don't think we've done—speaking of we, meaning the Black community, the left community—have done an adequate job in terms of analyzing that phenomenon, which might be useful to our own liberation.

CS: Thank you very much. As you were talking about the effect of mercenaries, you wrote, "Mercenaries should not be viewed as a sidebar," they were "the principal carriers of 'whiteness' on the ground in southcentral Africa."[11] As you pointed out there is this coalescing of anti-communism, of a lot of mercenaries from the US who are disillusioned from the Vietnam War and saw this as the last fight against communism. Then there was the legacy of white supremacy that also drew a lot of people over there. I'm wondering

11. Ibid., 24-25

if you could break that open more—speaking about your research and some of the things that you discovered?

GH: Well first of all, there's this Pan-Europeanism, which in many ways morphs into a kind of whiteness and white supremacy. In my 16th century book, I trace its roots to the dilemma faced by Protestant London in the 1500s after King Henry VIII succeeds from the bulwark of Christianity, speaking of the Vatican, and then that leads to religious wars on top of London seeking to compete with the Iberians for the produce of the colonial feast unfolding in the Americas.[12] The looting and plundering of the Americas, not to mention the looting and plundering of Africa. That leads London to move away from the Iberian's focus on religious sectarianism as a qualification for settlement to Pan-Europeanism. That is to say, from religion to race.

Recently in *The Nation*, I wrote a piece where I pointed out that in the 1500s you had Catholics burning Protestants at the stake.[13] By the end of the 1800s, you had in North America, you had Protestants and Catholics sometimes even joined by Jewish Americans, burning Africans at the stake, oftentimes in the most ghoulish manner, throwing gasoline on them, and oil on them and with thousands of settlers attending. As if this was some sort of religious ritual, or even some sort of pre-radio, pre-television entertainment. That, of course, was solidifying the bonds of whiteness—this joint enterprise of seeing this poor Black person go up in flames and that solidifying their own self-identification.

The juxtaposition of the extinguishing of life—of this Black person's life—and their continued life, and they would hope their continued or even their continued flourishing or even the beginning of their flourishing. So, this was not just a North American phenomenon. You see the same phenomenon transposed to Southern Africa. I point out—maybe in the Zimbabwe book, but certainly in my 1776 book—I point out that Ian Smith, recall that he was the leader of the racists in Rhodesia, when he executed, he and his comrades executed Unilateral Declaration of Independence from the British Empire in November 1965, because they thought London under pressure was moving towards African majority rule, which they

---

12. Gerald Horne, *The Dawning of the Apocalypse: The Roots of Slavery, White Supremacy, Settler Colonialism, and Capitalism in the Long Sixteenth Century*, New York: Monthly Review Press

13. Gerald Horne, "The Politician-Scholar: Eric Williams and the Tangled History of Capitalism and Slavery", *The Nation*, October 5, 2021: https://www.thenation.com/article/society/eric-williams-capitalism-slavery/

opposed staunchly.[14] Ian Smith said, as quoted in my 1776 book, perhaps the Zimbabwe book, that he saw himself as walking in the footsteps of 1776, not only in terms of trying to preserve a kind of white supremacy and a kind of settler colonialism, but also repudiating the aspirations of Africans for majority rule.[15]

Of course, in 1776 we're talking about repudiating the aspirations of enslaved Africans to be free from slavery, which has been hinted at by Somerset's case in 1772 in Britain, which illegalized slavery in England, there was an apprehension it might leapfrog the Atlantic and rather than accede to that, the settlers in both cases declared independence. Although there are those who would seek to deny this in the United States, at least today, the point is that the settlers in North America then went on to establish a kind of minority rule that persists to this very day.

What I mean is, if you look at the sacred US Constitution, or the would-be sacred US Constitution, it inscribes minority rule. I mean, at least that's the way this constitution has been interpreted with nine unelected politicians in black robes having the final say on women's reproductive freedom and the ability, for example, to have a country where there are more weapons than people—330 million people, conservatively 400 million guns. An Electoral College, whereby a Donald J. Trump can come in number two in terms of accumulating votes, but the elected president because of the machinations of an electoral college. Or a US senate, whereby your neighbor Wyoming has 2 percent of the 40 million population of California, and yet it too, has two US senators, as does California, which means a vote in Wyoming is worth more than a vote in California.

Of course, this is a form of minority rule. That's why I've suggested of late that the slogan of the 1% versus the 99% really needs to be revised because it's a kind of class essentialism and class reductionism. More accurate and more bespeaking the pernicious nature of settler colonialism, which involves class collaboration across class lines—that is to say poorer and richer Europeans from the inception of settler colonialism in North America, you have this class collaboration—it would be more accurate to say the one-third versus the two-thirds with the one-third being comprised of the economic

---

14. Gerald Horne, *The Counter-Revolution of 1776: Slave Resistance and the Origins of the United States of America*, New York: New York University Press, 2014

15. Ibid.; Gerald Horne, *From The Barrel Of A Gun: The United States and the War against Zimbabwe, 1965-1980*, Chapel Hill: University of North Carolina, 2001

royalists, the captains of industry with a significant sprinkling of Euro-American workers and middle class. So, of course, this is the same kind of class lineup that you had on January 6, 2021, when there was an attempted coup with the outgoing President Donald J. Trump, according to press reports, sharing the slogan "Hang Mike Pence," his own vice president and comrade, because he wasn't going along with the plot. They constructed a gallows on the grounds of Capitol Hill. Excuse that digression but I think in a certain sense it follows from this discussion about minority rule in Zimbabwe.

CS: Thank you for that digression. It all ties together and helps paint this picture. As you were talking about the mercenaries, they were a precursor to the US wars that would later follow, especially with Iraq and the US entering this phase of privatization. In Zimbabwe, then Rhodesia, there were these other groups, there was a group called RIGHT. There was a group called HISTORY that had the worst acronym for history I've ever seen in my life, which was "Hooray for Ian Smith, Titan of Rhodesian Yearning" that you wrote about.[16] There was the El Kamas Enterprises and the Military Advice Command International and a lot of these were propped up and recruited by the *Soldier of Fortune* magazine from Boulder, Colorado, which was really interesting to read about in your research.

GH: Yes, *Soldier of Fortune*—they had quite a crew in Boulder. The magazine was glossy, full of color pictures. It had correspondents from the battlefields of Southern Africa. It was used to recruit military veterans to head across the Atlantic to fight and at times die, and certainly kill. As the footnotes of that Zimbabwe book suggests, the minority regime in Rhodesia had support at the highest levels in the United States of America, not least in the US Senate with Senator Strom Thurman of South Carolina—who served in the US Senate and in public office for decades, ran for president in 1948 on a Jim Crow ticket—despite his apartheid leanings and sympathies.

It turns out—as it sadly and tragically so often happens—he fathered a child by a Black woman, who as I recall was a housekeeper in his family's home. Interestingly enough, if you visit Clemson University in South Carolina, his Alma Mater, there is an edifice erected in his honor. As you walk in, there is a picture of he and his so-called white family and his Black daughter, Black as defined in the United States of America. That is to say, very similar to the one drop rule, one drop of so-called Black blood in the United States still means you're Black.

---

16. Ibid., 102

This legacy of slavery—but it wasn't just Strom Thurmond; of course throughout Dixie, Senator Richard Russell of Georgia. Now, if I'm not mistaken there's still a Senate office building on Capitol Hill in Washington named for this arch segregationist. Certainly, if you visit the University of Georgia in Athens, Georgia, you can sift through his massive archive, which has thorough documentation of his close ties to minority regimes in Southern Africa.

The same holds true for Mississippi. Senator James Eastland and his archive at Ole Miss, University of Mississippi at Oxford, which you may recall had a major conflagration when one Black student James Meredith sought to integrate or desegregate that institution in 1962. As a matter of fact, people were killed in an attempt to have just one Black student go to class and there was a perception on this side of the Atlantic, which may not have been mistaken, that if the racist had to accede to majority rule in Southern Africa, then their comrades here would have to accede to an erosion of Jim Crow and US apartheid. It turns out that there was something to that. However, of course, we on the other side of the barricades, speaking of people like myself, also realize that— which is why it was appropriate to begin our conversation talking about events in Manhattan, in the 1970s, in solidarity with Southern African liberation.

CS: I wanted to start off this next question with a quote by James Baldwin, which is, "the great force of history comes from the fact that we carry it within, are unconsciously controlled by it in many ways, and history is literally present in all that we do."[17] I really saw a lot of these dreadful repetitions such as the American Women's Club in Saulsbury, which had a confederate flag displayed.[18] I also thought about when the white mass murderer entered the church in Charleston, South Carolina, June 17, 2015, he had pictures wearing a Rhodesia patch and also this connection to the growing right wing fascist movements now.

GH: Well, it is troubling I must say. As you were going through that litany, I was thinking of January 6, and the early allegation that some of the seed funding came from Europe. I was thinking of the fact that the Conservative Political Action committee, CPAC, one of the more extremist ultra-right groups in the United States, has close ties with the right-wing populist leader in Hungary, speaking of

---

17. James Baldwin, "The White Man's Guilt," *Ebony* 20, No. 10, 1965, 47-48
18. Gerald Horne, *From The Barrel Of A Gun: The United States and the War against Zimbabwe, 1965-1980*, Chapel Hill: University of North Carolina, 2001

Viktor Orban in Budapest. There is obviously a kind of brotherhood, if you like, of the races.

That Brotherhood has existed from the inception of settler colonialism—reference my earlier remarks about Lüderitz, for example, of Texas and Southwest Africa, for example, and it exists today. Unfortunately, we have not had sufficient digging, that I've suggested should be done, that would expose how and why it is that we've had the rise on these shores of Elon Musk and Peter Thiel and Roelof Botha and others too numerous to mention.

In trying to puzzle this out it reminds me of your mention of Roxanne Dunbar Ortiz and her book, *Not A Nation of Immigrants*, one of her recent books.[19] I think that that mythology about the United States being a so-called nation of immigrants helps to rationalize and justify the arrival on these shores and the subsequent plundering by Peter Thiel and Elon Musk and the like. Whereas, if we saw the United States as a settler colonial project, which of course it is, it would lead to viewing such arrivals with more skepticism, to put it mildly.

CS: Speaking of that—kind of those ripples of history on the other side—there's also the Black Power movement, which was influenced by Zimbabwe and Malcolm X and the Black Panther Party had an influence in Zimbabwe as well. You point out, especially the Lumumbas, along with that I was wondering if you could talk about your experience teaching at the University of Zimbabwe, your experience researching over there and some things that you found surprising and some breadcrumbs as well.

GH: I used to walk from the residence where I was staying in Zimbabwe to the archive where I did research, and it was a mile or two, and I would walk by the residence of Mengistu Haile Mariam who was the leader in Ethiopia after the overthrow of Haile Selassie circa 1974. This is 1995 when I'm taking my walk. His home was guarded by what appeared to be some volley of soldiers because when the struggle in Zimbabwe heated up in the mid-1970s, he was in power in Addis Ababa and provided military training and military assistance to the fighters in Zimbabwe. When they came to independence in 1980, they felt indebted to him. So, after he was ousted from power, shortly thereafter, they provided him refuge. As far as I know, he's still there. Although I can't vouch for that all together.

---

19. Roxanne Dunbar-Ortiz, *Not "A Nation of Immigrants": Settler Colonialism, White Supremacy, and a History of Erasure and Exclusion*, Boston: Beacon Press, 2021

I also arranged to donate many books to the library at the University of Zimbabwe. In fact, in my will—to bring up a morbid topic—my library is supposedly going to be shipped to the University of Zimbabwe, just as whatever funds that I have will be sent to Cuba, for the medical school for the training of African and Caribbean medics, doctors, physicians, etc. Of course, Cuba has done an outstanding job in that respect. It has trained a number of doctors from this country as well on scholarship.

Now, I recommend the Zimbabwe archives. Actually, in terms of archives, when I was doing that book on Zimbabwe, the archives, the African National Congress has not been established, which it has been established now. Fort Hare, which is the Howard University of South Africa, the alma mater of Nelson Mandela. Zimbabwe's Robert Mugabe and others hadn't been established because independence only comes in 1994. The archive was established years later.

I really recommend the ANC archive. I have to say, I mentioned a moment or two ago that the ANC had its office in Manhattan, the United Nations office, the address 801 Second Avenue, if I'm not mistaken. I have to say, I didn't see that office as being that well organized. I used to visit it all the time. But I was so mistaken, when I got to that archive I guess in December 2016, I found meticulous recordkeeping. I was shocked. And that recordkeeping and letters and correspondences is then reflected in the footnotes of my book *White Supremacy Confronted*. So, there was a lesson there somewhere I'm not sure what it is. Maybe I underestimated the comrades.

CS: Thanks for sharing that and as you mentioned in the book, that's good to hear because you pointed out that many of the archives on Zimbabwe were destroyed when the regime fell. I really liked that you said that researchers take breaks and compare notes at the University of Zimbabwe. As you mentioned before this book came out in 2001 and there's probably a lot of new records that have been released since then as well.

GH: Oh, absolutely there is. That's why history always has to be refreshed and updated. Just like our knowledge needs to be refreshed and updated. I noticed this tendency in the United States. People sometimes feel they know enough. But the problem is that knowledge does not stand still. I mean, new insights are constantly being created and perpetrated. Not least because new records are constantly being released. We all have to be lifetime students, that's the bottom line.

CS: I love that. Thank you and you're a great example of that and always inspire me to keep learning and sharing knowledge.

Chapter *11*

South Africa, Cuba, and Anti-Apartheid Solidarity
July 3, 2022

CS: This interview is going to focus on some of the history of your involvement in the anti-apartheid movement and your book *White Supremacy Confronted*.[1] You write about Elizabeth Benson and how she stood in Chicago's frigid weather and picketed First National Bank to protest apartheid because they were selling the Krugerrand, the South African coin. She said, it was "the feeling of collectivity that propelled her."[2] I wanted to dig into more of your perspective on the direct actions that took place and some that you were involved in as well. I would like to start with 1966 when South Africa's UN Mission in Manhattan was invaded by protesters and shortly thereafter, when you were involved in the 1968 Princeton protest, where there was an occupation of the building.

GH: Well, I've only written about the 1966 action. I participated in the 1968 action. This was taking place in the context of turmoil, not only in the United States, but globally. I'm sure you recall the activism of French students in particular, and the French working class, which helped to bring the government in Paris to its knees. There were many student protests erupting across the United States then, many of them having to do with the question of the curriculum. For example, installation of Black Studies, more hiring of Black professors, more admission of Black students.

At Princeton, people were protesting the university's investments in its endowment, and corporations, with holdings in apartheid South Africa, and as you know in succeeding years that question of divestment swept campuses across the United States, up to and up

---

1. Gerald Horne, *White Supremacy Confronted: U.S. Imperialism and Anti-Communism vs. the Liberation of Southern Africa, from Rhodes to Mandela*, New York: International Publishers, 2019

2. Ibid., 36

through the 1990s, the early 1990s before the election of Nelson Mandela in 1994. We occupied the financial center of the campus. I must say that the occupation was not greeted with equanimity, either by the administration or by students, at least Euro-American students, some of whom amassed at the building, chanting: "go home, go home." Of course, I'm not sure if they meant go back to your dorm. They may have meant go back to St. Louis, in my case, or perhaps even Africa in other cases.

Speaking of Africa, I think one of the triggers of this protest was the fact that on campus there was a complement of African students from Nigeria, from East Africa, in particular. I think that their presence helped to sensitize us to the horrors of what was going on in the southern cone of Africa. That triggered as suggested the protest and ultimately, I think the protest was successful, not in the short term—it's not as if when we left the building the university decided to divest. But certainly, in the long term, in terms of helping to put pressure for the passage of the comprehensive Anti-Apartheid Act of the mid 1980s, which in an anomalous sense put the United States to the left of many nations in the European Union, which is quite unusual, even unusual to this very day. I think a lot of it has to do with the chord that was struck in Black America in particular by the terrible nature of exploitation and oppression in Southern Africa. I think that that helps to explain those events.

CS: Thank you for laying down those threads. Zooming back in the book you mentioned. A bastion of white supremacy and settler colonialism was the Berlin Conference in 1884-85 where you write that the African "continent was carved up like a turkey by European powers."[3] I was wondering, when did apartheid first hit your radar, when did you first start getting active? Was it in the 1968 occupation, I imagine it was before?

GH: Well, it's hard to say. I mean, I think I've mentioned, not in interviews with you, but with others that from an early age, I'd been following the news—to the extent that you could follow the news by reading the *St. Louis Post Dispatch* and the *St. Louis Globe Democrat*, the two main corporate newspapers in St. Louis. I'm trying to recollect when I began to pay acute attention to apartheid and I'm not really sure. The answer might rest in my papers at the Schomburg. It may rest with articles that I wrote then, but I now don't recall, because it's so long ago. Or letters that I wrote, because there are

---

3. Ibid., 58

some of my correspondence going back to that era too. So, it's hard me to answer that question.

CS: I would love to research that down the road. I'd like to move to some of the work you did in the 1970s. I believe, with the "100,000 signatures gathered" "demanding the expulsion of South Africa from the U.N." and also your work with the National Conference of Black lawyers, where you lead a study on the "'needs of South African refugees in Angola, Mozambique and Zambia.'"[4]

GH: So, in 1973 I attended a conference in Chicago of an organization that came to be known rather awkwardly as the National Anti-Imperialist Movement and Solidarity with African Liberation (NAIMSAL). Obviously, that name was the result of many committee meetings attempting to get every possible adjective and noun included. By that point, I had graduated from law school at Berkeley. That summer, which I guess is an emblem of a kind of internationalism, I decided to go to South America, to Chile, because of an interest in what was going on with the election of Salvador Allende and the Socialist government that he was trying to construct. I left a few weeks, fortunately, before the coup on September 11, 1973.

I came back to St. Louis for a brief respite, and I think when I went to that conference in Chicago, I was enroute to New York where I stayed from late 1973 to 1988, at which point I moved to Southern California to teach at the University of California Santa Barbara. But in any case, a signature campaign, literally and figuratively, of the organization we called NAIMSAL was this petition campaign to collect signatures against apartheid South Africa.

I was involved in that. I used to go out on the streets in New York and gather signatures. I recall some interesting encounters. I recall this Euro-American woman, rather elderly woman, rather proudly, interestingly enough, telling me that she had never heard of apartheid. She seemed to be proud of that. It was striking. Now, on the one hand of course, people in the United States for whatever reason oftentimes tend to be insular and provincial. But I sensed something else, which is a pride in being unaware of the horrors of racism in Southern Africa, which then could lead into a pride of being unaware of racism of the United States? I don't know, maybe I'm making too much of the incident. But in any case, we gathered signatures.

At that point the African National Congress (ANC) had an office at 801 Second Avenue in Manhattan right around the corner from the United Nations. Because of course this was their mission to the UN.

---

4. Ibid., 536, 594

The Southwest Africa People's Organization (SWAPO), now the ruling party in Namibia, also had an office in the same building. Also in the same building was this Black talk radio station WLIB AM, where we, speaking of activists, ANC folks, SWAPO folk, oftentimes commanded the airwaves, speaking over the radio, this is pre-internet of course, to a mostly Black audience in the New York City metropolitan area.

The station was controlled by Percy Sutton, who was a Black American man with roots in San Antonio, Texas, who had relatives who resided in the former Soviet Union. He was former borough president of Manhattan, former member of the New York State Legislature in Albany, defeated in an attempt to become mayor of New York City. He was a progressive person generally and obviously he acquiesced to us coming on his radio station, talking about colonialism and imperialism, etc. That helped to put wind in our sails. The fact that we had access to this radio station, and then, of course, we had access as well to the Pacifica station, WBAI FM, as you know is part of the Pacifica network with stations in Washington, Houston, Los Angeles, Berkeley, and then affiliates across the country. I was quite active, as I am now with Pacifica. I was active then just with WBAI. We were often on the airwaves.

CS: Can you talk more about your work with the National Conference of Black Lawyers?

GH: I worked with the National Conference of Black Lawyers, too. Its office was at 126 West 119th Street in Harlem. It was a progressive organization of Black lawyers and legal workers. This was at a moment where I think that many people probably including myself sort of misjudged the political climate in the United States. What I mean by that is, that beginning in the 1950s the United States was under pressure to address US Jim Crow apartheid, not least because African and Caribbean nations were surging to independence. Washington found it difficult to compete as long as Jim Crow stalked the land.

So that creates a dynamic for the erosion of Jim Crow and there was a bit of unrest and turmoil unfolding in the United States as a result. You have the rise of the Black Panther Party, for example, in 1966, or at least the major iteration of the Black Panther Party in 1966. You had the activism generated by the arrest and trial of Angela Davis, who was tried for, supposedly, her complicity in an August 7, 1970, attempt—what eventuated was that a judge was killed, and others were wounded. The people who were involved in this action were killed as well. So, there was all this activism at that time and many people thought that the revolution was nigh.

I think that that led to the National Conference of Black Lawyers being organized in 1968 and my working with them. But I think we misjudged the moment because what swiftly follows that chapter of activism was brutal repression, as represented by the killing of Black Panthers, and the jailing of some individuals who are still in prison as we speak. But in any case, that was what we were thinking at that time. The National Conference of Black Lawyers, particularly my role with them, was to try to generate anti-apartheid activism. Eventually I became the leader of the National Conference of Black Lawyers in the mid-1980s. In which instance, I was able to work with the United Nations in raising money to bring to the shores a founder of SWAPO, Andimba Toivo ya Toivo, for a national tour and also to gin up interests in anti-apartheid legislation.

Namibia, just to digress, larger territorially than California and Texas combined, but with a contemporary population of a few million, had been illegally occupied by South Africa up to its independence in 1990. Interestingly enough, Toivo ya Toivo, during that tour, he met a Euro-American woman who became his wife who was still in Namibia; he died a few years ago.

I should also say that I was able to raise money from Congressman George Crockett of Detroit of the Congressional Black Caucus and there hangs a tale as well. I'll digress because I find it interesting. Tomorrow I'm going to be on WPFW, the Pacifica station in Washington for two hours. So, Crockett, this is a story that I'm going to talk to about tomorrow because it's illustrative of the era. Crockett, he was a lawyer with the United Auto Workers, then fell victim to the anticommunist purge. Then by 1949, he was lawyering the Communist Party case where the leadership of the Communist Party was put on trial. His advocacy was so militant that after the trial, not only were the defendants jailed, so were the lawyers. He was jailed by Judge Medina in New York City during this trial. A reason I raised that in this context and the reason I'm going to raise it tomorrow is because Crockett was very angry about the fact that he couldn't get support from the NAACP, particularly Thurgood Marshall, who of course, went on to become a justice of the US Supreme Court. The NAACP was deathly afraid of associating with people to their left.

The reason I'm going to mention that tomorrow is because tomorrow's forum is entitled "A Farce of You Lie or the Fourth of July." Part of the problem that has the United States on the cusp of fascism as we speak—despite all of this propaganda about this sturdy democratic experiment inaugurated in 1776—is that if you look on the right like in your own Colorado. As a matter of fact, I just read a long article in the *Washington Post*—you should read it—about this group, you probably know about it, FEC United: Faith, Education, Commerce.[5] These folks are serious. Their leader is threatening violence against the governor and talking about constructing gallows. They're far out, man.

So, the Republicans, the Republican Party, in a sense has a de facto paramilitary wing—the Three Percenters, the Oath Keepers, the Proud Boys. The Republican Party obviously is not afraid to consort with those to their right. The Democrats are nervous, to put it mildly, about consorting with those to their left. Now, on the one hand, this fills in instability or it tips the scales towards the right, obviously. On the other hand, to try to explain it because I think we not only need to judge we need to explain. I think it's because, obviously, the Republicans have a stranglehold on the Euro-American vote across class lines. They have had that stranglehold since the Voting Rights Act of 1965.

The Democrats are existing in a settler colonial society that initially was based upon white supremacy—to a certain degree, of course, it still is. Yet the Democrats have within their ranks the descendants of enslaved Africans whose plight was the fulcrum on which the nation was constructed in the first instance.

So, in any case, that's a long digression before I get back to the National Conference of Black Lawyers, and so I raise money for Crockett. It was a very rich and fruitful experience. I recall going to international conferences in Lisbon, Portugal, and in Puerto Rico. I was part of a National Conference of Black Lawyers delegation to South Africa in the interregnum between Nelson Mandela being freed and the elections in 1994. So, this is probably 1992. As a journalist, I traveled to Namibia right before independence in 1990 and did a series of articles. I recall attending an international conference in Arusha, Tanzania. This is probably in the late 1980s. For me, it was a very productive period. At the same time, I was working on my doctorate in History at Columbia and also working with the Hospital Workers Union as well, doing cases. So, it was a very busy time.

CS: You were working on the Bakke case at this time as well, too, right?

GH: Yes. Working on the Bakke case, because I was head of the Affirmative Action Coordinating Center that arose in the 1970s, that

---

5. Rosalind Helderman, "With Violent Rhetoric and Election Denial, Podcaster Becomes GOP Force," *Washington Post*, June 27, 2022, https://www.washingtonpost.com/politics/2022/06/27/with-violent-rhetoric-election-denial-podcaster-becomes-gop-force/

was sponsored by the NCBL, the National Lawyers Guild, and the Center for Constitutional Rights. I was writing articles on a weekly basis for the Black press. I probably had a radio show at WBAI, which I've returned too. I now have a regular radio show on KPFK Los Angeles. The more things change the more they remain the same. It was a very busy time.

CS: Thank you for giving that history. I'd like to go into your book *White Supremacy Confronted*. You wrote, "Yet of all these landmarks, it is difficult to overstate the importance of the overthrow of fascism in Portugal in April 1974 as a factor in laying the groundwork for democratic elections in South Africa two decades later."[6] In 1980 you helped to organize Remember Soweto, a mass demonstration in Manhattan. Speaking of right-wing violence, you wrote about the Free South Africa Movement in 1984 where your comrade Adrien K. Wing was photographed with Yasar Arafat, and your office was bombarded with bomb threats.[7] I was wondering if you could talk more about this era?

GH: Well, certainly. What happened in Lisbon was of profound importance because Portugal had colonized Angola in the 16th century. In fact, I talk about that in my 16th century book and given Portugal's relationship to London, Angola became a happy hunting ground for enslavers.[8] I would suggest that a disproportionate percentage of Black Americans have ancestral roots in both Angola and Congo due north as a result of the relationship between London and Lisbon.

So, with the coming to independence of Mozambique and Angola in 1975, the fighters in South Africa have a rear base and also the fighters in Namibia, as well. Of course, they were supported by the Cubans, which I spent a lot of time talking about. Of course, I was in and out of Cuba quite a bit then, as well.

You mention 1980, I recall that we organized this fundraising concert for the liberation forces in Zimbabwe on the eve of the elections in the spring of 1980. We raised I think $15,000 to $20,000 and split it evenly between two wings of the liberation movement. As I recall, Hugh Masekela the South African trumpeter and singer then an exile

---

6. Gerald Horne, *White Supremacy Confronted: U.S. Imperialism and Anti-Communism vs. the Liberation of Southern Africa, from Rhodes to Mandela*, New York: International Publishers, 2019, 493

7. Ibid.

8. Gerald Horne, *The Dawning of the Apocalypse: The Roots of Slavery, White Supremacy, Settler Colonialism, and Capitalism in the Long Sixteenth Century*, New York: Monthly Review Press, 2020

performed. It was at the St. John the Divine Church on 112th and Amsterdam Avenue in Manhattan. Actually, at that time I was living on 112th and Amsterdam, in Manhattan, so it was very convenient.

In 1984, the Free South Africa Movement erupts in Washington under the leadership of TransAfrica, and Randall Robinson, where you have these choreographed demonstrations and arrests at the South African embassies, and I coordinated the arrest in Manhattan at the South African consulate. Interestingly, I'm still as you see from that book, some of the citations are to my papers at the Schomburg because I kept a lot of material. I recall keeping a list of everybody who had been arrested at these demonstrations, but I couldn't find it in my papers. They're probably there somewhere because at the time I was researching in my papers, they weren't organized by the librarians of the archive. So maybe that list can be found. In any case, that turned out to be a turning point in terms of generating pressure because it became quite fashionable to be arrested. All the celebrities wanted to be arrested. You know you've made a breakthrough when celebrities want to be arrested. We accommodated them, of course. We weren't sectarian to that degree.

CS: Can you speak about the incident with Adrien K. Wing?

GH: Adrien and I were good friends. She's teaching at the University of Iowa Law School now. As a matter of fact, I think it was 1985 Adrian and I went to Sudan to become involved in a mediation effort of the Sudanese Civil War. I have to confess, in retrospect, I was in way over my head. Although I don't think I realized it, because as you know, South Sudan ultimately does secede under the administration of George W. Bush.

On the one hand, I think it was worthwhile to try to keep Sudan together and so I don't criticize my effort to mediate the civil war. But what I will criticize was, I don't think I was sufficiently knowledgeable about the history of Sudan. I mean, I was knowledgeable to a degree of the post-independence history of Sudan. That is to say from the mid-1950s, over the next 30 years, and so the day I arrived in Khartoum, but I wasn't necessarily aware of the conflicted history between North and South with the South, basically being sort of like when I spoke of Angola as being the happy hunting ground for enslavers of Lisbon and London, South Sudan was the happy hunting ground for enslavers of the Ottoman Empire. Now, of course, meaning Turkey, the difference—I mentioned this to a friend a few days ago, he wasn't impressed.

The difference is that the Ottomans enslaved Europeans, too. Now my friend didn't see that as being exculpatory. I don't see it as being exculpatory either, but certainly it's a difference between the North

Atlantic countries. A lot of that history, which I think was generating the civil war, I was blissfully unaware of, which bespeaks being in a situation when you're in over your head. In any case, so Adrien— you know, we're all internationalists, we're all pro-Palestinian. I wound up in Lebanon. I was actually photographed with Yasar Arafat, too, but for some reason, Adrien's picture was picked up by the *New York Post*, which is the right-wing scandal sheet in Manhattan. They unleashed it and it was quite bad for a while. They got groups to denounce us. It was not a good time. It was not a good time at all.

CS: Wow. Thanks for sharing that history. That sounds really scary.

GH: I recall Adrien was on this trip. We met on a trip as journalists— Arafat and the PLO were then in exile in Lebanon. This is during the height of the war in Lebanon, in Beirut actually. It was like a movie when we met him because they came to pick us up in the middle of the night, and then drove us around on this circuitous route before depositing us in an underground bunker, where we met with Arafat and his comrades. I recall writing some articles about it for the Black press. That was quite a time I must say.

CS: Speaking on that time, I wanted to see if you could open up more about China and its support for apartheid at times and the tension of Cuba in Angola. You wrote that you "rebuked the poet Amiri Baraka" for "pro-China orientation" and I was wondering if you could talk more about this and Cuba's presence—that you called a "cul de sac for apartheid from which there was no easy exit."[9]

GH: Yes. That was also a very contemptuous time. I think I wrote my first article criticizing China in Africa in 1975. It's certainly in my papers and it's quoted in the book by Robeson Taj P. Frazier at the University of Southern California his book, *The East is Black*, which deals with Black Americans and China published by Duke University Press.[10] Initially in the 1950s, China began to criticize the international Communist movement over issues such as the devaluation of Stalin, who had died in 1953, the question of peaceful coexistence. That was a line of the international Communist movement. Of course, now China is all for peaceful coexistence. They have to deal with these imperialists who are willing to blow up the world, rather than give up power.

---

9. Gerald Horne, *White Supremacy Confronted: U.S. Imperialism and Anti-Communism vs. the Liberation of Southern Africa, from Rhodes to Mandela*, New York: International Publishers, 2019, 534, 562

10. Robeson Frazier, *The East is Black: Cold War China in the Black Radical Imagination*, Durham: Duke University Press, 2015

This isn't anything new, but at the time China was criticizing the left. Ultimately what happens is, perhaps inevitably, China cuts this deal after Nixon's trip—we're marking the 50th anniversary in 2022—to China. So, part of the deal, of course, was that China—after the United States was ignominiously ousted from Vietnam in 1975—China attacked Vietnam. China carried a lot of water toward US imperialism, but it got a sweet deal because what happens is that US imperialism begins to invest in cheap labor in China, and entire physical plants float across the Pacific, now creating this juggernaut.

China's economy by some measures is already larger than the US economy. Of course, the United States would like to turn that around, which explains why you had this NATO meeting in Spain just a few days ago, where the North Atlantic Treaty Organization let the other shoe drop by suggesting that it's not only Russia and Ukraine that it's concerned about but China. So, we're in the midst of another titanic struggle, whether people realize it or not.

By 1975-76, when I was writing these articles, China was opposed to the now ruling party in Angola. The Popular Movement for the Liberation of Angola, MPLA, and because it was close to Moscow—because if you were close to Moscow that meant that you were a revisionist. China was in this objective alliance with US imperialism and apartheid South Africa. As I said, China carried a lot of water, but they get paid off handsomely. If I were Wallstreet, I would rue that deal. I would say that China got the best of the deal.

In any case, the Cubans were the rescuers. They dispatched thousands of troops to Angola to beat back the South African apartheid invasion. That turned the tide. It was like 1974, Portugal all over again. With the Cuban intervention, it has profoundly important significance. Cuba, of course, paid a heavy price, too. Cuba's a small country. It's only about 11 or 12 million people. On the one hand, it is dangerously close to US imperialism. On the other hand, it reminds me of a basketball player, an older basketball player, someone like Tiny Archibald, who was a point guard, he led the league in both scoring and assists. He oftentimes thought that when he was going to the basket, he wanted the big guys close to him because then he could create angles to get the shot off over them.

So that's an analogy to Cuba in the sense that it's close to US imperialism, obviously, geographically, but US imperialism has to tread carefully, because you can see from what's going on in Central Europe right now, having missiles that travel 90 miles, they're not that hard to find. In any case, Cuba would often send its best troops across the Atlantic. It left itself exposed to invasion, or worse, from

US imperialism. That was a very dangerous time that we were able to overcome.

CS: Thank you for that background. My next question has to do with the intricacies of South Africa and Nazism, but also its relationship with Israel as well. I see a similar contradiction with the Proud Boys and the far-right in the US. It seems to be that they all kind of meet with settler colonialism. It's how they find union. I was wondering if you could talk about this relationship. Just to give a litany of examples you wrote how in the 1940s there were swastikas in Pretoria. You write about Oswald Pirow, who tormented Mandela. He was known as the "'Little Hitler of Africa.'"[11] How Nazi sympathizers sabotaged railways and set fires in Pretoria. You talk about the horrific pro-Nazi "'race riot'" in Johannesburg in 1945.[12] Even the guards with dogs sometimes wore "swastikas on their wrists" at Robben Island.[13] You also wrote that "South Africa was the first Dominion within the British Empire to recognize the state of Israel."[14] Can you talk about this dynamic?

GH: What's interesting about South Africa, even about the title *White Supremacy Confronted*, is that as I suggest throughout that book, part of the downfall of apartheid is that in a sense they were really not authentic white supremacists. I think that the white supremacists in the United States have been much more authentic. What I mean by that is that those who promulgated apartheid in South Africa, at root were Afrikaner nationalists. That is to say, they wanted privilege to those who had roots in the invasion of 1652, mostly Dutch settlers, who then were supplemented by an infusion of French Protestants in that century and subsequently, the so-called Huguenots—you've had Huguenots involved in North America as well. There is a graveyard in Charleston, South Carolina, today, where if you stroll through it you'll see that many of the headstones are inscribed with French names. They're French Huguenots buried, six feet under.

An ethical turning point in the history of South Africa comes with the so-called British Boer War of about 120 years ago. Recall that earlier in the 19th century, Britain had ousted the Dutch from rule in South Africa. As a result, you saw that Britain then tried to expand

---

11. Gerald Horne, *White Supremacy Confronted: U.S. Imperialism and Anti-Communism vs. the Liberation of Southern Africa, from Rhodes to Mandela*, New York: International Publishers, 2019, 127

12. Ibid., 182

13. Ibid., 698

14. Ibid., 197

and extend abolitionism to South Africa. Recall that the Boers, as they're called, the Afrikaners, they were enslavers. They were in alliance with their comrades—comrade enslavers in North America. They enslaved not only Africans, particularly Mozambicans, but as well as those with roots in that other massive Dutch colony, speaking of Indonesia, thousands of miles to the east.

Indeed, the colored population as it's called in South Africa, is not only like Trevor Noah, European and African, but it's also those who are African and what we would call Indonesian, or that was then called Malay. As a result of the British takeover in the early 19th century and the extension of abolition per the decree of 1833-1834, you saw that the Afrikaners began trying to move away from British jurisdiction—the Great Trek, as they called it. They could not move far enough because they began to wage war on one another in the late-1890s, early-1900s. Britain emerged triumphant. But there was still this lingering antipathy towards the British by the apartheid rulers, that is to say the Afrikaners, which made the creation of a synthetic white identity problematic.

For example, here's one example that illustrates the point. You're probably familiar with the well-known US writer Norman Mailer—of Jewish descent. His ancestors first migrated from Europe to South Africa but found the climate so hostile that they moved to the United States where, of course, he becomes this celebrated writer. So, what that also serves to do was drive many of the Jewish and non-Afrikaner, and to be fair some Afrikaners as well, but mostly Jewish South Africans, into the Communist Party.

The leader of the armed wing of the African National Congress in the run up to independence in 1994 was Joe Slovo, who of course was of Lithuanian Jewish descent. In the 1930s, because of their antipathy to London, the Afrikaners were in bed with the Nazis, because they thought the Nazis were going to prevail and they shared ideological sentiments with the Nazis. There's a lot of detail, as you know, in that book about that particular relationship, which as you see is based upon US records. The US authorities were well aware, very familiar with this inglorious history, which makes curious the comment by US President Ronald Wilson Reagan in the 1980s, that the United States could not turn its back on apartheid rulers because supposedly, they were united during World War II.

As you know, the rulers in South Africa, in Pretoria, they wanted the Nazis to win. World War II was a very interesting episode for South Africa because on the one hand, they wanted the Nazis to win. On the other hand, the apartheid rulers were deathly afraid of imperial Japan, which was in alliance with Berlin. There was a lot of hysteria about imperial Japan because as I said in other books, imperial Japan had decided to steal a march on the North Atlantic powers by proclaiming itself as the champion of the so-called colored races. That's one of the reasons they had so much purchase amongst Black Americans, for example. They had a certain amount of purchase amongst Black South Africans as well, which frightened Pretoria to its wit's end. I have to say, just thinking about that again, it almost makes me want to tackle the subject again, because I find it endlessly fascinating.

CS: Yes, you really show a lot of those markings in the book like the Boer War, anti-English sentiment and how that threw them to the Nazi side even further. My next question: Cornel West has this verb he uses, the "Santa-Clausification" of MLK and Nelson Mandela.[15] The US narrative often pivots these personalities into a more one-dimensional story of being nonviolent messianic figures. The author Peter Gelderloos wrote the book *How Nonviolence Protects the State* and points out spots from history where a diversity of tactics is needed to fight fascism, such as civil disobedience, or militancy, or ideologies and writings, such as what was seen with the ANC, or the Black Consciousness Movement.[16] I was wondering if you could speak more about this?

GH: Well, I'll speak to it, but if I don't address the point, just raise it again. One of the points I want to insert—I think I inserted in the book, I'm almost sure I did—which is one of the problems in Southern Africa, even today, is that the apartheid rulers intentionally chose to negotiate with the African National Congress as the Berlin Wall was collapsing. The fighters in South Africa, they relied enormously upon not only the Cubans, but the German Democratic Republic, East Germany, Soviet Union, etc. The apartheid rulers, under F. W. de Klerk, were sufficiently sophisticated to recognize that once the socialist camp was weakened, that the ANC would be weakened, so you always want to negotiate with a weakened bargaining partner. It would be difficult for South Africa, a country of only about 55 million, to move aggressively towards socialism once the socialist camp was eroded.

---

15. Kevin Bruyneel, "The King's Body: The Martin Luther King Jr. Memorial and the Politics of Collective Memory," *History & Memory* 26, No. 1 (Spring/Summer2014 2014): 75–108. doi:10.2979/histmemo.26.1.75; Cornel West, "Reflections on the Life and Legacy of Nelson Mandela," *Cornelwest. com*: http://www.cornelwest.com/nelson_mandela.html

16. Peter Gelderloos, *How Nonviolence Protects the State*, Cambridge: South End Press, 2007

So, what happens, of course, is that the option, in a sense is forced. In a sense, it is voluntary. We'll leave it to future historians to figure out the balance. The option taken is—rather than the state taking over large sections of the economy and, of course, the state does control a large section of the economy in South Africa, particularly compared to the United States—the idea was the so called Black economic empowerment that leads to Cyril Ramaphosa, the President of South Africa. Cyril Ramaphosa, was a lawyer for the mine workers, and the leader of the ANC.

After the ANC decides that Thabo Mbeki will succeed Mandela after Mandela steps down in 1998, then Cyril moves into the business world, becomes a billionaire and now is embroiled in a scandal. Because apparently, when he was at an African Union meeting, some guys broke into his estate and walked away with a few million dollars in foreign currency, maybe he had it stuffed in the couch. I mean, those of us who knew Cyril in the early 1990s would have been shocked by such a story but that's the way the situation has evolved.

In any case, with the emerging disillusion, or erosion of the socialist camp, the ANC negotiated a deal where they were not necessarily in the driver's seat. At the same time, as you know, the apartheid rulers, unleashed a reign of bloody terror against the ANC—up to and including the assassination of one of their leaders, Chris Hani—which was a real turning point in the struggle. There's this old saying that the cemeteries are full of indispensable people, which is something I ascribed to. When Chris Hani was killed it was a blow to the indispensable progressive leadership of the anti-apartheid forces.

Now, I would also argue that the erosion of the socialist camp also had negative consequences here in the United States. I mean, recall what I said a few moments ago about how the process of desegregation and retreat from US apartheid took place in the 1950s precisely because of the existence of a socialist camp. Now, the United States does not feel as much pressure, which is one of the reasons we're talking about being on the cusp of fascism.

By the way, as I'll say tomorrow, a leading indicator to watch for—if you're concerned about the rise of fascism—will be an increase in attempted political assassinations. In that context, consider the testimony that Mr. Trump on January 6, 2021, knew that the protesters were armed, that he wanted to lead them on their assault on Congress. We're lucky that more people were not killed that day. The only thing that was surprising about the testimony—Mr. Trump has a flair for the dramatic—I'm surprised he didn't have a white horse stashed off stage that he would leap on and lead the protesters down

Pennsylvania Avenue on his white horse, but somehow he forgot that bit of scenery.

CS: Can you elaborate about what Cornel West calls the Santa-Clausification of Nelson Mandela and the rewriting of history.

GH: Well, see the problem with the United States is, they get involved in all of this mischief, to speak euphemistically, supporting apartheid, backing Jim Crow, and then it falls apart, apartheid is eroded, Jim Crow is eroded. Then they have to create a narrative that shows that they were anti-Jim Crow all along. They were anti-slavery all along. They were anti-apartheid all along. Then they hire their court historians to write that story, which throws dust in the eyes of people to put it mildly. It's very confusing and disorienting. I think it lulls constituencies here that will be the victims of fascism into a false sense of complacency. Then it misleads the international community as well because then the international community tends to see the United States as being more progressive than it actually is, believe it or not, because they accept these narratives, for example, about July 4th, that it was the creation of this so called democratic experiment, even though most of the rights in the Bill of Rights did not apply to the Indigenous population or the African population. That's a small detail there's oftentimes ignored.

CS: That's the value of the work that you do and many others as well. It's so important. Speaking of July 4th, I found it interesting in your book you mentioned how in 1966 African Americans in Tanzania "boycotted the iconic July 4th U.S. national holiday."[17] This is my last question. You write about how "The spring of 1994 did mark the beginning of a new era" that still needs to be measured. I was wondering if you could talk more about the ongoing plight for South Africa's liberation or Southern Africa. Positive moments you've seen since and also ongoing colonialism from China and the US, such as AFRICOM as well.[18]

GH: AFRICOM is obviously a dangerous intervention by the United States. That is to say, this idea of a branch of the Pentagon that focuses on Africa. It's quite dangerous because what it does is that it allows French imperialism to lean on US imperialism through AFRICOM. That is to say, US satellite assets, for example, are essential for propping up French imperialism in Mali, Senegal, Burkina

---

17. Gerald Horne, *White Supremacy Confronted: U.S. Imperialism and Anti-Communism vs. the Liberation of Southern Africa, from Rhodes to Mandela*, New York: International Publishers, 2019, 419

18. Ibid., 815

Faso, Chad, Republic of the Congo, Gabon, Togo, Benin, all the way to the southeast of Madagascar.

Just as a footnote, I'm not sure if I'll find the time but somebody needs to write about the French role in Madagascar and here are two footnotes. One is that Andy Razaf, who was known as a Black American composer—"Ain't Misbehaving," "What Did I Do To Be So Black and Blue?" —his roots were actually in Madagascar and you had Black Americans who moved there who mated with the Indigenous and then that helped to produce Andy Razaf. Then in the late 1940s, French imperialism, they massacre—it was almost like Rwanda in April 1994, though it hasn't received as much publicity— tens of thousands of people. People were killed to keep, to maintain this bloody rule. I'm not sure if I'll get around to it, but somebody needs to write about that.

In any case, post-1994 and the rise of AFRICOM and its connection to France, it also compromises France, because France, left, right and center, particularly after the elections where you saw a surge of the left, they recognize that it's dangerous for France to be yoked to US imperialism, particularly when NATO has just put China in the cross-hairs. But at the same time, France is dependent upon AFRICOM to maintain its neo-empire in Africa. So, it's trapped between two fires, as they say, post-1994. It's been a very difficult road for South Africa.

The comrades need to engage in some self-criticism with regard to the ditching of Thabo Mbeki and his replacement by Jacob Zuma, who studies have shown—including studies by the ANC—the ANC government, engaged in state captures, leading to the looting of billions. And I just mentioned what Cyril was involved in. Despite the fact that you have these powerful unions in South Africa, the Congress of South African Trade Unions, you have a South African Communist Party, probably the largest in the continent with about 330,000—400,000 members, which is not negligible. There's still a long, long way to go.

But then I look at neighboring Zimbabwe. Zimbabwe is illustrative in the sense that it engaged in land reform, seizing the land of the European invaders, many of whose roots only went back to 1945, unlike South Africa, with roots to 1652. This unleashed sanctions against the regime seeking to drive the economy into the ditch and that has not been unsuccessful. What's striking to me is the fact that many people who should know better, even in the Black community, were not supportive of land reform and joined the sanctions band-wagon. In fact, there was a quasi-debate between myself and one of the people I'm talking about on *Democracy Now!* a few years ago, you can easily find online.[19] What happens in Zimbabwe, in a sense, was a signal because that was basically a classic redistribution of the wealth, and there was hell to pay as a result. See, to me it's hypocritical and contradictory to oppose redistribution of the wealth in Zimbabwe and then wonder querulously, why redistribution of the wealth hasn't taken place in South Africa? I mean, come on people, you saw the beatdown that was administered to Zimbabwe. That's a signal. So, the struggle continues. I'm certainly more optimistic about Southern Africa than I am about the United States.

---

19. "Zimbabwe and the Question of Imperialism: A Discussion," *Democracy Now!*, June 26, 2008: https://www.democracynow.org/2008/6/26/zimbabwe_and_the_question_of_imperialism

Chapter 12

Reflections, Futurism, and the Waning of US Empire
August 7 and 14, 2022

CS: The theme of this interview is going to be your books, *Blows Against the Empire: US Imperialism in Crisis* and *Fire This Time: The Watts Uprising and the 1960s,* but also some reflections, projections, and futurism based on your research.[1] My first question is, you wrote *Blows Against the Empire* in 2008, what has and hasn't surprised you most since then in regard to the continued waning of US Empire?

GH: Well, I think the trends I sketched in that book are still relevant. What I was trying to point out is something that apparently has escaped the attention of quite a few liberal intellectuals. That is, that the deal cut with China by US imperialism in 1972, a half century ago, supposedly, was a masterstroke of diplomacy by the United States. Certainly, it contributed to the eventual implosion of the Soviet Union in 1991. Certainly, in the short-term US imperialism garnered certain dividends and benefits. For example, after Washington's ignominious ouster from Vietnam in 1975, China waged war on Vietnam, and the relations between the two countries still are not ideal, even though both are governed by communist parties.

We know that in the 1980s, China collaborated with Washington in terms of destabilizing a left leaning regime in Kabul, Afghanistan. But we also know that those were short-term dividends because what happened as we all know—following the ouster of that regime and the ouster of the Soviet troops—we saw that the successor regime was apparently complicit in terms of housing, al Qaeda, which then was accused of bombing New York and Washington on September 11, 2001. Before that, bombing US embassies in Tanzania and Kenya, and even with the killing of Mr. al-Zawahiri in Kabul just recently,

---

1. Gerald Horne, *Blows Against the Empire: U.S. Imperialism in Crisis*, New York: International Publishers, 2008; Gerald Horne, *Fire This Time: The Watts Uprising and the 1960s*, Charlottesville: University Press of Virginia, 1995

it's apparent that Washington has not heard the last of al Qaeda, to put it mildly. In fact, some South African authorities, amongst others, have been saying that the United States might not be able to kill its way out of this problem with al Qaeda, that it would be well served to examine the root causes for the rise of al Qaeda, but as of yet, that particular point has not dawned.

Back to the thread, it's apparent that now China is in the passing lane as a result of the massive foreign direct investment that poured into China as a result of that 1972 entente. The current conflict in the South China Sea between and amongst the United States, Taiwan, and China, and China breaking off all contact with the United States—military contact, climate change talks, cross border crime talks, everything—it seems as if these two superpowers are headed for some sort of showdown.

Then you might have heard that the Russian authorities have offered, have suggested, to the Chinese that if they need assistance in confronting Washington, well, Moscow is all ears. The point that I'm making is that one of the themes of that book in 2008 was that the relation between Washington and Beijing were not ideal, obviously the backdrop was the financial crisis on Wall Street, which in many ways has been a turning point in terms of relations between Washington and Beijing. So that would be my major response to how that book has held up over the years. Although since I wrote it 14 years ago, there may be some points that I'm missing.

CS: Thank you. Yes, the threads are all there with you talking about China becoming a world economic power. You also touch a lot on climate change in the book as well, which was something I wanted to expand more on in this conversation. In the book *Climate Leviathan: A Political Theory of Our Planetary Future*, it talks about how as climate change continues to create havoc, governments will continue to become more authoritarian.[2] With your research on oppression, what do you foresee?

GH: Well, we already know that there is a phenomenon known as climate refugees. That helps to shed light on these stunning population movements, particularly from south to north. We know that in places like Italy, where you have Africans, in particular, trying to cross the Mediterranean on rickety vessels—oftentimes drowning in these choppy seas—where we see they're subjected to atrocious prosecution. You might have heard or even seen the video of the

---

2. Joel Wainwright, *Climate Leviathan: A Political Theory of Our Planetary Future*, London: Verso, 2018

Nigerian being killed on camera in Italy, just days ago, without any intervention by a passersby. We know that with the collapse of the government of Prime Minister Mario Draghi in Rome, that there is a distinct possibility that neo-fascists will be coming to power in Rome, perhaps within weeks.

In that light, I would be remiss if I failed to acknowledge a theme that if I were writing this book today, I would have to enunciate. I'm not sure if in that book, I foresaw this but as I said, I wrote it 14 years ago. So, I can't be sure. That theme is that if one were writing a book about the Republican Party right-wing in the United States today, a title might be from conservatism to counter-revolution. That is to say that one of the lessons of January 6, 2021—in particular, the recent revelations about missing texts from Secret Service agents, Pentagon chiefs, and all the rest—is that the attempted coup went further up the chain of command then many of us imagined. When we see these candidates who are being put forward for office—such as Blake Masters in Arizona, for example, or JD Vance in Ohio, both senatorial candidates—they are backed by the Silicon Valley billionaire, Peter Thiel, who, of course, spent some of his youthful years in what is now Namibia, I think it was during the illegal South African occupation, but you may want to check that detail, and, of course, his roots are in Germany.

We do see in the North Atlantic countries, this movement towards—to use Mr. Biden's term—autocracy, and it does not bode well to put it mildly. I don't even know why I'm laughing. I mean, this is very serious. I guess it's what might be called dark laughter, but in any case, I think that the pressure that's being placed upon the ruling classes in the North Atlantic countries is having a predictable result, which is sort of tossing overboard all of this rhetoric about democracy and reverting to the iron fist. I guess what I find particularly troubling is that I'm not sure if those who will be most affected by this turn are aware of what is happening as we speak.

CS: We've really seen an increased militarization on borders and there's this right-wing, fascist internationalism, which you see from the continued militarization on the US-Mexico border, then the recent speech by Hungary's Prime Minister Viktor Orbán. You mentioned what is occurring in Italy, and climate refugees is just going to keep increasing as you mentioned.[3]

---

3. "Hungary PM Viktor Orbán Addresses CPAC as American Right Embraces His Authoritarian Rule," *Democracy Now!*, August 04, 2022: https://www.democracynow.org/2022/8/4/hungary_viktor_orban_cpac_nazism_race

GH: I should also mention as well, that at the same time that the right wing welcomed Viktor Orbán into their inner sanctum in Dallas, recall that just days previous to his appearance one of his inner circle had resigned, because she objected to his invocation of rhetoric from fascist Hungarians of the 1930s. Specialists suggested, and I find this particularly chilling and sobering, that it was not a coincidence that he made this attack on so called race mixing, before he traveled to Texas, because the specialist felt that he was trying to make a particular appeal to his audience in Texas, believe it or not.

Then, in terms of this right wing international—what might be called the neo-fascist international—you have the spectacle of the Israeli lobby interfering in US elections—helping to defeat Nina Turner in Cleveland, and Donna Edwards in Maryland, both running for US Congress. They even helped defeat Andy Levin, a sitting member of Congress, one of the more progressive members of Congress from Michigan, despite the fact that not only is he Jewish but was the leader of his synagogue. However, he was defeated because he was seen as not necessarily in sync with the right wing in Israel.

At the same time, as you have this right-wing internationalism, you saw just a few days ago, that in St. Petersburg, Florida, and St. Louis, Missouri, the African People's Socialist Party, and their affiliated grouping, the Uhuru Movement, were routed and rousted by the FBI, because it was alleged that they have connections to Moscow. So, the message is that the right-wing can be internationalists. If you're not right-wing, you cannot be internationalists. In other words, the right-wing can fortify their ranks and replenish their ranks by joining upon global connections, but we're not allowed to do the same thing. It's quite unfortunate and I must say, I was disappointed that the African People's Socialist Party and the Uhuru Movement did not receive more support from the left from established Black organizations, etc. That does not bode well for the future.

CS: My next question was about the African People's Socialist Party and the threads from *Blows Against Empire*. You point out in the book that when imperialism is in crisis, you see an increase of police violence, authoritarianism, and surveillance.[4] These examples of these threads go from Chicago to Abu Ghraib to George Floyd to the recent murder of Jayland Walker, up to The Uhuru Movement, can you break open those threads as well?

---

4. Gerald Horne, *Blows Against the Empire: U.S. Imperialism in Crisis*, New York: International Publishers, 2008, 18

GH: Well, in that context, and I hope I'm not focusing too much on contemporary events because that may date this particular talk, but I'll plunge on unless you restrain me. I found it remarkable that just in the last 48 hours, the Chinese authorities in their battle with the United States have said to paraphrase: "we're not George Floyd." Now some people I've talked to in the Black community, they thought that that was a bridge too far to invoke this martyr.[5] But I understand what they were trying to convey. What they were trying to convey is, don't try to bully us. Don't try to intimidate us and also to look at it in a historical panorama. I've oftentimes suggested and written—I'm not sure if I wrote it in that particular book—that there is a connection between the mass genocide against Native Americans, the mass enslavement of Africans, and then exporting that model overseas, in terms of overthrowing the Hawaiian Kingdom in the 1890s, one of the more sophisticated polities in that part of the world, to the assisted genocide in Central America in Guatemala, particularly beginning post 1954, to assistance to South African apartheid and neo fascism in southern Africa, in the 20th century.

So, I think that there is an ineffable linkage between domestic and foreign policies. I think that's one of the lessons, I'm not sure if our domestic movements have absorbed. But I interpreted China's invocation of George Floyd as suggestive of the point that they did recognize that connection and they're warning US imperialism to back off. I'm afraid to say that I see little evidence that US imperialism is willing to back off, because despite the conflict with Moscow, it seems that their conflict quota has not been exhausted. So now you have this conflict with Beijing, which, as they say in Washington has received bipartisan support. Once again, this does not bode well. The only ray of sunshine that one might be able to detect is that as these events were unfolding in the past week or so with Speaker Nancy Pelosi's trip to Taiwan, igniting a controversy. You saw that these indirect talks with Iran over the nuclear question were resuming in Vienna, Austria. The US negotiator, Robert Malley jetting to Austria in the last few days. Perhaps there's a recognition in Washington that taking on China and Russia simultaneously is more than enough without adding Iran to the mix, which was the import of Mr. Biden's trip to Israel and Saudi Arabia. Just a few weeks ago where Iran was clearly on the table in both countries.

---

5. Sam Cabral, "Taiwan tensions: China halts co-operation with US on key issues," *BBC*, August 5, 2022: https://www.bbc.com/news/world-asia-china-62438262

So, let us hope that my supposition is accurate, because I don't think that US imperialism will survive, quite frankly. By that meaning the country, meaning yourself and myself, as well, because we happen to be trapped on this ship of fools and so taking on, Russia, China, Iran simultaneously, could be quite damaging and fatal for many people who live in this country, including constituencies that we purport to represent. The fact that all three countries are also yoked together in the Shanghai Cooperation Organization, which is the kind of counterpoint to NATO, the North Atlantic Treaty Organization, is quite sobering.

Speaking of the North Atlantic Treaty Organization and staying on this theme of recent developments—which I'll continue to illustrate, unless I'm told otherwise—we also have the spectacle of President Erdogan of Turkey showing up in Sochi, Russia, to confer with President Putin. Now, it's apparent that Turkey—a member of NATO, a supplier of drone warfare fighting contraptions to Ukraine, which have been quite effective on the battlefield, —is not altogether on board with regard to North Atlantic policy, which is understandable because Turkey has been a candidate member of the European Union since 1999.

When you had the Brexit vote in 2016, with Britain exiting from the European Union, one of the demagogic issues on the table were conservative politicians, Tory politicians, suggesting that if Britain remained in the European Union, that Britain would be deluged with refugees from Turkey. I think what that illustrates is a point that I made in my 16th century book, which, of course, we're aware of today, this underlying tension between so called predominantly Christian countries and countries that are not predominantly Christian, that are predominantly Muslim like Turkey.[6] I think that has led to Turkey, the NATO member, feeling not necessarily embraced all together by its alleged comrades in the North Atlantic Treaty Organization. So, it's going its own way and that helps to illuminate the persistent contradictions in NATO.

CS: Thank you for breaking that open. The massive threat of nuclear annihilation in any of these conflicts, and even the ongoing conflict with Russia and Ukraine, is frightening as well. I'd like to move to your book *Fire This Time: The Watts Uprising and the 1960s*. You describe the carnage that the National Guard and LAPD took.

---

6. Gerald Horne, *The Dawning of the Apocalypse: The Roots of Slavery, White Supremacy, Settler Colonialism, and Capitalism in the Long Sixteenth Century*, New York: Monthly Review Press, 2020

And we're nearing the 57th anniversary of Watts.[7] I was wondering what differences and also connections do you see between Watts 1965 and the George Floyd insurrection and some of those ongoing threads?

GH: Well, the first thing that comes to mind are what might be called negative parallels. That is to say by 1965, the Red Scare had taken quite a toll on the Black community with the sidelining and marginalizing of the tallest tree in our forest, Paul Robeson—and those who stood by him and those who sought to emulate him—and that helped to puncture the internationalism in our community, which I was just making reference to, concerning the attacks on the African People's Socialist Party.

However, at the same time, you had the US escalating the conflict in Vietnam and already in Los Angeles and elsewhere there was gathering anti-war sentiment that then reached a kind of efflorescence with the formation of the Black Panther Party in California, in 1966, which was prefigured in south Los Angeles by the rise of the Community Alert Patrol, which was organized to police the police so to speak. That is to say, to send our young brothers and sisters out with walkie talkies and radio communication so that they could intervene when they espied the police, as the Panthers used to say, snapping on brothers and sisters on the streets. So that's kind of a mixed record with regards to 1965 and Watts.

Now if you fast forward to 2020 and George Floyd, we see that by 2020 the Black Panther Party is basically dead but at the same time, internationalism is not dead. But internationalism, in order to be vibrant and viable should be filtered through organizations, particularly militant organizations like the Black Panther Party, which of course had a legation in Algeria. It almost had a legation in Congo-Brazzaville, the current Republic of the Congo, formerly the People's Republic of the Congo, to be distinguished from the larger Congo, which is its neighbor across the Congo River. It sent delegations to Vietnam and to North Korea. So that's the sort of internationalism, which was arising from the ashes of Watts, that by 2020 had been virtually smashed by the authorities. We all know the story, it has been even captured on celluloid, with the killing of Black Panthers in Chicago in their beds on December 4, 1969. The killing of Black Panthers at the UCLA campus in January 1969. The killing of

---

7. Gerald Horne, *Fire This Time: The Watts Uprising and the 1960s*, Charlottesville: University Press of Virginia, 1995

scores, some estimate hundreds of Black Panthers during a few years period, from about 1966 to 1971-72.

With the movement around slain Black teenager Michael Brown, in Ferguson, Missouri, in 2014, just outside of St. Louis, you saw an effort to internationalize that struggle going to the Human Rights Council in Geneva of the United Nations, for example. Since that time, you've had human rights investigations by both the United Nations and international bodies of attorneys of the United States and that's all for the good. I salute those who have been involved in those efforts, but we must realize that the virtual liquidation of the Black Panther Party was a very profound blow, because again, that internationalism flowers and reaches new heights when it's filtered through militant organizations like the Black Panthers.

As of now—with all due respect to the Black Lives Matter movement—I think it was structured intentionally on a decentralized basis because they saw what happened to the Black Panthers when you have a centralized leadership. What happens is that the authorities try to cut off the head so that the body will die. So, if there's decentralization, there's less of a possibility of that particular gruesome model working. The downside of course, is that with all of its virtues, decentralization is not necessarily the ideal model for pursuing a national and international strategy. Centralization is much more effective in that regard.

So, from 1965 to 2020, I would give a mixed verdict. However, I would encourage readers to focus on the positive aspects of my autopsy. That is to say, the surviving internationalism, the surviving militancy as reflected in the massive demonstrations that unfolded from May 25, 2020, throughout the summer, in the midst of a pandemic. At the same time, there was a random comment in *The New York Times*, I think it was a month or two ago, where the hypothesis was floated that there are those in the United States who get outraged by the spectacle of these mass protests against racist police brutality and that leads to a backlash, a backlash that may have contributed, I'm afraid to say to the January 6, 2021, insurrection and the rise of this neo-fascist trend simultaneously.

CS: Thank you. When you're talking about these surviving and thriving trends, I've really seen the Copwatch groups continue to grow. Since George Floyd, there was the whole movement for abolition of prison and police has grown, and then as well there were US embassies protested all around the world after George Floyd was murdered, which were some promising threads.

GH: Yes. That last point really needs to be highlighted. That was one of the more heartening aspects—that global solidarity—and

I think that helped to fuel these international delegations from the United Nations and bodies of lawyers that I mentioned. As I said, we need to concretize that sort of international solidarity through international networks, because to a certain degree there was a certain amount of spontaneity, with regard to these protests, with people spontaneously marching in Australia and Western Europe in particular, in outrage after seeing the video of what happened to Mr. Floyd.

Once again, we really need an organization that has dues paying members that meet in conventions, that has chapters and branches in major cities from the Atlantic to the Pacific and that puts out consistent propaganda. I don't mean that in a negative sense, I mean that in the sense of literature, and not just the usual social media but perhaps even newspapers, magazines, and analog media as it's called. So that's what we're missing it seems to me.

CS: I know you're doing some more recent research on the Black Panther Party in California. In your book *Fire This Time* you talked about how in the 1960s, "The philosophy of nonviolence was receiving a direct challenge in Black LA." You write about how Dick Gregory was shot in the leg when trying to talk to the Bloods and how this was a precursor to the Black Power movement.[8] I really liked one story you shared about when Bayard Rustin went to Watts and he urged people to stop rioting, and in response, the youth screamed: "'Go back where you come from. We are winning,'" and then, "One of them lit a match, held it up and said, 'This is our manifesto and it's winning.'"[9] Can you talk about that transformational time that you found in your research?

GH: Well, on the one hand it had deep roots. It had deep roots in terms of slave rebellions. If I'm not mistaken in my 1776 book, I talk about arson as a political tool by disarmed and unarmed enslaved Africans.[10] In my recently published Texas book, I talk about the so called Texas tariff, circa 1860-1861, on the verge of the US Civil War when the enslaved were accused of torching fields, so that they wouldn't have to toil in those fields, in 100 degree weather and basically take to the match.[11]

8. Ibid., 184

9. Ibid., 299

10. Gerald Horne, *The Counter-Revolution of 1776: Slave Resistance and the Origins of the United States of America*, New York: New York University Press, 2014

11. Gerald Horne, *The Counter-Revolution of 1836: Texas Slavery & Jim Crow and the Roots of U.S. Fascism*, New York: International Publishers, 2022

You see that as well in Los Angeles in 1965. Now, fortunately as noted, what happens following that is an attempt to channelize that energy into organization—in the Community Alert Patrol, in the Black Panther Party, etc. I dare say that an outgrowth of the Black Panther Party and its internationalism was a vibrant anti-apartheid movement and the Southern Africa Solidarity movement of which I was a part of.

Of course, I should mention too, that when I was living in Berkeley, in law school, circa 1970—well, actually, I should mention before I went to Berkeley, I had visited there in 1969 for the Panthers major conference, Combat Fascism. I'm going to write about it in this book. It was really a very significant event, bringing together people across class lines, racial lines, and gender lines. It was really one of the high points of the Panthers brief tenure. Then I returned as a law student, as I said in 1970, and I worked with the Panthers. I taught at this prison Vacaville Prison, cow town, just north of Berkeley. I recall, it's an interesting story. So, one of my students—I lent a copy of the book by Engels, *The Origin of the Family, Private Property and the State*, and I never got it back because that prisoner, Donald DeFreeze. He decided that the Panthers were not militant enough. So, he got involved in other actions, such as the kidnapping of heiress, Patty Hearst, and the organization of the so-called Symbionese Liberation Army. Of course, they all died in flames in Los Angeles a few years after. He was my student and then, of course, I never got my book back.

I stress organization because I think the dialectic is that militancy is a constant in this country, particularly from the descendants of enslaved Africans. I think that it has not been sufficiently theorized as a form of class struggle, because when you're a slave you're an unpaid worker, and being an unpaid worker generates militancy. That then helps to create a culture that's passed on even after slavery is abolished, which helps to explain why the Black community votes more heavily against the Right—eight-to-two or nine-to-one—than any other demographic. But the variable is organization, that fluctuates. The sweet spot is when there's a confluence of the militancy with organization. That's when we tend to make real progress. That's a lesson that I hope is ingested sooner rather than later.

CS: Thanks for sharing this story about teaching in the prison as well. You also wrote for the Black Panther newspaper for a time?

GH: And the Nation of Islam newspaper. As I recall, I might have written for the Black Panther newspaper with a pseudonym. I think I wrote for the Nation of Islam paper with my name because in 1973 after I graduated from law school I went to Chile, because those were the times of Salvador Allende. I wanted to witness up close that experiment. I recall coming back to the United States and writing articles for the Nation of Islam newspaper about South America. I also wrote for the Communist Party newspaper as well. Sometimes using a pseudonym, sometimes using my name. Those articles can be found.

CS: Awesome, thanks for sharing that. You talk in *Blows Against the Empire* how future wars with the US may take place in Asia, which is what we talked about earlier. You write, "Unfortunately, scholars and critics in the humanities have failed to consider that the shift in the literary canon away from the 'Eurocentric' curriculum is a reflection in the shift in imperialist strategy—and not solely the product of the demands of African Americans."[12] You're talking about how "white supremacy" is in an "agonizing retreat," can you expand on this thread[13]?

GH: I think it's useful to keep an eye on Australia in order to understand that, because, you know in my book *The White Pacific*, I talk at length about US Australian relations, and how London and Washington were in many ways the parents of Canberra, and that Australia has been tailing behind Washington, certainly since 1945 with the eclipse of the British Empire.[14] Even before that, and you see that with regard to Australia moving away from its white supremacist policies in 1967, at the same time that the United States is doing the same thing.

Australia of course, faced a stiff challenge during World War II. Northern Australia was bombed by the Japanese military. You had some of the Indigenous Australians who flocked to the banner of Tokyo. That frightened many in Canberra. So, what happens post 1967, with the official move away from white supremacy, you have a companion attempt to engage Asia. You might have noticed that the current Foreign Minister of Australia is Penny Wong, who is of Chinese descent. Asian languages are taught quite heavily in Australian curriculum, probably more so than in the United States of America. Now of course, there's no comparison in the sense that Australia only has a population of about 30 million, perhaps nine percent of the population of the United States of America but still, traveling through Asia one oftentimes encounters Australians who

---

12. Gerald Horne, *Blows Against the Empire: U.S. Imperialism in Crisis*, New York: International Publishers, 2008, 62-63

13. Ibid., 63

14. Gerald Horne, *The White Pacific: U.S. Imperialism and Black Slavery in the South Seas After the Civil War*, Honolulu: University of Hawai'i Press, 2007

are speaking Thai, who are speaking Vietnamese, who were speaking Pǔtōnghuà, or Chinese language, etc.

To a degree—I would say to a lesser degree—you see a similar phenomenon the United States of America now. Australia has Asia as a neighbor. One of its closest neighbors of course is Indonesia, which it has fraught relations. For example, routinely, one of the first visits that an incoming Australian Prime Minister makes is to Jakarta to confer with their Indonesian counterparts. In the United States, as I said, you've had a similar trend, not to the same degree, as noted, that one has seen in Australia. Although, I must say I was living in Chapel Hill, North Carolina teaching at the University of North Carolina some years ago and Chinese, Pǔtōnghuà was taught in the public schools. My daughter started taking Chinese when she was five years old and now she's 22 and still taking Chinese. I think that that's an emblem of, it's a reflection not just of a push from below, although it is certainly that, but it's also a recognition of the changing correlation of forces globally.

With China being one of the major purchases of US Treasury bills—the People's Bank of China helps to keep the US government afloat, everything from the Pentagon to the post office. US farmers and agribusiness are heavily dependent upon the Chinese market, to sell commodities. Now, and all that of course, is up for grabs right now, with this downturn in relations over Taiwan. But at the same time, you see that the United States is going to have to rely upon South Korea and Japan in order to corral Beijing. That too, has led to a deeper engagement with those countries. You can see that in terms of popular culture with the popularity of BTS for example, the boy band in South Korea.

CS: I'm a big fan!

GH: Oh, you're a BTS fan?

CS: Yes. BTS Army

GH: Right on. The Army as you know, they were accused—I'm not sure accurately—of sabotaging Trump's appearance in Tulsa, Oklahoma.[15]

CS: Oh yeah, by all signing up to be there in the crowd that was all fake tickets?

---

15. Taylor Lorenz, Kellen Browning and Sheera Frenkel, "TikTok Teens and K-Pop Stans Say They Sank Trump Rally," *The New York Times*, June 21, 2020: https://www.nytimes.com/2020/06/21/style/tiktok-trump-rally-tulsa.html

GH: Right, exactly. So, this is part of this changing correlation of forces, which as noted has led to a push from below and also a recognition amongst elites that there need to be certain kinds of changes. It's just like the often quoted, Italian novel—I think it's called *The Leopard*, it was made into a film—where one of the characters says to paraphrase, "For everything to remain the same, everything has to change." I think that for a certain wing of the US ruling class, that's their mantra. Obviously, they want everything to remain the same in terms of their rule, but they also recognize that there needs to be change, if things are to remain the same.

CS: Thank you. That also reminds me of the increased attack on critical race theory even though a lot of critics don't know what it means. My next question is looking at the long view of the writing and research you've done of Indigenous resistance and Black resistance. Where do you see the movements for reparations? In the context of Indigenous communities, where do you see the discussion of Landback moving? Do you see a breakpoint moment for possible radical change?

GH: Well, with regard to Indigenous movements, I detect progress. I hope I'm not being naive. I mean, I think for the longest, I'm afraid to say, is that people who consider themselves radical and progressive really ignore the Indigenous movement. You see that in their narratives of the founding of the United States of America, where which basically involves massive land theft and set the stage for even more massive land theft but was saluted by many who consider themselves progressive and radical. But of late that is not happening to the same extent, I can't say it's not happening at all, that would be a bridge too far, but it's not happening to the same extent and that's a positive sign.

Certainly, with regard to the literature, there's been an explosion of writing and analysis of Indigenous history. I think of Roxanne Dunbar Ortiz's book. I think of Kyle T. Mays of UCLA. His book *An Afro-Indigenous History of the United States*.[16] I think of Benjamin Madley of UCLA. His book on the genocide against the California Indigenous. [17] My own work of course. Particularly the recent books I've written. Particularly the one I wrote on Texas, where the Indigenous question is front and center.

---

16. Roxanne Dunbar-Ortiz, *An Indigenous Peoples' History of the United States*, Boston: Beacon Press, 2014; Kyle Mays, *An Afro-Indigenous History of the United States*, Boston: Beacon Press, 2021

17. Benjamin Madley, *An American Genocide: The United States and the California Indian Catastrophe, 1846-1873*, New Haven: Yale University Press, 2016

So that augurs well. I think that the visit of the Pope to Canada—insofar as it may lead to a kind of reparations from the Vatican and a returning of artifacts belonging to the Indigenous of Canada—hopefully, that's a positive sign. You've had descendants of enslaved Africans also visiting the Vatican of late receiving audiences, not necessarily from the Pope, but from his aides. That's a positive sign. But at the same time, I mean, we shouldn't go too far, because these troubling neo-fascist trends, which have been generated in no small measure by this idea that their romanticized view of the United States is coming under attack.

We mentioned in passing critical race theory, which has been coming under assault. We see the attacks on school librarians, the purging of libraries of certain books. We see the pressure on teachers as a result of legislation, particularly in Texas and Oklahoma, and Arkansas, for example. So, it's a very curious confluence that we've reached right now. Where on the one hand, there seems to be steps forward, which there certainly are, but on the other hand, there's been aggressive pushback, which we would be foolish to ignore.

CS: Thank you. We've been seeing increased attacks on the transgender communities as well with the right-wing trying to interrupt the transgender story times that they do with children at bookstores, which has been protected by the community which has been an inspiring story. Through your research can you talk about some moments of Black and Indigenous solidarity over time and threads from past acts of solidarity that should be highlighted and brought back to the present?

GH: Well, there's so many. My Texas book just came out so it's fresh on my mind.[18] The Caddo of East Texas, West Louisiana, that vicinity, had an interlocking directory with Black people. You can say the same thing for the people we refer to as the Seminole of Florida, who of course fought the United States in some of the bloodiest conflicts the United States has ever been involved in—that includes being involved in Vietnam, for example—wars circa 1818-1819, in the 1830s, and again in the 1850s. Many deported from Florida, and then that resistance, in many ways goes back to the first glimmerings of settler colonialism.

I'm speaking of the arrival of the Spanish in what is called St. Augustine, Florida, in 1565. My book on the 16th century is replete

---

18. Gerald Horne, *The Counter-Revolution of 1776: Slave Resistance and the Origins of the United States of America*, New York: New York University Press, 2014

with detail about the Indigenous resistance, African resistance, joint resistance.[19] That has been a major theme now of course, once again, there have been contrasting trends. In my Texas book I talk at length about the so-called Civilized Tribes, which includes the Cherokee Chickasaw, Choctaw, Creek, and some wings of the Seminole, who of course, were involved in slavery. But of course, the enslavement of Africans I should say, but still were forced to evacuate their property and their land in the southeast quadrant of North America and walk on the Trail of Tears in the 1830s to Indian Territory, so called today's Oklahoma.

What happened of course, in Georgia is a sobering lesson because the Cherokees in particular sought to assimilate by enslaving Africans, by professing Christianity, by dressing like the settlers. They still had to go. That's a very sobering lesson because it's really one of the more graphic illustrations of white supremacy and how it was executed in North America, because emulating the white supremacist did not save the Cherokees. In fact, it led to more significant losses for them. So, these sorts of stories are trickling out. I mentioned some of the literature, I could have mentioned more but there's much more that needs to be done in this realm.

CS: Thank you so much for those stories. Now, moving from the past into the present and thinking about resistance today, I was wondering who are some groups, collectives or organizations that inspire you today? Who do you think we ought to be paying attention to and amplifying or who are some thinkers or ideas that inspire hope in you today?

GH: Well, I think of Roxanne Dunbar Ortiz. I think of the Haitian filmmaker Raoul Peck. His documentary *Exterminate All the Brutes,* which draws up on the work of Roxanne Dunbar Ortiz. I think of the workers at Amazon and Starbucks organizing a union. I think even of the auto workers who have been going through some difficult patches in recent decades trying to regain their footing, maybe going on strike shortly, of course, as their home base in Detroit suffered.

I also think of Detroit, the largest predominantly Black city in the United States, about 90 percent Black and also helping to produce historic figures. I think of their former Congressman George Crockett, who was a leader in the anti-apartheid movement from the halls of Congress. I actually solicited a donation from him of $5,000

---

19. Gerald Horne, *The Dawning of the Apocalypse: The Roots of Slavery, White Supremacy, Settler Colonialism, and Capitalism in the Long Sixteenth Century*, New York: Monthly Review Press, 2020

to bring recently freed Namibian political prisoners to the states. Before that, he was a judge who refused to toe the line when asked to engage in mass detention of those in rebellion in Detroit in 1967 and those who were part of the so-called Republic of New Africa, who were routed and rousted by the police. Before that, he was a lawyer in Mississippi during the hottest days of the move to register voters. Before that, in 1949, he was the lawyer for the Communist Party defendants who were convicted and because of his vigorous advocacy, he was imprisoned, too. Before that, he was a lawyer for the United Auto Workers fighting racism within the union. I think Crockett—I'm about to review a book about him that's why he's fresh on my mind—he's a figure people need to know more about because he's of course passed away now, but his life can be quite inspirational.

CS: This question is about Palestine. You've written about when you interviewed Yasar Arafat in the 1980s in a bunker in Lebanon.[20] I was wondering if you can talk about some of your work in solidarity with Palestine over the years, your assessment of the Boycott, Divestment and Sanctions Movement (BDS), and hopes for Palestine's liberation?

GH: Well, things are rather complicated right now because, obviously, in the right-wing atmosphere that prevails in the United States specifically—and I would say the North Atlantic corridor, generally—the Israeli lobby has gained strength. You know about their interference in US elections—on defeating Andy Levin, a progressive Jewish American as sitting congressman from Michigan, defeating in primaries Nina Turner, in Cleveland, and Donna Edwards, in Prince George's County, Maryland, both Black women. So, they're on the march, and there have been laws passed to circumscribe the activities of the BDS movement.

Things are rather complicated. Over the years I've been involved intermittently in that solidarity movement, not only with regard to that trip that you mentioned, which was in conjunction with the National Alliance of Third World Journalists. I think it was in the 1980s, probably in the 80s that I served as book review editor of *Jewish Affairs* under the leadership of Herbert Aptheker, the communist historian. In that capacity, I reviewed numerous books concerning Palestine, Israel, Zionism, antisemitism, etc. And *Jewish Affairs*—sort

---

20. Gerald Horne. "One Historian's Journey." *The Journal of African American History* 96, No. 2, 2011, 248–54. https://doi.org/10.5323/jafriamerhist.96.2.0248

of obscure, but I doubt if every issue has been deep-sixed, I mean, I'm sure there are some issues around somewhere.

When I was with the National Conference of Black Lawyers, we oftentimes got into hot water because of our pro-Palestinian positions. In fact, I talk about that in my book I wrote on Southern Africa.[21] There's a vignette about that, in that particular book that involves myself and one of my colleagues in the National Conference of Black Lawyers. Perhaps for that and other reasons, I felt compelled to explore what used to be called the Jewish question, which you can find in my book on the 16th century, for example, as well as you can find aspects of that in some of the 20th century books that are wrote on Black communists.

CS: These next questions are more reflective. I was wondering, how do you think about time as a radical historian, and the effect the work you've done and are doing is having on the future? One example is your work changed my present in history and it's something I've shared with others and has changed their worldview and working towards justice?

GH: I think the work that I've done, what I've been trying to do is do work that I feel will benefit current and future generations in understanding this country and the world. I mean for example, in doing this research on the Black Panther Party, it's apparent that they were rather misled, shall we say about the nature of the United States of America. That is to say that all of this propaganda—which in no small measure has come from the left, that speaks of this grand revolution of 1776 and the so called liberal progressive traditions as embodied in the Bill of Rights—I think that that propaganda ill prepared many, including the Panthers, for the right-wing nature of the United States. It ill prepared them to understand settler colonialism, which has a central component of class collaboration between and amongst those of European settlers. Of course, you find that class collaboration amongst settlers in historic Palestine as well. So, part of my work has been to try to puncture that balloon of illusions so that people can be better prepared to confront this difficult reality that we face in the United States.

CS: When you're talking about the strong mythology of the US, that settler colonial mythology that really wasn't seen for what it

---

21. Gerald Horne, *White Supremacy Confronted: U.S. Imperialism and Anti-Communism vs. the Liberation of Southern Africa, from Rhodes to Mandela*, New York: International Publishers, 2019

was in a lot of realms, that mythology even pervaded Ho Chi Minh as well.

GH: Yes, I talk about that in my 1776 book.[22] I tried to explain it by dint of the fact of relations between and amongst nations. That is to say, if the left, right, and center say that the creation of United States is a great leap forward, well then Ho Chi Minh says, "Well who am I to tell these people they don't know what they're talking about," because a central principle—although people in the United States might find this hard to believe—is noninterference in the internal affairs of sovereign states. Particularly if you're trying to curry favor with that state, that gives you more impetus to accept what they say about themselves. But now, I think it's time at least for the left to break ranks and for the Black community to break ranks, so that a Ho Chi Minh arriving in the 21st century will not feel compelled to adhere to US propaganda.

CS: You've provided so much inspiration and support for so many of us over the years and I'm wondering who are some people who have helped you along the way and that you're grateful for?

GH: Oh, I guess my family, my sisters, my mother, high school counselors. In terms of example, people like W.E.B. Du Bois, Shirley Graham Du Bois, Fidel Castro, I could go on. Other than the foregoing, the people who helped to create this foundation, my foundation, that is to say, family, high school counselors, etc. Then there are historic figures you might never have met but who you've read about who you feel set an example that you strain to emulate.

CS: Thank you and your sister has a memoir out as well.[23]

GH: She reminds me of some things, growing up I used to read comic strips all the time. Actually, I still do although it is mostly just Doonesbury nowadays. I used to read this comic strip called Li'l Abner, which was really a stereotypical view of Euro-Americans in West Virginia, or places like West Virginia, what we imagined West Virginia to be. So, we were poor. She says in her memoir that she once asked me when we were kids to lend her some money. Then I quoted a line from Li'l Abner. I guess in retrospect it was sort of a right-wing populist cartoon, although I didn't realize that at the time. My response to her was straight out of Li'l Abner: "No more

---

22. Gerald Horne, *The Counter-Revolution of 1776: Slave Resistance and the Origins of the United States of America*, New York: New York University Press, 2014

23. Malaika Horne, *Mother Wit: Exalting Motherhood while Honoring a Great Mother*, Pittsburg: Dorrance Publishing, 2018

foreign aid to Lower Slobbovia." In other words, the cartoonist was referring to these poor Euro-Americans as slobs, Slobbovians. That was my response to my sister straight out of a right-wing populist cartoon. It wasn't one of my finest moments. But anyway, it's in black and white so I don't mind, I mean it's in her book [laughing], even though it doesn't leave me in the most positive light.

CS: That's funny. This is my last question. It's been a pleasure and honor to dig deep into your work over the years and have these conversations with you. I want to thank you. I've learned so much about how to look at history differently and in a deeper way, and how to bring it into focus today. I was wondering what learning lessons can you offer radical historians and who are some of your favorite radical historians from the past and today?

GH: Well, in terms of the past, of course, Marx and Engels, Nkrumah, Du Bois, Alphaeus Hunton, some of the work of Shirley Graham Du Bois. In terms of lessons, of course I still start every day by going through numerous newspapers. I think that's important, because in many ways the past is just a reflection of the present, and vice versa. I think the more you learn about the present the more you'll understand about the past.

For example, I have a couple of Washington DC projects. One that I'm writing on Washington in the 20th century and another on Washington in the 19th century. I find that *The Washington Post*—perhaps because it abuts the former slave owning territories of Maryland and Virginia; of course, it covers the Black community, which does not tend to accept conservatism—it really has some very useful articles for all my historical research, almost on a weekly basis of some aspect that will illuminate my history projects.

Likewise, I think in terms of trying to influence public opinion, it's very important to be up to date and up to speed on current events because you're trying to influence people, you're trying to give them a narrative, a story that they find legitimate, they find compelling, that they find illuminating. For example, if you look at the latest Trump scandal, the taking of the documents to Mar-a-Lago. One of the interesting twists, of course, is that some of the documents related to President Macron of France. Of course, we know that one of the startling photographs from the Trump era was when he and Macron shook hands and Macron did the macho thing and the squeezing of Mr. Trump's hand and wouldn't let go. I thought of that when I saw the paper the other day. It said that some of the documents he had taken related to President Macron. Now, of course, my first instinct was to think that Mr. Trump probably wants to blackmail Macron.

Obviously, I'm entering the realm of speculation. It's very important to separate facts from speculation, but one has to wonder why these documents on Macron?

So, what I'm trying to suggest is that as a political person—and I would say as a teacher, also—you're trying to be in a position to illuminate what's going on today. I mean, that's why I not only read numerous magazines and newspapers, part of which I think is reflected in the *Journal of African American History* issue that dealt with my work.[24] That explains also why I read *Rolling Stone* and *People Magazine*, because young people in particular, as you know, oftentimes are besotted by popular culture. I feel it's important for me to be aware of popular culture so I can use that as a window or as an avenue through which I can help to influence them by my knowledge of the ins and outs of popular culture, for example.

CS: Thank you. I read a conversation between Cornel West and bell hooks. That was a big point that they made as well—of integrating pop culture references and current ones into their teaching and philosophies.

GH: Yes. For example, Bruce Springsteen's charging $5,000 a ticket for his latest concert. It really makes one think.

CS: Wow. That book with Obama added some inflation.

GH: Yeah, well, that's another thing, too. When they did that book, *Renegades*, the conclusion it led me to was the devaluation of the term Renegade. When a rock star who may be worth a billion dollars—you know, he just sold his back catalogue for over a half billion—and a former US president are Renegades? I mean, it's like the devaluation of the term revolutionary. It's applied to Thurgood Marshall, for example, who sabotaged communists for his tenure with the NAACP. So, there's this rapid devaluation. Inflation makes the deflation in the Japanese economy seem tame by comparison.

CS: Maybe they are renegades from the International Criminal Court for war crimes?

GH: Yes, right. Alright, sounds good and good luck to you.

---

24. Gerald Horne. "One Historian's Journey." *The Journal of African American History* 96, No. 2, 2011, 248–54. https://doi.org/10.5323/jafriamerhist.96.2.0248

www.ingramcontent.com/pod-product-compliance
Lightning Source LLC
Chambersburg PA
CBHW031510270326
41930CB00006B/343